Revolution Televised

Revolution Televised

Prime Time and the
Struggle for Black Power

Christine Acham

University of Minnesota Press   Minneapolis / London

An earlier version of chapter 4 was previously published as *"Sanford and Son*: Televising African American Humor," *Spectator: USC Journal of Film and Television Criticism* (Spring/Summer 2000).

Published by the University of Minnesota Press
111 Third Avenue South, Suite 290
Minneapolis, MN 55401-2520
http://www.upress.umn.edu

Library of Congress Cataloging-in-Publication Data

Acham, Christine.
    Revolution televised : prime time and the struggle for Black power / Christine Acham.
        p.   cm.
    Includes bibliographical references and index.
    ISBN 0-8166-4431-4 (alk. paper)
    1. African Americans on television. 2. Television broadcasting—Social aspects—United States. I. Title.
    PN1992.8.A34A28 2004
    791.45'652996073—dc22

                                                        2004009969

Printed in the United States of America on acid-free paper

The University of Minnesota is an equal-opportunity educator and employer.

12 11 10 09 08 07 06 05 04   10 9 8 7 6 5 4 3 2 1

*This book is dedicated to Ailsa Jeanne Acham
and the memory of John L. Acham*

Contents

Acknowledgments

Revolution Televised: Prime Time and the Struggle for Black Power
began while I was a graduate student at the University of Southern California, and I would like to thank my dissertation committee (Todd Boyd, Tara McPherson, and Darnell Hunt) for support through the PhD program and in completing the dissertation. I especially thank Todd for his belief in my abilities and his encouragement and guidance throughout the process.

Before I get too far, I must recognize those who got me to graduate school in the first place: those who helped me through my somewhat chaotic undergraduate career at Clark University. There was a chance that I might not have obtained a bachelor's degree at Clark because of financial concerns, and for their support I would like to thank my family: Jeanne, John, Roger, Lee Jay, and Gina-Marie. I would not have graduated from Clark without the guidance, support, and assistance of the dean of students at that time, Kevin McKenna. Whether running interference with financial services, signing off on forms to allow me to take extra units, or just giving me a shoulder to lean on, he always managed to be there for me, and I am forever grateful. I also thank Marvin D'Lugo for his inspiring classes and for encouraging me to apply to film school.

To get back to the book at hand, I thank Steve Hanson and the staff of USC School of Cinema-Television Library, the staff of the UCLA Film and Television Archive, and the Museum of Radio and Television in Los Angeles. Even while bogged down in her own research, Sharon Sekhon read early versions of this work and helped to organize my thoughts and ideas. Jennifer Healy, my very first editor, took my often disorganized, run-on sentences and chapters and got them into shape for presentation to the dissertation committee. I also thank both her and her family, Tom, Bill, and Diane, for providing a second home during my graduate work and the writing of this book.

The real transition from dissertation to book began when I took an appointment at the University of California–Davis. Kent Ono and Sarah Projansky helped me to unhinge unnecessary "dissertation language and structure" and think through the direction of the project. They provided and still provide true mentorship. I would like to thank members of the program committee of African American and African Studies for their support as well as the Office of the Dean of Humanities, Arts, and Cultural Studies and the Vice Provost's Office for the faculty development award and publication assistance grant that greatly benefited the completion of this book. Kathy Littles, Kahala Crayton, and Leslie Madsen, cultural studies graduate students at UC Davis, helped with fact checking, indexing, and numerous other tasks. Richard Edwards at the Institute for Multimedia Literacy at USC offered the assistance of Ted Kupper in obtaining frame grabs for illustrations. Catherine Lieuwen went with me from shop to shop on Hollywood Boulevard foraging for stills. Bill Harting, with his expert photographic skills, took my picture for the book jacket. I also thank Andrea Kleinhuber and the staff of the University of Minnesota Press for their interest in the project.

Last but definitely not least, I acknowledge appreciation for those friends and colleagues who supported me through the past years: Carol Povenmire, my sounding board, adviser, coach, and cheering squad; Elizabeth Ramsey, who not only gives me literal shelter in Los Angeles but also senses my moments of desperation and forwards copies of books with such titles as *The Survivor's Guide to Getting It Published*; Jenny Healy and my mother, who listen to my countless phone calls from miles away; Sergio de la Mora, who befriended me upon my arrival in Davis and has been a source of support and friendship at UCD; and Lori Fuller, who provided shelter, transportation, and friendship during this process.

I would like to send a special shout out to the following friends and family: Wendy, Tyler, Jordan, Brenda, and Morgan Acham; Liesl Charles; Sohail Daulatzai; Michael Eric Dyson; Enid, Keith, Marilyn, Alana, and the rest of the Lee Wo clan; as well as all Trini friends and family.

Introduction

Dy-no-mite!
What's happening?
Peace, love, and soul
Elizabeth, I'm comin' to join you.
What you see is what you get.
The devil made me do it.

Anyone up on 1970s television trivia will recognize these phrases; spoken frequently by television characters, they became part of the American popular lexicon. This was a vibrant time for blacks on network television, and as a child I enjoyed watching black television shows such as *Good Times* and *What's Happening!!* with my family. I obviously was not able to contemplate such critical concepts as the "ramifications of the images" or the "state of minorities in the television industry"; I simply liked the shows for what they were to me—often humorous, sometimes over the top, and occasionally poignant.

Good Times was my show, and as the youngest child in my family, I empathized with Michael's plight as the underdog. I remember in particular the episode in which he refuses to apologize to his teacher for calling George Washington a racist and willingly faces the wrath of his father, James, in order to stand up for what he believes. His sister, Thelma, and mother, Florida, attempt to convince him to change his mind before James gets home. J.J., as usual, tries to be the center of attention and comes up with numerous silly suggestions to help Michael.

At the time I did not comprehend the mixed politics of the show. Michael argues for the incorporation of black history into the curriculum and refuses to accept the textbook's simplified explanations of the founding fathers of this nation. He opens James's eyes to the fact that he, too, was miseducated. These are important statements about the education system and its exclusion of African Americans, but at the end of the episode James asks Michael to compromise his values and apologize to his teacher so that he can return to school. Also, as clearly illustrated in Marlon Riggs's film *Color Adjustment* (1991), in both his dress and demeanor J.J. replicates the old coon images from early cartoons and minstrel shows.

Watching these shows decades later I understand why critics responded to many of them with such negativity. Indeed, some of these late 1960s and 1970s black-cast shows used historical stereotypes modernized to the new decades. Academic studies of the black television programs of the era usually see them simply as negative representations; the shows are reduced to merely kitsch or viewed with a level of disdain. Although these shows aired during the Black Revolution, a period of much turmoil and political protest, the few scholarly analyses of them have generally been limited and reductive, dwelling primarily on perceived stereotypes in what are considered antiprogressive television texts.[1]

I could not so easily dismiss the pleasure gained by myself and numerous African Americans who not only watched the shows at that time but also do currently in reruns and with newly released DVDs. Staying within this positive/negative binary prevents a deeper understanding of these texts. When I began to research the black-cast television shows of this period to find an alternative story, I discovered numerous instances of black agency. African American actors and producers disrupted television's traditional narratives about blackness and employed television as a tool of resistance against mainstream constructions of African American life. Actors challenged the development of the story lines and their characters, found ways of covertly speaking to a black audience within typical television genres, opened up television for the inclusion of more African Americans, and used other media outlets such as mainstream magazines to question the motives of television producers.

Of the many 1970s television shows rooted in blackness, certain texts were chosen for particular reasons. *Julia* (1968–71) is a milestone in television history, the first show to star an African American since *Amos 'n' Andy* (1951–53) and *Beulah* (1950–53).[2] *Black Journal* (1968–77) and *Soul Train* (first broadcast in 1970) are landmark nonfiction programs that specifically address the African American community. *The Flip Wilson Show* (1970–74), *Sanford and Son* (1972–77), and *Good Times* (1974–79) were enormously popular within both the black community and mainstream society. Why were such shows able to garner mainstream popularity when other black programs failed? Finally, the short-lived *Richard Pryor Show* (1977) represents critical black engagement with television in the late 1970s.

I begin, in chapter 1, with a review of the historical trajectory of African American participation within mainstream American society and how factors such as Jim Crow, segregation, integration, and de facto segregation led to the formation of black communal spaces. These sites often nurtured African American culture and resistant politics. The example of the Chitlin' Circuit, a group of theaters across the United States that catered to black audiences from 1907 until after World War II, demonstrates the importance of these spaces within African American society, culture, and politics. As these black sites of resistance have emerged politically and culturally, the mass media, especially television, have become significant tools in this transition and have promoted different aspects of a black political agenda.

In the early 1960s, network television turned toward documentary production, and television news and news documentaries eventually looked to black America as a source of its stories, given the ever-growing vocal protest of black Americans during the Civil Rights era and the Black Power movement. But what did these documentaries say about race? In chapter 2, I discuss the opposing constructions of black life presented by mainstream documentaries and by African American journalists in the PBS series *Black Journal*.[3]

I then go on in chapter 3 to examine two programs that debuted on television in 1970—the legendary music and dance showcase *Soul Train* and Flip Wilson's variety program. Under the guidance of Don Cornelius, *Soul Train* is a product of a Chicago UHF station and went into national syndication in 1971. Flip Wilson, who performed in the Chitlin' Circuit, brought his own brand of black comedy and characterizations of black folk to NBC. How did the individual politics of Cornelius and Wilson impact these shows' construction of blackness?

Chapter 4 focuses on Redd Foxx and the mainstream format of the situation comedy. Foxx is a crucial figure in the transition from black-only settings to a mainstream forum. A veteran of the Theater Owners Booking Association (TOBA, another venue for black performance) and Chitlin' Circuit, Foxx had a reputation as a blue comedian whose X-rated party records sold in an underground market for years. How did this comic move into the public forum of prime-time television?

Black women played an important role in publicizing the concerns of black artists within the television industry. Through interviews and comments in mainstream magazines, black actresses participated in a culture of resistance by critiquing their televisual images and the industry's approach to race. In chapter 5, I consider the question, Did their efforts impact the narratives of their shows?

The latest historical show included in the book is *The Richard Pryor Show,* and in chapter 6 I analyze Pryor's four-episode prime-time run. Pryor evolved from a conservative comedian into one of the most controversial black performers. Using street language, he portrayed characters from the black underclass to provoke insightful criticism of U.S. society. *The Richard Pryor Show* used both comedy and drama to address issues pertinent to the black community. Why was this show so short-lived?

Finally, I conclude *Revolution Televised* by reflecting on the possibilities and problems of using television as an instrument to impact social change. Focusing on Chris Rock's two comedy specials, *Bring the Pain* (1996) and *Bigger and Blacker* (1999), as well as his HBO weekly series *The Chris Rock Show* (1997–2000), I propose ways in which this medium is either successful or underutilized in vocalizing the continuing concerns of the African American population, and I suggest the role that African American artists play within this process. Does cable television offer the space for resistant black voices?

Influenced by African American historians and cultural critics such as Robin D. G. Kelley (whose book *Race Rebels* looks at areas often ignored by mainstream historians), I chose to follow suit with my study of black television. Kelley locates resistant culture in unlikely places, and because of its commercial nature television is typically considered an improbable space for an alternative culture— but *Revolution Televised* finds many oppositional strategies at work in black television. Herman Gray's *Watching Race: Television and the Struggle for Blackness* examines television shows of the 1980s and 1990s and provides another helpful framework for understanding television texts. Gray avoids the positive/negative dichotomy and instead considers how technologies, industrial organization, and political economy influence commercial culture and the representation of blackness. His work reveals that television is not black and white but a medium of slippage and contradictory meanings.[4] Critics such as Michael Dyson, Michelle Wallace, and bell hooks also present valuable methods of critique as they look at black images within popular culture. Each views popular culture and black media images through his or her own political position and with an understanding of the historical implications of such representations.[5]

For cultural critics and members of the African American population to ignore television's potential as a forum of resistance is to misread levels of vernacular meaning inherent in many African American television texts. What follows here is not intended to be a comprehensive social history of African Americans in television in the late 1960s and 1970s, but rather a new interpretation of key shows in a reassessment of black television history. For black society, improvisation has traditionally been essential for survival, and *Revolution Televised* illustrates how black television artists and producers have often used this skill to challenge the television industry and to locate effective resistance in an effort to control black images. This commitment to community and social change played out over television screens across the nation during this significant historical moment.

1. Reading the Roots of Resistance

Television of the Black Revolution

Growing up in the 1970s on a staple of black-cast television programs, I rarely considered that the face of television had ever been primarily white. Flipping through the channels, or I should say manually turning to each channel, brought black people into my living room on a nightly basis. I imagined myself on the Soul Train line, laughed at the antics of J.J. on *Good Times,* and although my mother loved the show, I wondered if (and hoped that) Fred would actually succumb to one of his famous heart attacks on *Sanford and Son.* Needless to say the 1980s were quite a shock when, although *The Cosby Show* ruled the airways and *Different World* became a college favorite, it was evident that black people had receded to the background of network television. I was aware of the black concern about the situation and also observed the interest and critique present when blackness reemerged in the late 1980s and 1990s and television, as Herman Gray argues, entered a stage of "hyperblackness."[1] During this time, black-cast television programs often ended up on the new networks, Fox leading the way, followed by the Warner Brothers Network (WB) and the United Paramount Network (UPN), creating a network ghetto in which fictionalized black people resided.

I became interested in this ebb and flow of black images on television and then more specifically in the first point of hyperblackness, the 1970s. I am struck by the ways in which cultural critics from the 1970s and in the present day have maligned television of the era. Authors who have chosen to document this period, such as J. Fred

MacDonald in *Blacks and White TV,* a politically disputable survey of African Americans in television, dismiss the era as "the New Age of Minstrelsy," suggesting a time of essentialized positive and negative imagery.[2] Donald Bogle's recent book, *Prime Time Blues,* although more detailed in its analysis, still categorizes television of the 1970s as "the Jokesters" and, as such, focuses on perceived stereotypes reinscribed by television.[3]

But 1970s black television cannot be reduced to such simplistic analyses. Falling in the period of the Black Revolution within the United States, this era of television goes further in helping us understand how television operates as a cultural site. This historical moment is of utmost importance, because the impact of African Americans in the political arena expanded exponentially. It was a never-before-seen uprising and demand for change, made more public by the use of television. The incorporation of these images of struggle inadvertently changed the face of the medium in both fiction and nonfiction genres.

Television of this time period has been ignored because of the shape of early African American cultural criticism, which considered black cultural works under the rubric of positive and negative representations. Media representations were often rejected as negative for the black community. This certainly has been a primary concern of African Americans, given awareness of the hegemonic influences of media representation. However, as critic and filmmaker Marlon Riggs notes in the response to his film *Tongues Untied* (1989), one needs to consider the notion of "community standards" when analyzing the appropriateness of a particular image.[4] In this case, who is given the power to decide what media products meet the standards for the black community? Is this process, indeed, a self-reinscription of the notion of the monolithic black community in which every black person reads a cultural product, gains pleasure or pain, in the same way?

In my attempt to show the flaws in this way of thinking, one of my key tasks is to rehistoricize, reconsider, and recuperate arenas of black popular culture such as television. African American participants in the television industry during the Black Revolution were often accused of engaging in acts of black self-oppression. Those who leveled such criticism ignored the history of black popular culture, in which residual resistance exists in what may seem on the surface to be antiprogressive texts. Those who assessed popular culture through what was then considered the lens of a middle-class black sensibility gauged the images produced in these texts as having a negative impact on the process of integration; they were therefore unable or unwilling to recognize any form of potential resistance that existed in television.

In order to avoid the positive/negative dichotomy of analysis, I choose to ask a series of questions that will guide this discussion of television of this era in a different direction. What social, political, and industry factors brought about this shift from invisibility to hyperblackness in the late 1960s and 1970s? Why were many of these shows treated with such disdain in the 1970s and continue to be dismissed within African American critical circles today? Should this era of televisual blackness be so easily reduced to kitsch or seen as negative representations of African American society? Can we consider that African Americans used television as a site of resistance during this critical era?

I place the television programs within the appropriate historical context, which gives the reader an understanding of how issues of race intersected with television as a medium during this volatile time. Indeed, I consider how fictional television conflicted with the image of African American society desired by mainstream black political organizations. Also included within the analysis are issues such as network versus public and pay television, genre, gender, and intertextuality. I challenge the continued perception of television as a "vast wasteland" and argue that during this era it was instead a site used to challenge hegemonic notions of race in America.[5] But how does African American society, which is historically positioned outside mainstream political power and certainly outside power positions within the television industry, oppose hegemonic aspects of the media?

Television, Uplift, and Hidden Transcripts

I certainly acknowledge that television has been used to oppress the African American population. For instance, shows such as *Cops* continue to reinscribe specific ideas about criminality and the black population.[6] Television during the Black Revolution was often within the control of white producers, and many of the fictional programs starring African Americans did seem to represent either idealistic images, such as *Julia,* or historical caricatures of black life, as seen in J.J. of *Good Times.* So with these "negative representations," or "sellout shows," how can I argue that television was a source of empowerment and/or resistance? In order to clarify this seeming inconsistency, one must look at two central factors: the multifaceted nature of the African American community and the ways in which the ideology of uplift operates within black society.

Mainstream television shows of the late 1960s and 1970s and the artists involved were often seen as sellouts by segments of the black community; that is, the shows and the performers involved were putting aside a race-specific agenda for the commercial payoff. Being a sellout was a concept that truly evolved in the 1960s and '70s with the possibilities of integration. But the meanings underlying the term *sellout* were gauged by the racial projects of the major black political organizations of the time.[7] Exploring the term and its meanings illustrates the diversity of ideas within the African American community.

The term *sellout* takes on a variety of meanings in the black community. For a Black Nationalist, mainstream integrationist organizations can be seen as sellouts. The Student Nonviolent Coordinating Committee (SNCC) eventually viewed the Southern Christian Leadership Conference (SCLC) from this perspective, as Martin Luther King Jr. and his organization promoted an agenda of passive resistance. In the context of film, Sidney Poitier was seen as a sellout, as he presented what many termed a colorless black man.[8] For an integrationist, someone who had taken advantage of the benefits of integration but sought to distance himself or herself from the black community was a sellout. For an Afrocentric person, maintaining a black American identity and distancing oneself from Africa was selling out. I do not intend to simplify the agendas of these black political organizations. I elaborate on this term to unpack the notions of a unified black community that existed in the pre–Civil Rights era. The black community has always been multifaceted, with class, social, and cultural differences. Nevertheless, despite the variety of applications of the word *sellout* within the African American community, a common thread of racial uplift emerges. Terming a person or black organization a sellout has been a tactic used to criticize those seen as prohibiting the progress or uplift of the black community. In turn, racial uplift determines the acceptance or rejection of any African American cultural product within the black community.

Rooted in African American slave culture, racial uplift has been a prevailing ideology evident in African American society since the late nineteenth century.[9] Uplift has had a variety of meanings within the black community. In his book, *Uplifting the Race,* historian Kevin Gaines suggests that "uplift ideology describes African Americans' struggles against culturally dominant views of national identity and social order positing the United States as 'a white man's country.'" During the antislavery campaigns, uplift in slave spirituality meant "personal or collective spiritual—and potentially social transcendence of worldly oppression and misery."[10] The notion of uplift was tied to issues of liberation and group advancement.

Another aspect of uplift is evident in the post-Reconstruction period, with the self-designation of a group of African Americans as middle class. Uplift in this case is intrinsically tied to the black leadership's struggle with racism by positing the notion of class differences within African American society. As Gaines explains, the black lower-class status was a result of cultural rather than biological racial differences:

> [T]he black opinion leaders deemed the promotion of bourgeois morality, patriarchal authority, and a culture of self-improvement, both among blacks and *outward, to the white world,* as necessary to their recognition, enfranchisement, and survival as a class.[11] (emphasis added)

Uplift can be seen as a struggle between the elitist groups and more popular forces evident in the push for education, economic rights, and social advancement.

Implicit in the concern of uplifting the race is African American scholar and activist W. E. B. Du Bois's notion of double consciousness. Du Bois argued that African Americans often gauged themselves in terms of how the white world viewed the black world.[12] This does not imply that uplift ideology necessarily involves a longing to be white; rather, the notion of uplift asserts a desire for a "positive black identity." However, operating within uplift ideology is "unconscious internalized racism," because African Americans who do not live up to these standards are blamed for not assimilating into the acceptable black middle class and therefore into mainstream white society.[13] Poverty and lack of a stable family are no longer seen as a result of the social reality; now they are seen as a result of personal failure. Although this can be more clearly seen as emanating from mainstream black political organizations, such as the NAACP, this idea of a positive black identity takes on a variety of forms depending on the politics of the black individual or group in subsequent history.

The concern with how the white world viewed the black world became even more critical when African Americans were represented on mainstream American television. The first shows to star black people were *Amos 'n' Andy* (1951–53) and *Beulah* (1950–53), which motivated African Americans, the NAACP in particular, to confront the television industry, because they believed these programs harkened back to stereotypical notions of blackness and would have a negative impact on the black community seeking full integration. The importance of having positive representations of African Americans on television became a part of the critical discourse from television's inception. After a period of relative invisibility in the 1950s, black civil rights images were given some emphasis in the 1960s in the news and in a few integrationist shows such as *I Spy* (1965–68) and *Julia* (1968–71). The 1970s proved to be the era in which African Americans were integrated into fictionalized television as never before. I illustrate the manner in which these racial projects and the concern with uplifting the race shaped the criticism of television in the 1970s. I argue that the harsh reproach and dismissal of fictionalized television characters from within segments of the black community in the 1970s arose from these underlying political ideologies.

In order to reinterrogate television of the Black Revolution, I follow the path laid out by such social historians as Robin D. G. Kelley. In *Race Rebels,* Kelley looks at the politics of the everyday and the "hidden transcripts" of cultural production in order to obtain a more detailed picture of a historical moment. Interpreting the work of political anthropologist James C. Scott, Kelley argues:

> [D]espite appearances of consent, oppressed groups challenge those in power by constructing a "hidden transcript," a dissident political culture that manifests itself in daily conversations, folklore, jokes, songs, and other cultural practices. One also finds the hidden transcript emerging "onstage" in spaces controlled by the powerful, though almost always in disguised forms.[14]

Using this framework, one can consider the hidden transcripts created by African Americans who participated in television's production. The hidden transcript is a way in which black people used the mainstream venue of television to communicate with a wider black American community. The black audience garners a different meaning from the television text because of its members' understanding of the conversations and cultural forms that are created within the black community. Although television on the surface appeared antithetical to supporting black life during the Black Revolution, reading the hidden transcripts helps us to gain a better understanding of the ways in which African Americans used television in political ways.

To advance the debate about television of the Black Revolution beyond this binary of positive and negative, sellout or authentic, we must understand historically the spaces in which African Americans socialized, were entertained, and discussed the social and political life that surrounded them. Communal black spaces have been essential for African American life. These spaces were dictated by law from the days of slavery, through slave codes, the black codes in the post-Reconstruction era, and eventually Jim Crow laws, which enforced segregation. However, considering the antagonistic and destructive atmosphere created by the enslavement of black people and the cultural differences in American society, we need not wonder why reprieve was to be found within these black communal sites. It was here that many black people found a sense of self-affirmation. They garnered the strength to cope with the harsh reality of their public life and critiqued the white society that enslaved them and refused to acknowledge their status as human beings. They also celebrated, relaxed, and enjoyed themselves away from the critical eyes of white society.

The Creation of Black Sites of Resistance

The trajectory of American racial politics, as it pertains to black people, is critical to an understanding of the American political climate in the late 1960s and the 1970s. In their book *Racial Formation in the United States,* sociologists Omi and Winant argue that "race has been the fundamental axis of social organization in the U.S."[15] Their paradigm of "racial formation" proves useful to this book. Pre–Civil Rights era America was a "racial dictatorship." This dictatorship defined the American identity as white and sought to marginalize African Americans and any other racial minority. The establishment of a slave-based economy and the eventual failure of Reconstruction validate this point. Reconstruction signals a period in which the tide of American racial politics could have turned to the benefit of black people. In its original formation, African Americans would have had the opportunity to participate in the American system of politics, economics, and social life and thus prevent the racial dictatorship that followed. Instead, the complete failure to maintain the basic tenets of abolition led to the continued preservation of the color line, the loss of life for African Americans, the abject poverty, and the social disorder that still exist today.

The maintenance of the color line was achieved through laws such as the Black codes, which arose during Reconstruction. Black codes, which "bore a remarkable resemblance to the antebellum Slave Codes,"[16] sought to reestablish control over the newly freed blacks and allowed for the fining, imprisonment, and death of blacks for numerous offenses, such as not going to work, quitting their jobs, owning guns, and insulting speech. The laws also limited where black people could live and prevented them from testifying in the trials of whites. With the overthrow of Radical Reconstruction, the efforts of the racial dictatorship were evident in the disenfranchisement of African American voters through violent acts, poll taxes, election codes, and other complications of the voting procedure. The establishment of Jim Crow laws, through which blacks and whites were kept separate in all public accommodations and intermarriage was made illegal in every southern state, accompanied disenfranchisement. Eventually, the federal policies such as the outlawing of the Civil Rights Act (1875) by the Supreme Court in 1883 and the upholding of segregation with the determination of "separate but equal" in *Plessy vs. Ferguson* (1896) determined that the racial dictatorship remained standing for decades to come.[17]

Indeed, the racial hostility evident in American society and the federally commissioned law of separate but equal led to the formation and development of communal black spaces. It was in these arenas that much of African American community life, politics, and cultural production flourished. As Robin Kelley describes,

> A number of recent studies have established that during the era of Jim Crow, black working people carved out social space free from the watchful eye of white authority or, in a few cases, the moralizing of the black middle class. These social spaces constituted a partial refuge from the humiliations and indignities of racism, class preten-

sions, and wage work, and in many cases they housed an alternative culture that placed more emphasis on collectivist values, mutuality, and fellowship.[18]

Out of necessity and camaraderie, these spaces became key locations for African American life.[19] The history and development of African American humor serve as a sound example of the workings of these sites.

Slavery set the stage for the form and content of African American humor. In his book *On the Real Side: Laughing, Lying and Signifying, the Underground Tradition of African-American Humor . . .*, Mel Watkins examines African American humor from slavery to the 1990s. Just as the underlying motivations of uplift are concerned with the way the white world sees the black world, a similar process works within the context of black humor, according to Watkins's observations. He draws upon the ideas of W. E. B. Du Bois, who suggests that African Americans operate with a

> double-consciousness, this sense of always looking at one's self through the eyes of others, of measuring one's soul by the tape of a world that looks on in amused contempt and pity. One ever feels his twoness,—an American, a Negro: two souls, two thoughts, two unreconciled strivings; two warring ideals in one dark body, whose dogged strength alone keeps it from being torn asunder.[20]

Seen in this context, black humor's trajectory and significance can be situated around this duality: one type of humor in the mainstream public and another, private, humor used within all black settings. Both were operational in order to maneuver through the hostile American terrain. A division must be recognized between the societal view of blacks as inherently humorous and black humor. African Americans could be seen as humorous once they were contained within certain roles, ones implicated in childishness and naïveté. However, an ironic, realistic, sarcastic, and satirical black humor was reserved for the black community. As Watkins argues,

> African Americans . . . assume[d] dual social roles: one for a hostile white world, the other the natural demeanor they reserved for interactions among themselves. Humor was a crucial factor in dealing with a situation. In interactions with whites, it eased tensions that might otherwise have exploded into violence. . . . In the privacy of completely black settings, black humor was more acerbic . . .

surreptitiousness and trickery were the principal defenses against repression, and humor played a key role in this deviousness.[21]

The two sides of black humor were rarely combined during slavery and Jim Crow because of the obvious possibility of violence.

During slavery, African storytelling, involving animal and trickster tales and folk humor, though often misinterpreted by the white mainstream culture, actually held the seeds of African American humor.[22] These forms of oral culture often related the incongruities of American society. "[M]any of these animal tales depict the triumph of physical weakness, hypocrisy, mischievousness, trickery, and cunning over brute strength and guilelessness."[23] Less covert tales were those of the trickster, who, although not always idealized, was often regarded as a hero who outwitted his master and was able to gain rewards or freedom. Signifying and satire were present in African American society, but they were publicly veiled. White people were not privy to the criticism of mainstream society often expressed in these forms.

The public image of African Americans as inherently happy, frequently singing and dancing, was often created from a mode of interaction necessary to literally survive adversity in pre–Civil War America. Often African Americans performed dances such as the cakewalk for the white plantation owners. White owners were so pleased with the entertainment, they failed to realize that the mode of dress and exaggerated displays of airs and graces were a critique of white society. As a slave maxim notes, "Got one mind for white folks to see, 'Nother for what I know is me."[24] There is much evidence that songs and dances were methods of protest and often used as signals for escape and insurrection.[25] White America embraced this image—the slave as naive, simple, and essentially happy, which allowed in part for the enduring justification of slavery. African Americans saw themselves ridiculed and distorted in mainstream popular culture through forms of minstrelsy and blackface. Minstrelsy was known for the mimicry of black dialect and the stereotypical physical characteristics—huge eyes, wide mouth, painted lips—the essential lack of intelligence of the characters, and the notion that they were happy with plantation life.

African Americans participated in this form of entertainment when they rose in popularity as blackface minstrels at the end of the nineteenth century. Ironically, African Americans also became the predominant audience for black minstrelsy. Though some may interpret this participation as an acceptance of white America's perceptions of African Americans and a case of self-oppression, as Watkins argues, the amusement could also have emanated from an acknowledgment of the ridiculous and exaggerated nature of the minstrels' behavior.[26] Because of segregation in most forms of social interaction, African American humor was given a separate space to develop its specific characteristics. African American blackface minstrelsy for segregated black audiences established venues for professional black performers and the development and expression of black humor. By the early 1900s the evolution of the black road show, which also catered to African American audiences, gave way to the Theater Owners Booking Association (TOBA, or Toby Circuit) and eventually to the Chitlin' Circuit.

Starting in 1907, the TOBA provided a circuit of theaters that showcased black performers. The circuit included playhouses in the South and the Midwest, primarily in the black areas of major cities and in smaller towns. Many African American musicians and comedians, such as Bill "Bojangles" Robinson, Dewey "Pigmeat" Markham, Count Basie, Ethel Waters, Bessie Smith, Moms Mabley, and Sammy Davis Jr., developed their skills on the TOBA Circuit. Although the TOBA provided steady work for black performers and assured them payment, the theaters were often rundown. Performers had to help with the setup of the theater and performed at least two shows a day, seven days a week. Watkins states:

> [T]o many black entertainers, the acronym TOBA became widely known as "Tough on Black Asses." Still, TOBA looms as one of the most important chapters in African American entertainment history. It provided the principal transition from minstrelsy's rigidly maintained stereotypes to a performance style that more accurately reflected the majority tastes of the black community.[27]

The TOBA was a black communal space, the comedians of the TOBA practiced black humor, and the audiences were active participants, openly showing their pleasure or annoyance with an act. As Watkins describes, "Audiences would greet unpopular acts with derisive catcalls, invective, and an occasional flying missile."[28] Using the tradition of African American cultural practices such as call-and-response, the audiences were as much a part of the act as the onstage performers.[29]

Comedians of the TOBA were known for their situational routines that reflected on black everyday realities. Comedians' subjects ranged from home life and food to sex and rarely addressed the nonblack community. The TOBA comedians very seldom directly addressed the audience; they worked in pairs of a straight man and a comic. Although the audiences were primarily black, white bystanders, it was always understood, would not tolerate direct address by a black comedian, which suggested some sort of equality between the audience and the performer. The comics' humor also generally excluded addressing political issues. Remembering that they performed in an era of lynchings, we can understand why these sentiments were veiled.[30]

The following skit between Spo-Dee-O-Dee and Moms Mabley, who played a washerwoman, exemplifies comedy typical of the TOBA. The story is told from Spo-Dee-O-Dee's perspective.

> Hey, woman! Where's the money?
> She would reach her hand out and I would say in a stern voice,
> Bring it over here, woman.
> She would try to hide some of the money from me and say, I need the money for food.
> You ate yesterday. You want to eat every day?[31]

Spo-Dee-O-Dee portrays a voice of authority and, as a black man, does not directly implicate white society. However, his character's relationship to the black woman can be seen as a thinly veiled portrayal of the relationship between black and white society. The comedy of the TOBA, in addressing everyday issues of black folks, such as the inability to find employment or the lack of access to resources, formed the basis of a political comedy. Although it did not directly address the emotions resulting from these circumstances, this comedy can be considered an everyday political act—a "hidden transcript" formed, in a communal setting, from a group's acknowledgment of its public reality.

Interestingly, many middle-class African Americans rejected the comedy of the TOBA. Black comedy, like many critical African American cultural forms, developed within the working-class black communities. Indeed, in their desire to uplift the race, middle-class African Americans rejected African American comedy because they felt it did not conform to their image of blacks as respectable members of mainstream American society. By holding and expressing these beliefs, middle-class African Americans rejected cultural practices and black folk culture, which had helped to develop the roots of African American society. Middle-class black Americans believed that in order to fit into mainstream white American society, African Americans needed to emulate white America. This involved showing America how well the African American could mimic white cultural forms. Their embarrassment over comedians and jazz and blues musicians represented this division between middle-class acceptability and what had become working-class black culture.[32]

This schism crystallized in the workings of the Harlem Renaissance, which coincided with the performances of the TOBA. Looking at the key text of the Renaissance, the Alain Locke–edited tome *The New Negro*, one can recognize what was designated as appropriate black culture by what was included in the text, poetry, literature, and gospel music. Jazz and comedy, which were also very popular among working-class black people, were considered folk culture and thus an embarrassment to the middle class. This process of selection and rejection recurred as African Americans eventually moved into mainstream exhibition outlets.[33]

The Depression brought an end to the TOBA, because many southern theater owners could no longer afford to keep venues open. Black audiences, who were often unable to access government aid, were even more intensely affected by the Depression. They were thus less likely to spend their limited funds on entertainment outside the home. Many of the southern theaters, which formed the TOBA, closed their doors. The rise of the American economy caused by the start of World War II, as well as the continued black flight from the South to northern cities, concentrated many African Americans within large urban centers. As such, theaters and exhibition outlets catering to black audiences became centered in the North. The Apollo in Harlem, the Howard in Washington DC, the Royal in Baltimore, the Uptown in Philadelphia, the Regal in Chicago, and other black theaters made up the Chitlin' Circuit and became important settings for African American performers and audiences. On northern doorsteps, members of the black middle class continued to fear the impression of black life that black performers gave to white audience members. Interestingly enough, within comedy acts, the topic of racial prejudice based on skin tone and experienced *within* the black community was a visited theme.

The Depression and eventually the post–World War II era brought more aggressive social commentary and satire to the forefront of African American comedy. The extreme level of poverty during the Depression created a level of despair, and the lack of response to the needs of African Americans exacerbated their anger. Again in World War II, African Americans were promised that their participation in the war effort would assure community acceptance within U.S. society. The "double V" symbol, victory abroad and victory at home, signaled the African American belief that the fight against racism in Germany would guarantee the end of racial prejudice on U.S. soil. When civil rights were not forthcoming, frustration and anger continued to fester within the black community.

Within comedy circles, performers began to address openly such issues as southern racism and color prejudice within and outside the black community. Political sentiment or political activities on a small and large scale, in hidden transcripts or more vocal renderings, were components of these segregated spaces. The following segment of an act performed at the Apollo by dance and comedy team Patterson and Jackson represents this more assertive attitude and the emergence of a political voice, reflective of the social circumstances:

> Got on the train in Tampa, Florida, on the way to New York. Conductor came around, said, "Give me your ticket, boy." Gave him my ticket, he punched it and gave it back. Came around again in Richmond, Virginia, said, "Give me your ticket, boy." Gave him my ticket; punched it and gave it back. In the Lincoln Tunnel on the way to New York City, conductor came around and said, "Give me your ticket, boy." Turned around to him and said, "Who the hell you callin' boy?"[34]

In this case the black man is very aware of his status as a secondary citizen in Florida and Virginia—states that openly exhibited racial segregation and, more important, where lynchings were a distinct possibility. The deference to the white power structure, although a necessity at that moment, is not an accurate gauge of the feelings of the black man. When crossing into northern states, and into New York City in particular, the attitude of the black man is expressed more directly. A place in which African Americans had formed a solid social and cultural community, New York provided the space for the black man to confront the racist white population. The skit demonstrates that black political consciousness, although veiled out of necessity, is never far from the surface and, in the proper place and time, will rise.

The Transition of Black Political Humor

World War II and its outcome for black Americans on the domestic front served as a catalyst for profound social change for African Americans. The hope that the United States would acknowledge the inconsistency between its explicit policies of world freedom and its own domestic and repressive racial practices was crushed. The realization that freedom was not forthcoming was a wake-up call to a more vocal positioning of African American people and their political organizations. The postwar U.S. economic and social climate fostered the continued emergence of black political voices.

The arrest of Rosa Parks on December 1, 1955, and the publicized Montgomery bus boycott that followed proved to be memorable moments of a movement in transition from politics that existed in all-black settings to overt confrontation with the mainstream U.S. population. These events are illustrative of the multilayered protests of African Americans to their status as secondary citizens. As social historian Robin D. G. Kelley posits, "[T]here is a long history of black working class resistance that has remained unorganized, clandestine and evasive."[35] In his discussion of the Birmingham, Alabama, public transportation system, Kelley notes the many ways in which black people resisted Jim Crow laws during World War II:

> Despite the repressive, police-like atmosphere on public transportation, black passengers still resisted. Over the course of twelve months beginning September 1941, there were at least eighty-eight cases of blacks occupying "white" space on public transportation, fifty-five of which were open acts of defiance in which African American passengers either refused to give up their seats or sat in the white section. . . . the total number of reported incidents and complaints of racial conflict reached 176.[36]

Young African American passengers sabotaged trolley cables and threw rocks at streetcars. Zoot suiters and military servicemen had confrontations, and there were physical altercations with bus drivers and other white passengers. Sometimes they simply talked loudly to disturb whites as a critique of Jim Crow practices.[37]

The reaction of working-class blacks was not always as dignified as one's collective memory might suggest. Many black women were unhappy with bus segregation and were involved in numerous verbal and physical disputes with bus drivers and other passengers, and as Kelley discovered, "most black women's opposition tended to be profane and militant."[38] Yet, in the collective American memory, these everyday acts are lost, and the quiet and dignified image of Rosa Parks with her connection to the NAACP replaces the everyday humiliations of and reactions to the Jim Crow South. These seminal moments cannot be seen in isolation from the larger workings of the black community, which, in its separation from white society, inevitably politicized those who participated in organized struggles and those who chose not to but whose lives were examples of resistance.

The work of African American comedians and performers, who were politicized by their existence in a racist American society, may not as readily be considered part of the political projects of the era. Yet, to ignore these underlying venues is to deny many alternate sites of resistance open to African Americans. By the 1950s, African American comedians continued to bring their brand of improvisational folk humor to black audiences on the Chitlin' Circuit or in a variety of small clubs, bars, and cabarets. With the cancellation of *Amos 'n' Andy* and *Beulah* on television in 1953, African American comedians were generally disregarded for starring positions in mainstream U.S. circles and performed almost exclusively for all-black audiences. Mel Watkins describes how the Chitlin' Circuit showed marked differences from the TOBA and placed itself outside the range of acceptability for middle-class black society.

> [B]y the late fifties profane denunciations of white bigotry and graphic sexual jokes were common in chitlin' circuit showplaces—particularly the numerous gutbucket cabarets "where good Negro folks would never venture and stepping on a brother's Florsheims has meant hospitalization."[39]

Although rejected by the middle class, working-class black people used these sites for their own cultural production and for their own underground purposes. This public discourse contributed to an ongoing critique of racist white society. When clubs had more restrictive policies as to what could be said, the comedy took on veiled aspects. At other times, white club owners were simply happy to make money, and performers were free to express their sentiments. Comedians who eventually crossed over into mainstream U.S. entertainment venues, such as Redd Foxx, Moms Mabley, LaWanda Page, Nipsey Russell, George Kirby, Richard Pryor, Dick Gregory, and Flip Wilson, performed and honed their acts within these black communal spaces.

Some African American comedians, such as Russell, Slappy White, Kirby, and Gregory, crossed over into integrated and white clubs and performed on television variety shows in the 1950s. However, the comedians had to dilute their edgier material that had become popular on the Chitlin' Circuit in that decade. Mainstream white audiences overlooked Redd Foxx and Moms Mabley, who maintained their acts within the folk and profane. However, these performers remained popular with black audiences.[40]

Although many comics made adjustments to their comedy so that it was understandable to a white audience, a different cultural community, they did not change it to the point where it was unrecognizable to those who shared its black roots. Often comedians used these adjusted acts to gain a place within white venues and, after obtaining a level of acceptance, began to integrate more caustic material. A good example of this can be seen in the career of Dick Gregory. Gregory had worked many of the smaller and more exclusive black clubs and a few white working-class clubs. He got his first opportunity to perform in a white establishment at Chicago's Playboy Club in 1961. Gregory was called in at the last minute to replace another performer, Professor Irwin Corey, and was confronted by a convention of southern businessmen. An excerpt of his routine that night follows:

> Last time I went down South I walked into this restaurant, and this white waitress came up to me and said: "We don't serve colored people here." I said: "That's all right, I don't eat colored people. Bring me a whole fried chicken."
>
> About that time these three cousins came in, you know the ones I mean, Klu, Kluck, and Klan, and they say: "Boy, we're givin' you fair warnin'. Anything you do to that chicken, we're gonna do to you." About then the waitress brought me my chicken. "Remember, boy, anything you do to that chicken, we're gonna do to you." So

> I put down my knife and fork, and I picked up that chicken, and I kissed it.[41]

A similar story was often told on the streets of black America, although there the story often ended with kissing the chicken's ass.[42] Here, Gregory removes a bit of the edge to the story but keeps it within the mode of the trickster.[43]

Gregory's success at the Playboy Club launched his career within mainstream America. Within a year he was featured in *Time* and *Newsweek* and on many television shows. Although he avoided the sexual content of other Chitlin' Circuit acts, Gregory still expressed the social satire and ironic observations of traditional African American humor. Rising in popularity during the 1960s at the time of vocalized black political activity, Gregory focused on topical humor and moved from more observational jokes, as demonstrated by the aforementioned performance, to sharp social satire.

> You gotta say this for whites, their self-confidence knows no bounds. Who else could go to a small island in the South Pacific, where there's no crime, poverty, unemployment, war, or worry—and call it a "primitive society."
>
> Reagan is "Nigger" spelled backwards. Imagine, we got a backward nigger running California.[44]

Gregory became more of a social activist, giving up his career as a comedian to follow these political causes. However, he paved the way for many of the older comics previously ignored by mainstream white society as well as many new black comics.

It is this transfer from the black underground to the mainstream that is often perceived as selling out, yet African Americans have always made some compensations because of America's hostile racial climate. As Gregory shows, there were ways of using the mainstream for one's own purposes. By finding entry into mainstream society, he was able to express to those white audiences the frustration of the black person in the United States and influence some social change. For this reason, it becomes necessary to observe the hidden transcripts apparent in these performers' works and take them into consideration when making any assessment of African American cultural production. For our purposes here, and for an understanding of African Americans on television, it is relevant to realize that many of the black performers on 1960s and 1970s television evolved from a tradition of performance in black communal spaces. Television was the most significant way of crossing over into the mainstream U.S. milieu. More effective than any other venue, television broadcast African Americans to a mainstream U.S. audience as no medium had done before.

Television and Blackness

It is this transition that I choose to focus on: from black cultural production within communal black sites to the very public moment of mainstream American television in the late 1960s and 1970s, when black performers appeared in large numbers on network television. The implications of this transition are numerous and are discussed throughout the book. The central question is: How does one choose to interpret the cultural production nurtured within the black community, which then crosses over into mainstream cultural production outlets such as television?

At television's inception, many in the black community perceived it as an impartial space for African American representation in the media. *Ebony,* the "black *Life* magazine" and a major proponent of the black bourgeois lifestyle, reported in 1950 that roles for African Americans on television were a "sure sign that television is free of racial barriers."[45] As early as 1951, network television shows also espoused a treatise of tolerance. The *Texaco Star Theater* presented a musical revue called "The United Nations of Show Business," hosted by Danny Thomas and Milton Berle. The following is a segment of their introduction to the program.

> THOMAS: Let me put it this way, Milton. In the past three years the
> great performers who have appeared here on the Texaco Star
> Theater have represented a cross section of the world. I mean
> Italians, Spaniards, Australians, the white man, the Negro,
> the oriental, the Protestant, the Catholic, the Jew—they've all
> shared the spotlight on this stage.
> BERLE: Well, Danny, if I may interject, that's the way show business
> operates. Danny, there's no room for prejudice in our profes-
> sion. We entertainers rate a brother actor by his colorful perfor-
> mance, and not by the color of his skin.[46]

Although network television executives openly promised nonbias in television production, their rhetoric was overwhelmed by a reality in which black participation was minimal at best and roles were typecast—a trend that has continued in much of network television. African Americans, including Harry Belafonte, Ella Fitzgerald, Sammy Davis Jr., Dewey "Pigmeat" Markham, Duke Ellington, and Sarah Vaughan, appeared primarily as comedy and musical entertainers on variety shows such as *The Ed Sullivan Show (Toast of the Town)* and Steve Allen's *Tonight*. African Americans also appeared on sporting programs, such as boxing, as quiz show contestants, and on religious programs and local television shows, a few of which were produced and directed by African Americans. However, *Beulah* and *Amos 'n' Andy* marked the first appearances by African Americans in starring roles in network television's fiction genre.

The controversy surrounding the production of *Amos 'n' Andy* proves to be instructive in illustrating the issues at hand. *Amos 'n' Andy* premiered on radio in the 1920s and was very popular. Although the characters were supposedly African American, two white actors, Freeman Gosden and Charles Correll, voiced them. Amos and Andy were viewed as stereotypical caricatures, tied to the minstrel performances of vaudeville. The plan to bring these images to television was met with outrage by a segment of the African American population.

In his article, "Amos 'n' Andy and the Debate over American Racial Integration," Thomas Cripps discusses the political struggles over televising the program in 1951. He argues that the growing NAACP, an essentially black middle-class organization, primarily spearheaded the rise in political activism after World War II. Many African Americans, especially those who had enlisted in the war effort, expected an improvement in civil rights after the war. Broadcasters sought out the wealthy black market, whose rise was touted by such publications as the trade magazine *Sponsor* and the publication of *Ebony*.

The arrival of *Amos 'n' Andy* appeared incongruous with the image of the upwardly mobile African American seen on the pages of *Ebony* magazine. "Led by the NAACP, the black middle class challenged what they took to be a parody of their historical struggle for social mobility in a hostile society."[47] They staged their complaints on the front cover of *Variety,* in letters to the sponsors of the program, and in various press releases. They also attracted the support of white liberal organizations such as the American Jewish Committee. Their central concern appeared to be the portrayal of the middle-class characters. There was a definite divide in the black community over *Amos 'n' Andy*. African American actors pointed out the opportunities for black artists in the burgeoning medium. Spencer Williams argued that the situations occurred to "real Negroes you and I know."[48] Other black viewers resented the NAACP and other white organizations for disrupting their viewing pleasure.

The show battled to avoid racist practices. They hired veteran African American TOBA and Chitlin' Circuit performer Flournoy Miller as a consultant on the set. The set decoration catered to so-called middle-class sensibilities through paintings, books, and apartment ambience. The main characters' motivations were also upwardly mobile, and supporting characters were often self-employed business owners. Criminals, when represented, were not African American. As Cripps concludes,

> Amos 'n' Andy arrived in full view of the television audience, complete with symbolic baggage from an older time in black history and broadcasting history. Solidly rooted in a segregated world, by its existence, even on television, it seemed to cast doubt over black social goals and to mock the newly powerful, organized black middle class.[49]

Thus, although *Amos 'n' Andy* had a large black following, the program was rejected by black activists as regressive.

The production and reception of *Amos 'n' Andy* indicate the level of contestation over images of African Americans. The debate over the show revealed how television was inscribed onto the African American program of uplift. In this case, middle-class black America believed that, to uplift the black community, integration was essential; one needed to represent African Americans as worthy of progressing into mainstream social and economic circles. These "regressive" black images, although entrenched in black folk culture, were impeding the process of integration. What this debate also points to is that the values of one segment of the black community could silence other black voices. I do not mean to argue that legitimate concerns did not exist in regard to the power of the medium in distributing images of a community. However, this production elucidates that a single black community has never existed and that the appeal of such binaristic positive/negative concerns leaves a gap in understanding the hidden transcripts of such productions.

Clearly, *Amos 'n' Andy* entertained many African Americans.

Many in the black community recognized its basis in the situational comedy routines made famous in the days of the TOBA. However, the middle class felt a sense of shame with respect to performers from these black communal working-class sites, an embarrassment that escalated with the movement of these performers into television. Outside of trying to negotiate the intent of the producers, one can still see this as a mainstream venue that publicly broadcast black images and created a sense of community across black America, derived from seeing black people on television. However, the show was pulled from production in 1953, and African Americans once again became practically invisible on mainstream network television, except for the short-lived *Nat King Cole Show* in 1956, in news stories, and in supporting roles. The mid-1960s signaled the reemergence of African Americans with the premiere of *I Spy* in 1965, the four-month-long *Sammy Davis Jr. Show* in 1966, and *Julia* in 1968.

The discourse surrounding *Amos 'n' Andy* allows us to understand some of the key concerns over black televisual images. The overwhelming desire to uplift the race again framed many of the discussions of 1970s television. Through an understanding of both the shift between performance in black communal spaces and performance in mainstream television and the clear class divisions in African American society, I propose that one look beyond the notion of positive and negative images. Although I certainly identify and consider the ways in which the media sought to quell black voices and often succeeded in doing so, I highlight the many ways in which black people used the media, specifically television, for community purposes, as a political voice for social change, for enjoyment, and for self-affirmation. As the following chapters reveal, television of this era is complex, and rereading these texts proves fruitful in unearthing a wealth of information about African American participation and resistance within the burgeoning medium.

This methodology promotes the recuperation and reassessment of African American popular culture and is applicable to the interrogation of the entertainment industry as a whole and television in particular. An elitist division continues between what is considered high and low culture. Many forms of popular culture are still seen as low culture and not worth serious discussion or consideration. This system of designation is class, gender, and race based and has to do with the levels of access to different arenas of culture and who speaks for the majority. Television is definitely positioned as low culture, yet perhaps more than any other cultural medium television enters the lives of people on an everyday basis. To dismiss television as a "vast wasteland" is to ignore the participation and investment of everyday people in this cultural site, different modes of reading a text, and the presence of resistant culture within this mainstream forum.

2. Was the Revolution Televised?

Network News and *Black Journal*

The 1950s and 1960s proved to be a period of political upheaval in the United States, especially concerning African Americans. The fallout from the lack of racial progress in the post–World War II era fostered the rise of grass roots political organizations that began to confront the American "racial dictatorship" head on. At this time some of the political practices developed in all-black settings moved aboveground into the mainstream U.S. consciousness.[1] Television played a central role in this transition. One does not need to delve far into the American collective memory to access images of African American protesters in the 1960s. Television covered the everyday struggles witnessed in the lunch counter protests, store boycotts, and the very public March on Washington. Television witnessed the eventual rise of the Black Power movement, the urban revolts, and the public protest of runners Tommie Smith and John Carlos at the 1968 Olympics.

The goal of this discussion is twofold: first, to illustrate how television, a medium in the process of transforming itself into a serious news vehicle, handled the challenge of covering the Civil Rights movement; and second, to analyze how television as a media source represented the rising Black Power movement to the American public, and therefore to analyze the role that nonfiction television played in negotiating the shift of these political movements into the public eye of mainstream America. I examine the myths of network news documentary practices, the differences between documentaries and the everyday news coverage, and finally the relevance of

Black Journal, a series that premiered on public television in 1968. *Black Journal* was created by African Americans, distributed by public television, and eventually seen in syndication. The show provided an alternative to mainstream news and incorporated various black viewpoints on contemporary incidents that affected the African American population.

Remembering the '60s

> Perhaps more than any other people, Americans have been locked in a deadly struggle with time, with history. We've fled the past and trained ourselves to suppress, if not forget troublesome details of the national memory, and a great part of our optimism, like our progress, has been bought at a cost of ignoring the process through which we've arrived at any given moment in our national existence.
>
> **Ralph Ellison, *The Shadow and the Act***

In the late 1950s and early '60s, television was arguably the most significant tool of entertainment, even while network television was struggling to position itself as a serious outlet for the news. As one-time reporter for CBS news Robert Schakne describes, "The whole process of changing television into a serious news medium happened to coincide with the civil rights movement."[2] Peter J. Boyer, a writer who covered television for the *New York Times* during the era, agreed, stating that the Civil Rights movement was

> the first running story of national importance that television fully covered. . . . Television brought home to the nation the civil rights struggle in vivid images that were difficult to ignore, and for television it was a story that finally proved the value of TV news gathering as opposed to mere news dissemination.[3]

With this focus on the Civil Rights era as a source of ready material, it is important to explore the political attitudes expressed by network television, the types of information that television disseminated, and how these attitudes changed over time with the evolving agendas of black political organizations.

A strong sense of nostalgia permeates American society for the newsmen of the 1950s and '60s, such as Edward R. Murrow and Walter Cronkite, involving a belief that this was a time when news was trustworthy, objective, and inspired social change. Indeed, as the chapter discusses, this was part of the rhetoric of the networks.

Yet, this era's major network documentary series such as Murrow's *See It Now*, *CBS Reports*, *NBC White Paper*, and ABC's *Bell and Howell Close-Up!* are not a part of our everyday experience in the way that reruns of *Bewitched* and *Father Knows Best* are.[4] So why as a culture do we retain these nostalgic connections between news and social change? This ongoing process occurs in two central ways: through television's contemporary construction of its past, and through the rhetoric of television news journalists in general and in that era specifically.

The United States is constantly involved in a process of mediation with its history, and television has played a significant role in this negotiation and recuperation of our national memory. Beliefs of the 1960s are often enmeshed in impressions garnered through contemporary media recuperations of the time, and the 1990s brought an increased interest in the era. Television shows such as *I'll Fly Away* (1991–93) and *Cronkite Remembers* (1997) and films such as *Mississippi Burning* (1988), *Forrest Gump* (1994), and *Ghosts of Mississippi* (1997) are contemporary imaginings of black America's racial past. These television programs and films work as revisionist history, modifying and often improving white America's role in the civil rights past. One of the common tropes of these shows is the incorporation of television news footage from the '60s. Through the use of the news footage, television is positioned in the role of catalyst to white individuals' action.

The NBC miniseries *The '60s* (1999) provides a clear example of this process. Released during February sweeps of 1999, the advertising for the program was aired weeks in advance and arrived with CD soundtrack and web site in tow.[5] NBC touted the production as "the Movie Event of a Generation," the story of two families—one white (the Herlihys) and one black (the Taylors). According to the network, "the story of these families is the story of America." In actuality the series spent more time on the lives of the white family and, in doing so, revisited black history from a white perspective.

Within the first thirty minutes, younger son Michael Herlihy, sitting in his living room in the North, is mesmerized by what he is watching on television. There is a clip of George Wallace's "Segregation now, segregation tomorrow, and segregation forever" speech, followed by a montage of images, identified as footage from Birmingham and Selma, Alabama, of black protesters marching peacefully and the infamous assaults with hoses and dogs. Each scene is intercut with a close-up of the increasingly horrified look on Michael's face. He confronts his parents the following day and demands that he be allowed to travel to the South to help with voter registration. "You saw those pictures on TV. . . . It is a chance to learn something about the real world. Isn't this what President Kennedy said, ask not what your country can do for you?" Michael soon boards a bus to Mississippi and is briefly introduced to the Taylor family. He is awakened to the horrors of segregation, and by the end of the program he becomes a self-professed freedom fighter.

Many other programs have employed this precise televisual device, using a liberal white character to assuage white America's guilt over its racist actions. Television critic Herman Gray suggests,

> [C]ontemporary television is constantly engaged in a kind of recuperative work, a kind of retrospective production of raced and gendered subjects who fit the requirements of contemporary circumstance. . . . television accomplishes this production discursively, by reading history backward.[6]

As with The '60s, the reincorporation of these images gives the impression of a liberal media body that documented and presented the horrors of racism to an American public and, indeed, inspired social change. Is this actually the case? Did television retain this objective as the Civil Rights movement evolved into the Black Power movement?

Certainly evidence exists to indicate that television coverage of civil rights protests and their brutal southern response brought home to the United States the plight of African Americans in the South as no other medium had heretofore. As mentioned previously, the Civil Rights movement occurred at a critical moment for television news. Beginning nine years after television news was established, this moment was seen as the opportunity to establish television as a legitimate news vehicle. As Robert J. Donovan and Ray Scherer argue in their book Unsilent Revolution: Television News and American Public Life, television kept the Civil Rights movement in the forefront of the American conscience.

> Only television, radio, the AP, and UPI regularly carried the daily news story from the South to all parts of the United States. Of these, television was by far the most compelling because of its visual impact. Doubtless, television news influenced northern newspaper

and magazine editors to keep playing the story year after year when they might have preferred to give readers something different for a change.[7]

Martin Luther King Jr. and members of the Southern Christian Leadership Conference became aware of the power of the television image. King understood the impact that the assaults on peaceful protesters had on a wider U.S. population. He therefore incorporated the presence of the cameras within the organization's protesting strategy. He was known to call off marches if it became known that cameras would not show up for the event.[8] Among other tactics, the SCLC scheduled its protests to take place when television crews would have time to get the footage to the networks for the nightly news.[9]

Furthermore these televised images and the outrage of segments of the American public directly impacted the Kennedy White House. Donovan and Scherer report:

On May 4, 1963, Kennedy said that the brutal televised attacks on women and children made him "sick." "I can understand," he added, "why the Negroes in Birmingham are tired of being asked to be patient." Public reaction against the southern militant segregationists was so great that Kennedy privately referred to his civil rights legislation of 1963 as Bull Connor's bill."[10]

Attorney General Robert F. Kennedy later wrote,

[W]hat Bull Connor did down there—the dogs and the hoses and the pictures with the Negroes—is what created a feeling in the United States that more was needed to be done. Until that time, people were not worked up about it or concerned about it.[11]

Another example of television's impact on the White House occurred on March 7, 1965. Martin Luther King Jr. had planned a march from Selma to Birmingham to protest for voting rights in Alabama. When the protesters arrived at the Edmund Pettus Bridge, Sheriff Clark and his police force, who were mounted on horses, attacked them. Television cameras were at the event, and ABC interrupted its regular broadcast to show images from Selma. When President Lyndon Johnson made his televised appearance before the joint session of Congress a week later to propose the Civil Rights Act of 1964, he referred to the Selma attacks in his speech. The bill eventually passed.

But what happened when African American political ideologies shifted from passive resistance to the more oppositional black power protests? Vast differences are evident in the medium's coverage of the urban rebellions and the Black Power movement. Black power, the political ideology, which arguably pushed America into complying with social changes, was often maligned in television coverage. Like shows such as *The '60s*, contemporary television does not reveal the questionable role that TV news played in the presentation and acceptance of the rising Black Power movement. This avoidance often leads the contemporary viewing audience to presume that television continued to be a vehicle for social change within the African American community and the United States at large during this continued period of social unrest.

Even with the passing of the Civil Rights Act of 1964 and the Voting Rights Act (1965), African Americans were confronted with the fact that laws did not necessarily result in change. In both northern and southern cities, African Americans were faced with continued racial hostility and lack of opportunities, and the frustration led many, especially youth, to question the efficacy of the agenda of the Civil Rights movement and its policy of passive resistance. Many black organizations, including the Student Nonviolent Coordinating Committee and eventually the Black Panther Party, inspired by the words of Malcolm X, Franz Fanon, and other third world revolutionaries, began to call for black power.

Evidence reveals that with the shift from civil rights to a black power agenda and the rising frustration of the black urban populations, television was no longer seen as an ally to the black community. As Donovan and Scherer argue, television indeed influenced the U.S. viewing population to fear and despise what the country considered the more radical aspects of the Black Freedom movement. The authors suggest that the urban conflicts dominated the news and were at times exaggerated. This became especially clear in the coverage of the riots in major urban centers, beginning with the Watts riots of 1965. They discuss the problems that occurred with the coverage of the riots, as exemplified by NBC executive William Corrigan's comments. Corrigan was called into Watts to cover the riots and stated that news helicopters "sent out some frightful reports that were totally unverified."[12]

Furthermore, by looking at news documentaries of the day, one can perceive the context constructed for the events and the ways in which documentarians and journalists sought to interpret and explain the historical moment to the American public. These programs are a gauge of the media's predilections and ideologies. There is perhaps no better way to disentangle revisionist history, nostalgia, and memory than to revisit texts from the specific historical moment and examine the social, economic, and political environment in which these documentaries were made.

The Golden Age of Television Documentary and the Myth of the '60s Newsman

Television in the 1950s concerned itself primarily with entertainment programming. In the late 1950s and early 1960s, network television turned toward developing its news coverage and journalistic depth. Documentary production was seen as one avenue to journalistic legitimacy. While public service and other non-entertainment programming was usually left to unpopular times on the schedule, such as Sunday afternoons, networks invested heavily in prime-time documentaries in the early '60s; this period is now referred to as the Golden Age of Television Documentary.[13] Numerous television critics have speculated about the motivations behind this change in programming, suggesting such reasons as atonement for the quiz show scandals of the 1950s and response to the government antitrust investigations. Many credit the impact of Newton Minow, the Kennedy administration's chairman of the FCC. In his speech to the National Association of Broadcasters in May 1961, Minow declared television a vast wasteland and thus gained notoriety within the industry as the first chairman of the FCC to actually deal with the content of television.[14] Minow's influence was a common concern of networks and producers because he held the power to revoke broadcasting licenses.

In *Redeeming the Wasteland*, documentary scholar Michael Curtin states that he initially believed that television's reliance on the documentary genre was a liberal investment in civil rights initiatives and a reflection of John F. Kennedy's political leanings. However, through an analysis of the flagship documentary series of the three networks, *CBS Reports, NBC White Paper,* and ABC's *Bell and Howell Close-Up!* Curtin asserts that documentaries of the Golden Age were produced at a

> distinctive and complicated moment when political and corporate leaders as well as network officials embraced television documen-

tary in an explicit attempt to mobilize public opinion behind a more activist [cold war] foreign policy. . . . like earlier mass media campaigns that accompanied the two world wars, this flourishing of documentary activity was part of an ambitious effort to awaken the public to its "global responsibilities" and thereby consolidate popular support for decisive action overseas under the aegis of the New Frontier.[15]

The international arena was seen as a burgeoning market for American television, and television documentaries were a vehicle to encourage public support of anticommunist foreign policy while promoting a positive image of America to a foreign audience.

New Frontier rhetoric contrasted sharply with the civil rights realities of the United States at the time. Yet these documentaries had to tackle this inherent contradiction and the advancing Civil Rights and Black Power movements. As one of the few writers to deal with African Americans in television in the 1960s, J. Fred MacDonald's reading of the Golden Age is worth considering. MacDonald asserts:

> If Newton Minow's new prescription for broadcasters was confusing and unnerving, President Kennedy's political priorities offered television executives a direction in which to exert their energies and placate the new administration: the civil rights movement. . . . these actualities brought home the necessity for, and intensity of, the black social movement.[16]

These comments suggest that civil rights became a key issue for network documentarians. In actuality, from 1959 to 1964, only 11 of the 147 documentaries of the flagship documentary series even dealt with civil rights, the majority targeting an international agenda.[17] The view of the documentary as bringing home the necessity for and intensity of the black social movement is, however, commensurate with the networks' rhetoric that documentary production was objective and had the ability to create social change. Thus, critics such as MacDonald are trapped in these beliefs about television news without thorough analysis of the situation. Consequently, a reading audience of this black television history is also left with false notions of these television documentaries.

This notion of objectivity is at the heart of American journalism, and it flourished in the Golden Age. Bill Leonard, who eventually ran CBS news, describes the producer of documentaries as follows:

He's got to care about the truth; he's got to care about the truth much more than he cares about the art. More about the truth than what looks pretty. He must be willing to ruin films, ruin stories, not rearrange them or throw them out, because he cares so much about truth. He must be willing to have things a little duller than he'd like them to be because that's the way they are. The trick, of course, is not to have things dull and yet still be right and still make it honest journalism. And that's not always easy.[18]

This rhetoric adds to the mythology of the era and the nostalgic recuperation of the moment. However, what often slips in the embrace of the notion of objectivity is the role of interpretation, something that journalists acknowledge is an active component in their capacity as professionals. As journalists, documentary producers know that analysis is a critical part of their work, yet in the Golden Age there was a belief that analysis could work in concert with objectivity. This is often not the case, because ideology is reflected within the analysis. In dealing with black subject matter, more often than not reporters did not have regular contacts within the black community and thus lacked an understanding of black perspectives. And the analysis provided within these documentaries reflects this.[19]

When documentaries dealt with blackness, what did they say? This was the moment of the emergence of a black voice on mainstream television, but were black people able to find a place within the documentary constructions of the Golden Age? I have chosen "Watts: Riots or Revolt?" from *CBS Reports* for analysis because it was produced during the Golden Age and because the subject matter is also of particular interest. The Watts rebellion symbolized for many the changing tides of politics from civil rights to black power. It was one of the first in a series of revolts in which African Americans expressed open discontent with the U.S. system and indicated that they were no longer willing to follow through with peaceful protests. A look at one of the documentaries of the period, especially one confronting the issue of urban revolt, will allow for a close examination of how network television handled the shift away from the more accepted strategy of passive resistance.

Riots or Revolution?

In December 1965, *CBS Reports* aired "Watts: Riots or Revolt?" As the documentary declared in its opening moments, the text sought to examine the "principal events and causes of the nightmare in Watts." This program illustrates the difficulty that this show and other documentary texts of the time had in overcoming the central contradiction between the United States' position as leader of the free world and the clear evidence of its human rights violations. The documentary also calls attention to the instances of what Bill Nichols terms "documentary excess," moments that are uncontainable within the "narrative structure."[20] These were times in which black people used the public venue of television to assert the politics that evolved within black society yet were not recorded or displayed in mainstream U.S. settings. Also central to our discussion here is the focus of "Watts: Riots or Revolt?" which, like many other documentary texts of the era, was on the conflicts of blackness within the urban space. This and other documentaries had an influence on the perceptions of the inner-city black community, especially when urban conflicts escalated in the late 1960s and 1970s.

Mass migration to urban centers began at the turn of the century. By the 1960s, large segments of the black population lived in enclaves of major urban centers across the United States. Many of these people, who had moved out of the South in hopes of finding better opportunities, were faced with new as well as familiar types of oppression in northern and western cities.

One such enclave of black life was Watts in Los Angeles. Many African Americans had migrated to Southern California with hopes of new jobs but were systematically excluded from work in construction and the rapidly expanding aerospace industry. Black unemployment between 1959 and 1965 increased from 12 percent to 30 percent in Watts, and the median income decreased significantly.[21] Efforts of civil rights organizations to improve the lives of African Americans in Los Angeles were curtailed. One such example of this occurred with the passage of Proposition 14 (1964), which was intended to repeal the Rumford Fair Housing Act. The Rumford Act, which passed into law in 1963, prevented racial discrimination in the sale of homes by allowing housing grievances to be handled by the California State Fair Employment Practices Commission rather than through the courts. This system was more accessible to minorities who could not afford expensive court proceedings when filing a housing discrimination claim.[22] Although later declared unconstitutional by the U.S. Supreme Court, Proposition 14 passed with 75 percent of the white vote.[23]

The hostility of white Los Angeles toward the encroaching black population was also reflected in the response of the Los Angeles Police Department to the black community. As LA historian Mike Davis explains, "Since the days of the legendary Chief William Parker in the early 1950s, the LAPD has been regarded by L.A.'s Black Community as a redneck army of occupation." Parker was a "puritanical crusader against 'race mixing,'" and there were raids of local black and tan clubs.[24] In April 1962, the LAPD raided the Nation of Islam Mosque without due cause, killing one member and wounding six. This reflected official agencies' fear of the politicization of black youth, one of the groups most disenfranchised by the racist practices of Los Angeles.

It is no wonder that the Watts rebellion of 1965 was sparked by a police incident. On August 11, 1965, at 7 p.m., a twenty-one-year-old African American male, Marquette Frye, was arrested by California Highway Patrol officer Lee W. Minikus for drunk driving. Because Frye lived only one block away from the arrest scene, his mother tried to convince the officers to allow Frye's brother to drive the car home. A crowd gathered, and, according to sociologist Raphael Sonenshein, the

> discussion soon turned ugly, and by 7:23 PM all the three members of the Frye family had been hustled into the CHP vehicle. The growing crowd objected vehemently to the arrests. As the officers were withdrawing from the scene, someone apparently spit on them. Using very questionable judgment, the enraged officer and his partner waded into the crowd to find the assailant. The officer grabbed a young woman wearing a barber's smock resembling a maternity dress, and with great force, dragged her to a police vehicle. To the increasingly agitated crowd, the police had brutalized a pregnant Black woman. As the officers left the scene, rocks began to fly. Soon young men in the crowd began to attack passing vehicles with rocks and bottles. The riot was under way.[25]

The hostile environment created by Chief Parker and the propositions and policies passed by white Los Angelenos had created a situation ripe for explosion.

"Watts: Riots or Revolt?" aired some four months after the Watts rebellion. This episode of *CBS Reports* is a disjunctive text, which reflects the aforementioned conflicting agendas of the Golden Age of television documentary. There are three central contradictions of the text: first, the conflicting voices of authority in the documentary; second, the opposing narration, sound, and images; and, finally, the varied use of the documentary "actors." As the key reporter, John Stout, begins to narrate the documentary, the camera pans down the street in Watts and reveals burned-out buildings. Stout states:

> Three months ago on this street in Los Angeles, California, violence produced all this. A local riot? Or a revolt? Part of a national social revolution? A carnival of hoodlum lawlessness? Or the product of a festering social illness?

Stout's questions suggest that the documentary will provide a detailed interrogation of the causes of the Watts riots. He sets up binaries of possibilities: riot or revolt, social revolution or hoodlum lawlessness. The last suggestion is that Watts was the product of social illness, and one may infer that this is the direction the reporter might take.

The documentary has four major sources of authority: first, the findings of the McCone Commission, a group of eight men appointed by the governor of California to investigate the Watts incident; Daniel Moynihan's then-recent report on the "Negro condition in America"; interviews with Los Angeles Police chief Parker; and finally, interviews with local African American leaders and residents of Watts. The sources of authority are placed in this order within the construction of the documentary, which illustrates the importance that each is given. So although the documentary's wide source of "experts" on the incident reflects the discourse of objectivity, the emphasis placed on the white authority figures and the relatively minuscule amount of air time given to the community members of Watts paint a far less clear picture of objectivity.

The McCone report, which provides many of the statistics used in the documentary and is read on-screen by the reporters, attributes the Watts incident to widespread unemployment, the difficulties in obtaining food, and the problems of the education system. In the end governor of California Ronald Reagan and Los Angeles mayor Samuel Yorty implemented few of the McCone Commission's recommendations.

The documentary provides long segments of one-on-one interviews with Daniel Moynihan, whose underlying theory on the riots was that they were a result of the breakup of the black family and the increasing number of female-headed households. Moynihan's published findings, "The Negro Family: The Case for National Action," otherwise known as the Moynihan report, was much disputed at the time, and its legacy has been debated by African American feminists, who have criticized the ways in which it demonized black women. Critics at the time also condemned the report for placing the onus of the black condition on black families while overlooking the root of the problems, which was the racism of the society.[26]

According to the report, the breakup of the black family began under slavery and became progressively worse with the migration to the cities and the discrimination experienced there. Although the premise is feasible in that it ties the conditions to some historical legacy of oppression, from this point on the report takes an insidious turn. Moynihan argued that after World War II, black men had an increasingly difficult time with employment, which led to the prominence of female-headed households. This in essence was a core problem according to the report.

> At the heart of the deterioration of the fabric of Negro society is the deterioration of the black family. It is the fundamental cause of weakness in the Negro community. Unless the damage is repaired all the effort to end discrimination, poverty and injustice will come to little.[27]

Moynihan further argued that the black man was more damaged than the black woman was by the legacy of slavery and discrimination. The problem needed to be rectified in order to reengage the black man with the family. Moynihan made recommendations that would position the black male at his rightful place as head of the household, because "[t]he very essence of the male animal, from the bantam rooster to the four star general is to strut."[28]

As noted, this report was controversial. Parts of it were accepted by established leaders of the Civil Rights movement, such as Martin Luther King Jr. (SCLC) and Roy Wilkins (NAACP), as a component of the War on Poverty campaign. Other portions of the report were highly contested by African American leaders such as George Wiley, of the National Welfare Rights Organization, and by sociologists and psychologists. They questioned the black matriarchy theory and the ways in which the report managed to place the blame for the black condition on black women. Some critics also challenged the reliance on the white middle-class family structure as the model for the American family in an age of successful untraditional families. As African American feminist Paula Giddings sums up,

> The thinking seemed to be: Just make Black men the lords of their own castles and everything will be all right. To reach this utopia, of course, Black women would somehow have to slow down, become less achievement oriented, give up much of their independence. By remaining assertive, they were running the family and so ruining the race.[29]

It is important to note that the controversy over the report did not receive any attention in the documentary and that Moynihan's findings were presented as undisputed facts. At no point does the journalist intercede with an alternate hypothesis or question Moynihan's argument. Therefore, while the statistics of the McCone Commission report, which are read on screen, may provide some idea of the institutional racism that led to the riot, the more personalized interview with Moynihan is centrally positioned within the text and structures the narrative. This suggests that the riots were a result of the problems inherent in the black family. A segment of Moynihan's interview also concludes the documentary, so his theories are further heightened in their level of authority.

Other contradictory elements include the opposing interviews of African American leaders and Chief Parker. There are several clips of an interview with Chief Parker, and he is described as "a man known for his integrity and bluntness of opinion." Yet, the documetary does not indicate that historically Parker had an abrasive relationship with the black community, and countless complaints of police brutality were registered under his growing militaristic regime. In order to justify his accrual of power and relentless policing of minority communities, Parker nurtured an image of black Los Angeles as criminal and barely under the control of the LAPD. An examination of police brutality in Los Angeles during this time describes Parker's appearance in front of the U.S. Commission on Civil Rights in 1960.

> A belligerent Parker characterized the LAPD as the real "embattled minority" and argued that the tensions between LA's minority communities and the cops had simply to do with the fact that Blacks and Latinos were statistically many times more likely than Whites to commit crimes. Indeed Parker assured the Commission that

the "established community thinks cops aren't hard enough on Black vice."[30]

In this regard, too, the documentary overlooks information that perhaps expressed a more objective understanding of the incident. Parker is presented without the contextual information about his relationship with black citizens of Los Angeles.

Perhaps in an attempt to gain a level of objectivity, the documentary intercuts Parker's interview with comments from John Shabazz, one of the many Muslim leaders in Los Angeles. Shabazz briefly discusses the feeling of repression within the community. However, even before he speaks, Shabazz's words are discredited. At the beginning of the segment, a voice-over indicates that the documentary will now interview John Shabazz, a Muslim whose "sect [is] built around the belief that all whites are evil." This preface not only calls into question the validity of his commentary but also ties Shabazz to the legacy of the media's negative interpretations of the Nation of Islam. This interpretation was most apparent in Mike Wallace's explosive five-part series for CBS, *The Hate That Hate Produced,* which discussed the so-called Negro racism of the Black Muslims.

These oppositions and conflicts are also mirrored within the visual and aural context of the documentary. The first segment deals primarily with the images from the August riots. The visuals are set up to intrigue, fascinate, and inspire fear among a white audience. The imagery is the product of hand-held cameras, which quickly dart around a darkened city, lit only by fires and a few streetlights. The use of such imagery heightens the reality of the situation, and the confused, quick, and abrupt movements give the impression that one has entered a war zone. After the opening credits and introductory narration, there is a quick cut to the fires burning with an alarm ringing, a voice is heard yelling, "Kill the white man. . . . Get the white man, get the white man," and the sound of laughter echoes over the soundtrack. The voice-over relates:

> It was the most widespread, most destructive racial violence in American history [forgetting, of course, slavery]. White people driving through the riot area were considered fair game, whether young or old, men or women. Their cars were battered, the drivers stoned, kicked, and beaten, and the cars were burned. The mobs might groan and curse in disappointment when a white got away and then cheer like a football crowd when a car went up in flames. The burn-

ing and the looting, the shooting and the beating, went on for nearly a week.

The sound bites of the black residents immediately follow this segment and illustrate that many of them are upset at police brutality. However, their comments are undermined by the narrator's following statement about the mobs attacking not only the police but also firemen attempting to put out the blazes. And as the narrator states, "The mobs hated authority, but more generally, they hated all whites."

Although African American "actors" within the text are often intentionally used for the aforementioned dramatic and dangerous effect, there are moments of "documentary excess."[31] Documentary theorist Bill Nichols suggests that

> the impossibility of perfect congruence between text and history stems from the impasse between discourse and referent, between the signification of things and things signified. Representation serves to bridge that divide, however imperfectly, self-consciously, or illusionistically. Explanation, like ideology, provides strategies of containment designed to account for historical reality. . . . In every case, excess remains.[32]

The excess of this documentary lies within the uncontainable acts of the Watts residents, who do not comply with the narrative structure of the documentarians. The narrative structure clearly shows a balance in the information presented, which highlights the relevance of the white authority figures over that of the black interviewees from the Watts community. However, in a few instances the black citizens of Watts move beyond the attempted containment of the narrators. They are then able to put the politics of the community into the public arena of television.

The clearest example of this within the documentary is a reporter's interview with a black female resident of the city. This woman has four children and no husband in the home, a typical Moynihan report case. The reporter talks about all of the welfare programs, suggesting that there should be no need to riot. The woman will not be assuaged by his suggestions and repeatedly insists, "I'd be proud to go to work." A crowd begins to gather around the reporter, who continues to remind them of all that is provided by the welfare programs. The crowd's frustration is clear, and a man stares at the reporter with a weary look on his face and simply responds, "We need jobs." This is a brief moment, but worth noting, as it is one of the few opportunities for black expression to escape the structure of the documentary, which attempts to mute the voices of the African American residents of Watts.

Texts such as "Watts: Riots or Revolt?" indicate that images and meanings, within documentary production in the 1960s, are conflicted and multilayered. At the same time, such analyses allow us to question the notion of the impassioned media, catalysts for civil rights, and dispassionate seekers of the truth. These documentaries could not quite contain the emotions and politics of a rising vocal black population. These individual African Americans are examples of television's potential to be used as a forum to express a politics often seen only within the black community. However, there were limits to this expression due to the construction by the networks. "Watts: Riots or Revolt?" is a representative documentary of the Golden Age, and an analysis of the text reveals the limits of the medium at this historical moment.

Indeed, because of the intense rioting of the late 1960s, in 1967 President Lyndon B. Johnson created the Commission on Civil Disorders. One of the tasks of the commission was to study both television and print coverage of the riots. The commission's conclusion was clear in its critique of the media. It stated that news reports helped to shape America's views of the riots. It supported the thesis that television gave more coverage to moderate African American leaders than to the so-called radicals.[33]

The commission's report specifically states that television news "too often do[es] not achieve . . . sophisticated, skeptical, careful news judgement. . . . the media report and write from the standpoint of the white man's world."[34] The commission also observed that the media did not frame their analysis of urban unrest within an understanding of the problematic race relations in the United States.

> They have not communicated to a majority of their audience which is white—a sense of the degradation, misery and hopelessness of living in the ghetto. They have not communicated to whites a feeling of the difficulties and frustrations of being a Negro in the United States.[35]

The limits of the network media coverage, expressed by the commission and observed in the analysis of "Watts: Riots or Revolt?" become even clearer when contrasted with programs produced by

African Americans. As they gained more control of the medium, programs such as PBS's *Black Journal* were produced with much different results.

Black Journal: Resistant News Coverage

> We are probably the only people in history who were Africans at one end of a boat trip and Negroes at the other end. The Irish got on their boat as Irish and landed in the United States as Irish. The Italians started out as Italians and got here as Italians. But we started on the boat [African] and got off Negro.
>
> **Tony Brown, in George Hill, *Ebony Images***

Black Journal first aired on PBS in June 1968 as a monthly news-magazine. Sponsored by National Educational Television (NET) with a budget of one hundred thousand dollars per episode, *Black Journal* was one of the few nonfiction programs focused on African American subject matter. Although initially run by a white producer, Alvin Perlmutter, the black staff demanded true control over the show, and by September, William Greaves, a black man, filled the position. Greaves led the show to an Emmy Award for excellence in public affairs in 1969. *Black Journal* also boasted a 75 percent black technical crew and a 95 percent black production crew, an unprecedented occurrence on a nationally televised program.[36] A film school was established to train the minorities, who interned with five New York production crews. The Ford Foundation, the Corporation for Public Broadcasting, and the Carnegie Endowment funded the school.

Because U.S. film schools generally did not accept African American students, Greaves was trained as a filmmaker in Canada before producing *Black Journal*. There he worked as an apprentice on films made for the Canadian Film Board and learned to consider documentary not only as an educational genre but also as a tool for social change.[37] Greaves assessed the state of television and the role of the *Black Journal* producer:

> In short, the search for candor, for honesty and truth—rather than hypocrisy and self-delusion—must become a basic component of television programming. . . . On such a foundation the Black producer of today and tomorrow will most likely build his programming. For him the mass media will be an agency for improving mass

mental health and social reform, will be a catharsis, a means of puri-
fying the emotional and spiritual life of this country.[38]

In order to truly understand the relevance of *Black Journal,* we
must consider the national landscape of television in the late 1960s,
especially as it pertains to the representations of African Americans.
Although African Americans were featured in news documentaries,
in that coverage they could be manipulated and shaped by political
agendas. On the other hand, African Americans were rarely depicted on fictionalized television in the 1960s. *Julia* premiered in 1968,
and actress Diahann Carroll was the first African American to star
in a television program since the cancellation of *Amos 'n' Andy* and
Beulah in 1953. Although *Julia* will be discussed in more detail in
chapter 5, it is relevant to note here that representations such as
Carroll's in *Julia* and Bill Cosby's in *I Spy* were primarily critiqued
in segments of the black press as problematic and one-dimensional.

In other words, when *Black Journal* premiered on public television, nuanced representations of African Americans were not a
common occurrence on national television.[39] PBS was not one of
the three major networks; however, the broadcasting system maintained a large viewership of both mainstream and black viewers.
Black Journal was a site of black cultural resistance because it was
positioned within this mainstream forum yet still produced critical
black news coverage, which was seen by a cross section of America.
The show's premiere episode illustrates how *Black Journal* used the
space of PBS to forward a black agenda into public discourse.

As the NET logo disappears, a black man dressed in overalls
(comedian Godfrey Cambridge), faces the screen and, using a roller,
covers the screen with black paint. Rhythmic drumming is heard,
and the title of the program *Black Journal* appears. Program topics of a broad range are painted onto the screen: Black Panthers,
Godfrey Cambridge, Poor People's Campaign, Harvard Class Day,
New Breed, Dateline, Graduation 68. Of relevance to many segments of the black community, these topics were often glossed over
or ignored by mainstream television. Host Lou House introduces
the program: "This is *Black Journal,* program number 1. It is our
aim in the next hour, and in the coming months, to report and review the events, the dreams, the dilemmas of black America and
black Americans."

The contrast between *Black Journal* and other mainstream news-magazines appears not so much in its aesthetics as in its content. As the show progressed, the hosts and guests at times wore dashikis and kente cloth and greeted the audience with jargon of the day. However, the program was shaped like a typical newsmagazine of its time, or even of today, divided into segments or stories, features that were new every week and others that were of a consistent format, airing regularly throughout the series. What is relevant is the manner in which each segment of the show, whether overtly addressing political issues or not, tied into the popular concept of uplift—the push for education, economic rights, and social advancement.[40] From its inception, *Black Journal* reflected the desire to uplift the black community. It did this through an explicit educational component as well as an underlying politics of advancement.

The premiere episode begins with a segment on the Class of 1968 and initially focuses on the Harvard University graduation, at which Martin Luther King Jr. was scheduled to speak before his death. Coretta Scott King, his widow, addresses the class instead, and black female reporter Ponchita Perez covers the event. Mrs. King discusses the need of the government to proceed on the recommendations of the Kerner Commission; she speaks out on Vietnam; the police buildup across the country; and the formation and persistence of the ghettoes.[41] What is particularly interesting is the length of the coverage of her speech. The viewing audience is allowed the time to listen to the words of Mrs. King uninterrupted for several minutes. This differs sharply from typical news reports, which, like the interview of John Shabazz noted in "Watts: Riots or Revolt?" couches sound bites within the commentary of the news reporters.

The reporter then travels to universities in the North and South—Harvard, Morehouse, Spelman, and Southern University of New Orleans—to see what black students are thinking about graduation and their goals for the future. The students raise and discuss a broad range of issues as the camera and the reporter take a back seat to these conversations. What is shared has the nature of a roundtable debate on the issues facing recent black college graduates.

The Morehouse and Spelman students discuss their postgraduation plans. One student talks about working in the black community on the South Side of Chicago, and another says that he wants to work with people in Africa. Immediately, a black female student questions his choice to teach in Ghana while the U.S. black population is still in need. The student responds that he needs to learn more about his blackness and Africa. This causes an uproar, as many of the others really believe that he needs to focus on black Americans. When another student expresses that he wants to work with SCLC, with all poor people, he is also challenged. By addressing the idealism of the Civil Rights movement, the opponent suggests that the race problem is so large that any black person with knowledge needs to use his or her education to build a black community.

Although the students are allowed free rein in discussing the issue, the editorial hand is visible in the reporter's closing comments:

> Unlike any other black graduating class in history, these young men and women must make up their minds about participating in the Black, and thus the new American, Revolution. Will their search be for middle-class detachment or insightful involvement? This is this mandate to the Class of '68.

The obvious appeal to the youth is the notion of group advancement suggested in the term *insightful involvement*. By posing this in opposition to the notion of middle-class detachment, *Black Journal* works toward promoting the popular views of uplift.

The second segment of the premiere episode serves as a historical survey of the black press. The birth of the black press is traced back to mainstream newspapers' refusal to print antislavery appeals. From here the viewer is taken on a virtual walk through history to learn the importance of *Freedom Journal* (1827), Walker's *Appeal* (1829), Frederick Douglass and the *North Star* (1847), as well as other black papers throughout history, ending with *Black Journal* as a present-day form of the black press. The words of the founders of *Freedom Journal,* "We wish to plead our own cause, too long have others spoken for us," remind the viewer of the continued relevance of the black press. *Black Journal* asserts that the black press gives full coverage to stories ignored by the white media.

Black-owned businesses are the subject of the fourth segment, another push for group advancement. New Breed Clothing, the example used in the episode, promotes itself as "an organization of some 150 Soul Brothers who offer new directions in men's clothing—the Afro-American look . . . designed for the black man of today incorporating elements of his past and present." In the words of New Breed president Jason Bennings, "We are quietly building a nation." The feature incorporates images of a male fashion show with discussions of the clothing design: the suits, jackets, dashikis, and, most impressive of all, the Breed-all—a "Soul Brother" take on the overall. New Breed got its start through selling stock to the black community at one dollar per share and to the Negro Industrial and Economic Union. The central idea of this segment is to impart the concept that, as one designer suggests, "the black man can do whatever he needs to do to be successful. . . . Blacks helping Blacks . . . the white man is an irrelevant person."

A later segment reveals the risks taken by *Black Journal*. Considering the political climate surrounding the Black Panther Party in 1968, the show's choice to tackle that organization within its first program is extraordinary. It again illustrates how *Black Journal* challenged the status quo, resisted mainstream constructions of blackness, and questioned the ruling powers. Again, within a media resource accessible to both black and white audiences, *Black Journal* was able to give an alternate view of the maligned Black Panther Party, which was specifically targeted by the Federal Bureau of Investigation.

Since the 1930s, the FBI monitored black political organizations, but the bureau increased its surveillance in the 1960s with the rising tide of black activism. Under order from President Lyndon B. Johnson in early 1968, COINTELPRO, the FBI counterintelligence program, was specifically charged with targeting the Black Panther Party. FBI director J. Edgar Hoover required agents

"to exploit all avenues of creating . . . dissension within the ranks of the BPP" and called upon field offices to develop and send to bureau headquarters "imaginative and hard-hitting counterintelligence measures aimed at crippling the BPP."[42]

In the *New York Times*, Hoover described the Black Panther Party as

the greatest threat to the internal security of the country. Schooled in the Marxist-Leninist ideology and the teaching of Chinese Communist leader Mao Tse-tung, its members have perpetrated numerous assaults on police officers and have engaged in violent confrontations with police throughout the country. Leaders and representatives of the Black Panther Party travel extensively all over the United States preaching their gospel of hate and violence not only to ghetto residents, but to students in colleges, universities and high schools as well.[43]

The media also actively attacked the Black Panther Party. *Black Journal*'s coverage directly responds to the mainstream media's portrayal of the Black Panther Party. The montage that begins the segment sets up the parameters of the story.

The trial of Huey P. Newton, accused of murdering a policeman, was scheduled to begin July 15 in Oakland, California.[44] The voice-over discusses the party's support of the use of guns in self-defense and its goal of "ridding the ghetto of police brutality and oppression." The segment shows footage of the Black Panther Party's armed entrance into the state Capitol in Sacramento. The narration explains how this incident brought the group to the nation's attention and then discusses a following series of armed confrontations that the police claim were initiated by the Panthers. The Panthers allege that the police were trying to "liquidate their leadership and destroy the party." The story follows one gun battle that led to the death of seventeen-year-old Bobby Hutton, who was shot while surrendering to the police. The journalists of *Black Journal* were not striving for the objectivity so sought after by news journalists of the Golden Age; however, the *Journal* does give time to Oakland Police Chief Gain, who argues:

> There have been many people in this city who have maligned this police department who, through some Mormon sentimentality or some other reason, sympathize with the Black Panthers and the peace and freedom movement. And what really . . . what real evidence is there to cause people to be so sick as to do that maligning? [Holding up a pamphlet] Take a look at this moral and unjustified junk that has been put out . . . Bobby Hutton . . . they try to deify one who tried to murder a policeman, and what do they say on this paper? . . . A black man who dedicated his life to defending the black community from racist oppression was murdered in cold blood by the Oakland Police. Ridiculous lies, ridiculous attempts to create prejudice. The Black Panther Party poses a real threat to the peace and tranquility of the city of Oakland.

However, compared with CBS's coverage of the Watts riots and its placement of Chief Parker as a person of unbiased authority, *Black Journal* goes to greater lengths to explore the other side of the story. The African American position is given more airtime with the interview of Newton from his jail cell and conversation with other Panther members in the Oakland community. What Newton says is worth quoting at length, because it allows one to see the importance of having this material aired on a national forum in counterbalance with the negative views of the organization that were primarily portrayed. The camera alternates between a close-up of Newton and a medium shot, which allows the viewer to observe the cell in which he sits.

COMMENTATOR: The Panthers have a different version of their role. Huey Newton, Panther leader, will soon be on trial for his life. We asked him about the origins of the party and their concept of self-defense.

NEWTON: We use the Black Panther as our symbol because of the nature of a panther. A panther doesn't strike anyone, but when he is assailed upon, he will back up first, but if the aggressor continues, then he will strike out and wipe out his aggressor, thoroughly, wholly, absolutely, and completely. I see the party as a second party rather than a third party, because we see very little difference as far as black people are concerned between the Republican and the Democratic Party here in the United States. We view ourselves as a colonized people, so we are in a situation of a mother country and a colony, and the politics of the mother country have not answered the needs of the black subjects in the colony. So therefore this is a black political party, and it is a vanguard group for the freedom of black people.

Originally our party was called the Black Panther Party for Self-Defense. The name now has been changed to the Black Panther Party, because many people misunderstood the scope of self-defense. The power structure, the establishment, has been aggressive towards us in every area: the social area, the economic area, and the political area. Therefore, we felt it necessary to erect a political party to defend and promote the general interests of black people. Aggression in the economic area is as real as aggression physically by the racist police that occupy our community, as a foreign troop occupies territory.

Bobby Seale, Black Panther minister of information, is interviewed on the streets. He reads the Panther 10 Point Program from the party's newspaper and shows how the group works to further community aims. He cites participation in a boycott of an Oakland grocery store because of unsanitary conditions and the lack of black employees.[45] There are discussions of the policing problems and suggestions that those who police the neighborhood should live in the neighborhood. Finally the *Journal* interviews Carlton Goodlet, a reporter from the *San Francisco Sun Reporter,* the local black weekly, who confirms what the Panthers assert: that the police were the provocateurs and that this situation would lead to the extermination of the Panther Party. The Black Panthers clearly did not receive positive or even fair press coverage from mainstream media sources. *Black Journal* empowered blacks to speak for themselves to a nationwide audience about the issues that have affected their lives.

The goal of empowerment and self-awareness was also conveyed with humor. In a skit entitled "Dateline," comedian Godfrey Cambridge and two white actors tackle the representation of African Americans in the media. The skit is set in Beverly Hills in the fictional "Equality Network—First with Color." Two white men discuss the ways in which they can diversify the network's programming and, in essence, lampoon Hollywood practices regarding black actors. There are jokes about what the average black man would have to look like (Sidney Poitier), how black men could not be next to white women on-screen, and how a nuclear black family could not be represented. By the end of the first show, *Black Journal* targeted issues critical to many parts of the black community with an overall message of uplift, black pride, and ultimately black self-empowerment.[46]

Over the years, *Black Journal* tackled various ways to create debate among black people and to air issues topical to African Americans. A 1969 episode featured blues musician John Lee Hooker, a story on black unions, and a roundtable discussion among major African American male sports figures from different generations: Jackie Robinson, Bill Russell, Arthur Ashe, Johnny Sample, and Harry Edwards. This episode allowed Jackie Robinson to express regret that his generation had not made more strides to change things, as he believed that this would have helped the present generation. In support of Harry Edwards's work with the 1968 black Olympic athletes, especially John Carlos and Tommie Smith, Robinson also mentioned how George Foreman made him "sick inside" when he waved the American flag after he won his fight at the same Olympics as the runners' protest.[47] One episode featured Sammy Davis Jr., who discussed, among other issues, his relationships with white women. Another show, dedicated to black women, featured an interview of Lena Horne by poet Nikki Giovanni.

One specific show exhibited the ways in which television was used to express the concerns of the multifaceted black community. It aired as a ninety-minute live special that featured twelve black commentators of varying viewpoints and sought to address the question, Is it too late (for blacks to survive in any form or capacity in the United States)? The panel was also asked to answer questions and listen to responses from a national audience, which contacted the show through regional call-in centers.[48]

While it is clear that *Black Journal* worked to express and provide an outlet for black politics, culture, and history, the fact that it was on public television did limit its reach.[49] In 1972, the operating budget for the Corporation for Public Broadcasting was approximately 140 million dollars, and the amount spent on programming averaged less than 5 percent of the total amount of money spent on television broadcasting in the country. The corporation's programming also made up only 15 percent of the nation's television programs. There were 700 commercial stations in the country compared with only 233 public television stations.[50]

In an article entitled "Blacks and Public TV," published in *Black Enterprise* magazine, writer James D. Williams, a member of the Advisory Committee of National Organizations to the Corporation for Public Broadcasting, noted that generally African Americans had shown less concern about the practices of the Corporation for Public Broadcasting than about those of commercial television. This was evident in the protests targeting network television over the types of representations. However, public television was primarily funded through tax dollars and therefore had a legal and moral obligation to serve the public. As of 1972, no blacks were in a position to truly affect policy decisions at the Corporation for Public Broadcasting, and only one black, Dr. Gloria L. Anderson, sat on the fifteen-person board of directors. This information supports the notion that broadcasting on public television limited the impact of *Black Journal,* because the forum has lacked the reach of the networks. To further hinder the impact, the show's budget was cut 80 percent after the first year and therefore had to air reruns instead of producing new material.[51] However, *Black Journal's* importance within African American society became even more evident when producers appealed to the audience in national black magazines to protest the loss of financial support of the show.

In the June 1969 issue of *Jet* magazine, William Greaves, then the only black producer in American television, stated that *Black Journal,* the "one oasis in a very large desert [will be dried up this fall for lack of funds;] if the black community across America wants to maintain the show on the air, it must demonstrate its concern through letters, petitions etc."[52] *Ebony* magazine followed in September 1969 with a feature article, "Black TV: Its Problems and Promises," noting *Journal*'s loss of underwriters, the problems faced by other local and independent black TV series, the lack of black sponsorship, black station owners, blacks in the field, and black technical control. Greaves noted here:

> Since the air waves legally belong to the public, they rightfully be-long to Afro-Americans as well. And since blacks share ownership, they should likewise share control. . . . Actually, it's an insult to the black community that 10 per cent of all network budgets aren't geared to black programming.[53]

When Tony Brown became the host of *Black Journal* in June 1970, he was the president of the National Association of Black Media Producers and at that time challenged the licenses of thirty-six radio and television stations in Detroit and several other cities, including Atlanta and Cleveland. Needless to say, Brown was very outspoken about the discrepancies in broadcasting policies and continued to make an appeal to the black public, as his predecessor had. In a 1971 interview, he stated, "Everyone making the deci-sions about what black people will see on TV today is white. That's institutional racism."[54] On that occasion, he noted that even when programs were in the hands of black producers, as *Black Journal* was, station managers could refuse to air a particular episode. This was the case with his episode entitled "Justice," which sought to explore the Angela Davis case and the lives of black prisoners. He received a "forceful letter" from the white program and promotion manager who, after previewing the program, refused to air it.[55]

The show began to realize the power of the viewing audience. NET and *Black Journal* received thousands of letters from the audi-ence, some agreeing, others angry at the viewpoints of a particular guest; some wrote in with suggestions for future shows. One fan wrote about the impact of the show on his life: "Black Journal has opened my eyes to a whole new way in which to live. Because of it, there's a brand new me. Can't thank you enough."[56] Others formed Friends of Black Journal clubs in various cities, which became a political force to be reckoned with. If stations chose to preempt *Black Journal* or change its exhibition time, the organization arranged letter-writing campaigns or other means of protesting the local affiliate. Tony Brown took advantage of this and called on the Friends of Black Journal to rally political support whenever he knew that a white television producer was going to preempt an episode because of content.

Perhaps the clearest example of this support occurred in December 1972. The Corporation for Public Broadcasting released the list of programs it intended to fund for the 1973–74 season. Conspicuously absent were the only two nationally televised black programs: *Soul,* a music-, poetry-, and entertainment-driven program, and *Black Journal. Black Enterprise* reporter James Williams observed that *Black Journal* had drawn the wrath of the Nixon administration and

> [i]ts producer Tony Brown, had become a thorn in the side of the establishment with his often bitter attacks against what he described as racism in public broadcasting. It was no secret that powerful forces in the White House were critical of "Black Journal" over what they regarded as its anti-administration attitude.[57]

Because the membership of the corporation's board had changed to a Republican majority, Nixon planned to use Henry Lomis, the new president of the board and his appointee, to cancel *Black Journal.* The situation was brought to the attention of many in the black community, who not only protested the cancellation of the two programs but also began to question hiring practices evident throughout the corporation, from its central headquarters in Washington DC to its local outlets.

Williams's article in *Black Enterprise* suggests that the Nixon administration grossly underestimated the reaction to its attempts to cancel *Black Journal.*

> It did not realize the importance blacks attached to "Black Journal," nor the even greater importance to them of the threat that a white-dominated, publicly-funded institution might get away with deciding, all on its own, what was best for black people.[58]

The corporation contended with complaints and protests from groups, which included the Friends of Black Journal, the Urban League, the Congressional Black Caucus, the National Newspaper

Publishers Association, as well as numerous individuals who sent letters and a line of picketers outside its offices in Washington DC. The protesters questioned not only the cancellation of *Black Journal* and *Soul* but, as indicated, the racial practices of the corporation as a whole. By February 1973, the corporation backed down and funded *Black Journal* for the following year at its previous funding level of $345,000. Soon after making this announcement, the corporation also declared that it would approach a "cross-section of the black community" in order to survey its members' ideas on the direction that public television should take with black programming. It also offered an additional $305,000 for new black-themed programming. In addition, the corporation was instructed by the board of directors to shape its equal employment practices and to institute an affirmative action plan. A minority-hiring project was also implemented in which fifteen minority people were employed in influential and potentially upwardly mobile positions in local stations, with half of their salaries picked up by the corporation and the rest by the local outlets.[59]

The problems for *Black Journal* were not resolved with the public's involvement, but this process reveals the ways in which the black public impacted the control of the industry. *Black Journal* remained on public television until 1977, although it continued to struggle with PBS over funding and the number of markets that opted to carry the show. For example, in 1974 as part of a new co-operative funding plan to finance public television programs, local stations were allowed to submit program ideas to the Corporation for Public Broadcasting, and ultimately stations were also allowed to decide whether or not they financed a particular show. A controversial show such as *Black Journal* returned to television in 1974 with fewer episodes and only 25 percent of the public broadcasting outlets.[60] The following year *Black Journal*, although again renewed, was programmed for only thirteen weeks and scheduled to air on only forty-two stations.[61]

These public broadcasting decisions may have encouraged producer Tony Brown to move *Black Journal* to commercial television in 1977, with the underwriting of the Pepsi Corporation. It was the first black show to make this type of transition.[62] The show then became *Tony Brown's Journal* but continued to deal with the controversial issues initiated on *Black Journal*. Brown eventually returned the show to PBS in 1981. As he explained, "We did well, but syndication has its own problems. We were in 60 markets, [moving back to PBS now] we will probably be in 200. We'll also appear in better time slots, out of the Sunday morning public affairs ghetto."[63] *Tony Brown's Journal* remains in production on PBS.

On a national level, *Black Journal* challenged the mainstream white imaginings of African American political and social issues; it also confronted the industry that sought to represent black society. Documentary programs such as *CBS Reports,* while touting themselves as objective, were produced in a time when America was attempting to contain rising black social and political movements. *Black Journal* provided a space for black people to speak for themselves in political, social, and cultural arenas.

3. What You See Is What You Get

Soul Train and *The Flip Wilson Show*

In the late 1960s a few more opportunities were created for black talent on television, and black faces were at times seen outside the news. *I Spy* debuted in 1965, and Bill Cosby's acceptability was arguably one of the factors that encouraged the networks to develop other black characters for network television. The networks were also under additional pressure from black political groups in Washington DC to improve and increase their representations of African Americans.[1] Black actors appeared in supporting roles throughout the late 1960s in shows such as *Daktari* (1966–69), *Star Trek* (1966–69), *Mission Impossible* (1966–73), and *The Outcasts* (1968–69).[2] *Julia* premiered in 1968, as did *The Mod Squad* (1968–73), which featured Clarence Williams III as Linc. According to his back story, Linc was taken into custody during the Watts riots and became an undercover police officer for the LAPD. Some episodes of *The Mod Squad* did address social issues, as did episodes of *Room 222* (1969–74), a show about an integrated high school in Los Angeles. *The Bill Cosby Show* (1969–72) cast Cosby as Chet Kincaid, a coach at another fictional Los Angeles high school.

As with *Black Journal*, black television producers at this time continued to carve out spaces for themselves within the industry. Many did not make it, but at the start of the 1970s two significant examples of shows that were produced by blacks and successful on television were *Soul Train* (beginning in 1970), which debuted on the local UHF Chicago station WCUI-TV, and *The Flip Wilson Show* (1970–74), which made its network debut on NBC. The success and failure of these early programs influenced black television artists and producers during the following decade. Unlike *Black Journal*, which dealt directly with political and current news issues affecting black America, *Soul Train* and *The Flip Wilson Show* were music- and entertainment-driven programming. Resistant culture may be more easily perceived in news programs such as *Black Journal*, which as a newsmagazine clearly spoke out against racism and its impact on black society and provided uplifting stories of advancement within the black community. However, entertainment-based programming also took on a critical role in expanding the position of black culture and politics within U.S. society.

Black society has traditionally improvised, finding alternate venues for and modes of political and social action; in the 1960s and 1970s, African Americans used television, among other sites, for such purposes. Outside of network television, avenues of access included local television outlets, arenas that enterprising African Americans such as Don Cornelius utilized for *Soul Train*. Other black performers and producers such as Flip Wilson forged their way into network television. The analysis that follows reveals an uneven legacy. There are moments when these programs are effective in reflecting at least some of the diversity of African American life in the 1970s, resisting narrow views of African Americans proposed by the mainstream U.S. media. At other times the muted voice and image of black life expose the ramifications of working within a white controlled industry at a politically hostile moment.

Peace, Love, and *Soul Train*

Five young African American children gather around a television set arguing about what to watch. The words and animated locomotive for *Soul Train* roar across the screen, and Aretha Franklin is heard singing in the background. The music emitting from the small screen disrupts the argument, and one brother shouts out, "Soul Train line!" Another responds, "Snap, my favorite part of the show." Three of the brothers get off the bed and begin to imitate the dancers on the TV screen, as they move rhythmically down the line.

The men and women in the Soul Train line sport naturals and are dressed in the hip accoutrements of the day—bell bottoms, broad-collared shirts, wide belts, all garments remarkably recaptured today by contemporary designers. The camera that is set up at the end of the line films the dancers as they move without compromise and confront the viewer with their style and rhythm, seemingly challenging the audience to question their ability. The younger sister provokes the boys when they try to perform the latest moves. "Y'all better move, somebody could get hurt . . . You can't dance." To which one of the dancing brothers replies, "Y'all got no soul." The brothers finally get it down and sing and move in time with one another and their onscreen counterparts. The father enters the room and asks them to turn off the TV, to which the boys respond in chorus, "Come on, Dad, we're watching the SO-O-O-U-U-U-U-U-UL Train."

This is a scene from Spike Lee's *Crooklyn* (1994), a moment undoubtedly played out in living rooms across black America in the 1970s, when Don Cornelius brought *Soul Train* to U.S. television. *Soul Train*—the music, the performances, and the dancers—has been a part of African American culture and the American television landscape for the past thirty years. During the 1970s *Soul Train* provided a community-forming locus, which allowed the show to cross the country and motivate a convergence of African American cultural expression and empowerment. As African American cultural critic Todd Boyd explains,

> [T]elevision can provide certain legitimacy, a form of cultural identity for those who see their image represented in an affirmative way. And in a society that had fully adopted the television set as a vital component in the domestic sphere, "Soul Train" assured a black presence when all other forms of representation were leaving something to be desired.[3]

For an accurate understanding of *Soul Train*'s role, it is perhaps best first to explain the significant position of oral culture in African American society, as expressed through radio and popular music in this era. Also, recognizing the influence of black music and culture on American culture as a whole will help to clarify how *Soul Train* became a forum for black cultural politics.

The Oral Tradition: Black Music and Black Radio

[R]adio has historically been so intimately connected with the consciousness of blacks that it remained their primary source of entertainment and information well into the age of television. Even in today's

VCR- and CD-filled era, black radio plays a huge role in shaping black taste and opinion.

Nelson George, *The Death of Rhythm and Blues*

African American culture is rooted in an oral tradition.

Ben Sidran, *Black Talk*

The African oral traditions of storytelling, the passing of myths, and music were used by slaves as a means of navigating the hostile environment of slavery. Music was used in work songs, as a means of subversion and escape, and as a mode of expressing the horror of their circumstances. As Amiri Baraka explains in *Blues People,* African American music developed from

> the most salient characteristic of African, or at least West African, music . . . a type of song in which there is a leader and a chorus; the leading lines of the song sung by a single voice, the leader's, alternating with a refrain sung by the "chorus."[4]

This was reflected in the early call-and-response structure of slave work songs, blues, and gospel. Cultural legacy and historical necessity continue to make oral tradition a crucial component of African American society and cultural production, across changing times and technologies.

In *The Death of Rhythm and Blues,* African American music and cultural critic Nelson George discusses the development of the African American oral tradition and describes the role of black radio and the deejay as central to this evolution. In post–World War II America, black radio stations became an arena for community announcements and black business advertisements and a platform for black independent music. The 1950s saw the emergence of the black personality deejays, "inheritors of the oral tradition."[5] These deejays embraced the role of the leader in the call-and-response structure. The African American audience is positioned as the chorus or respondents, interpellated by the news and the styles and personalities of the deejays. Al Benson, a Chicago deejay, was considered a forerunner of this style and one of the first deejays to avoid passing or sounding white on radio. His "black everyman's style" influenced deejays across America. The commercial success of Benson in Chicago led to the rise of black deejays ensconced in the oral tradition.

> A listener up on his black history might have realized that these nighttime motor mouths were very much the inheritors of the black oral tradition that spawned Br'er Rabbit, Mr. Mojo, and other rural tricksters created by Afro Americans during their forced vacation in the "New World." Yet for all the cornpone some laid on listeners, they were often as urban as the corner of Lennox and 125th Street.

The combination of these elements tapped into African American traditions and created a sense of community for the black audience.[6]

As the appeal of these announcers and the popularity of the music grew, white radio stations that had previously denied access to black announcers sought to move into the R&B market and began to hire blacks as consultants to help white deejays sound like the black deejays. The influence of black music was officially recognized with the release of the 1971 Harvard Report, which stated:

> The fact that 30 percent of the top 40 is composed of records which have "crossed-over" from soul stations underscores the strategic importance of soul stations as one of the most effective vehicles for getting on to the top 40. . . . In sum soul radio is of strategic importance to the record companies for two principal reasons: first, it provides access to a large and growing record-buying public, namely, the black consumer. Second, and for some of the record companies more important, it is perhaps the most effective way of getting a record to a Top 40 playlist.[7]

This report concluded what black people had known for a long time: that their music and culture as a whole not only had influence but also were constantly absorbed and co-opted by the mainstream. Even with the paradoxical nature of these situations, it was evident that black music and black style were continuing to make a major impact on American society.[8]

Other venues of absorption and co-optation included the film industry. In the mainstream venue, independently produced films such as *Sweet Sweetback's Baadasssss Song* (1971), *Shaft* (1971), and *Superfly* (1972) made strides toward a more empowered African American filmic image. Yet many of the films of the Blaxploitation movement that followed, although providing the audience a cultural catharsis and a release from the narrow roles of Sidney Poitier, were often scripted and directed by white Hollywood studio personnel.[9] Therefore, although the films often spoke the politics of black empowerment, because of the production environment they proved less exemplary of the mandates of Black Nationalism at its many levels.[10]

The significance of black radio was exemplified on the night that Martin Luther King Jr. was assassinated. Radio provided a source of calm and reason in the nation's black communities. As Del Shields, jazz deejay on New York's WLIB, describes:

> [O]n the night Dr. King was killed, all across America every black station was tested and everybody who was on the air at that time, including myself, told people to cool it. We tried to do everything possible to keep the black people from just exploding even more than what they were. . . . When America looked at black radio in that particular period, it suddenly hit them that this was a potent force. If, in every major city, a black disc jockey had said, "Rise up," there would have been pandemonium.[11]

The impact and influence of black radio, and the understanding of the strength and community created among deejay, music, and audience, brought Don Cornelius from black radio to television and the concept of *Soul Train*.

Soul Train: The Oral and Visual Tradition

Don Cornelius began his broadcasting career as newsreader and swingman, a deejay who covered open slots at Chicago's WVON in the 1960s. Frustrated by his inability to garner his own show, he began to look for another creative outlet for his work. As Cornelius explained, "It was with the advent of black radio that I thought black people would watch music television programs oriented toward themselves."[12] He began a second job at WCIU-TV, a local UHF station that was developing some minority programming. Cornelius worked as sports anchor on *A Black's View of the News* and formed a relationship with the station owners, to whom he pitched the idea of a black dance show patterned after Dick Clark's *American Bandstand*. Cornelius invested his own money to create a pilot for *Soul Train*, which he then took to the merchandising manager for the five Sears, Roebuck stores located in

Chicago's inner-city community. With Sears as a sponsor and with an agreement from WCIU-TV, *Soul Train* premiered in Chicago on August 17, 1970.

Whereas the combination of black dance and music was historically relegated to segregated or black and tan clubs, *Soul Train* brought this aspect of black life into the very public forum of television. Cornelius describes his vision of *Soul Train*:

> Our responsibility, as we see it, is to present to the black market visually what they've been hearing on the radio. And to give exposure to those artists that don't get invited to do any other free television.[13]

> I formatted it to be the radio show I always wanted to have. . . . To this day, it's still paced in the direction of a radio show. It never really slows down or engages in discussion or long interviews. . . . I started to interject some of the schtick I liked to use on radio. It came off kind of different for television, given what the eye and ear is used to.[14]

The low-budget technical aspects of the early series did not prohibit the show from hitting a nerve in Chicago. *Soul Train* filled the need for a recognition and celebration of blackness.[15] According to Cornelius, "Overnight, everyone in Chicago knew who I was. . . . the show was the talk of the town."[16]

Cornelius then made efforts to syndicate the show nationwide. Many sponsors ignored *Soul Train,* but Cornelius received the support and advertising dollars of Johnson's Products, the primary manufacturer of black beauty products. In October 1971, *Soul Train* made a debut in eight markets and was very successful. However, television stations were difficult to convince about the possibilities and profitability of niche marketing.

> Of the 15 markets we initially had tentative agreements with, only eight really came through. But we increased our projections gradually and within a year we were in 25 markets. In two years we were probably in 50 and after three or four years, we were up to a hundred markets. . . . The difference, was that our markets were just hard in coming. . . . It was simply because I [Cornelius and the show] was Black! . . . It took us three years or so to get New York. And you must have this market if you are to be taken seriously.[17]

With the major cities under his belt, Cornelius was able to take *Soul Train* to a truly representative national audience. The show caught on quickly and became the benchmark for style and hipness in 1970s American society. Boyd explains, "'Soul Train' was black style personified. . . . [It] offered blackness in its funkified essence. As the show's tag line suggested, it was "the hippest trip in America."[18] Elsewhere Boyd is quoted as saying, "'Soul Train' showed a generation what it meant to be cool. There's something about [the show] that suggested hipness. And if you wanted to be hip, you watched 'Soul Train.' . . . In the '70s, there was no other place to see this in the mainstream."[19]

Three central components of *Soul Train* established the show as a cultural and social institution in the 1970s: Cornelius as host and the politics he embodied, the Soul Train dancers, and the guest performers and their music.

Don Cornelius brought the vibe of black radio to the visual forum and, in doing so, became an African American cultural figure of significance. As hip-hop artist Mc'Shell NdegeOcello stated after performing on *Soul Train,*

> When Don came up to me, he said, "Me'Shell, um, um, that's a very unusual last name. But I love your music." I flipped . . . I was in heaven. That was like the epitome of black culture giving me his blessing. All I have to do is be in Jet magazine and I can die with a smile on my face.[20]

Cornelius also brought the politics of the historical moment to the screen, especially as it reflected the mandates of Black Nationalism. One of the key edicts of Black Nationalism, in any of its many renderings, is the importance of black self-sufficiency, especially blacks' ownership of their own businesses. *Soul Train* has been a black-owned enterprise from conception to presentation. *Soul Train* has bridged the concerns of black image and black control of a business. Cornelius staffed the program with a black technical and production staff and, through its formatting and advertising, targeted a black audience.

> I [Cornelius] had some pressure in the beginning to make it more mixed, to get more whites and to try to make it more of a crossover show. But I just instinctively resisted it. If whites come to participate, they come. We don't discourage them. And if they don't come,

we don't encourage them. . . . If a show is predominantly black in personnel [both] behind the scenes and in front of the camera, the nature of this country is that most white people are not going to be comfortable there.[21]

Second, the dancers were a significant part of this black address and what some may argue to be the key part of the show in its early decades. As Boyd emphasizes, "[T]he true stars of 'Soul Train' were the dancers. These dancers were 'real' black people, representing the common man and woman—doing the latest dances, wearing the hippest clothes and sporting those fly hairdos."[22] Cornelius was specific about the casting of these dancers. Although it may be part legend, a component of the show's lure was the absence of auditioning: there was only one audition to be a Soul Train dancer and that was for the first show. The only way to be on the show after that was through a recommendation from another regular Soul Train dancer. According to Cornelius, "People who dance well, dress well, are well groomed and know how to behave seem to know others who dance, dress and behave well."[23] The show's cast was therefore a close-knit family group, which was evident in the production.

Except for meals, the seventy or so high school and college students were unpaid. One weekend a month they taped four shows,

The Soul Train dancers are key to the success of the program.

back to back, at Metromedia's Hollywood studios. In 1974 an observer for *TV Guide* noted that the shows were filmed at these odd times because they were "the only time the real stars of the show can make it."[24] As he described, these nonprofessionals set the style for the American public.

> To the untuned-in observer it is audio-visual anarchy—every dance style from Golliwog's Cakewalk to Martha Graham. Ballet. Acrobatic. Eccentric. Jitterbug. Bugaloo. But mostly unidentifiable Free-style Soul. That is, until Pam Brown (Soul Train Dance Leader) points out couples doing the Robot, the Manikin, the Breakdown—three of the fad-dances that have originated on the show. Dress and hair styles are even more profuse. Bells, cuffs and tights. Tank tops, turtle necks, ruffles. Jeans, knickers, minis, maxis. Bow ties, scarves, stoles, chains and chokers. Unisex earrings and bracelets. Clogs, platforms, Adidas. Afros, cornrows, skinheads and pigtails. Sequined matadors, straight-arrow Harold Teens. Gatsbys, Po' Boys, Sportin' Lifes, American Graffitis. Rita Hayworths and Billie Holidays. Clothes out of the '20s, '30s, '40s, '50s, and '70s.[25]

In the 1970s the Soul Train dancers primarily performed to the music of contemporary black artists. As music critic Nelson George stated, "The potential of having an artist exposed to a mass market, which 'Soul Train' provided, made major record labels take black artists more seriously."[26] The list of guest appearances on *Soul Train* reads like a who's who list of black artists of that decade, many of whom have cultural currency today. Curtis Mayfield, B.B. King, Al Green, the Four Tops, Smokey Robinson, Kool and the Gang, Lou Rawls, Ike and Tina Turner, Barry White, the Temptations, Stevie Wonder, Aretha Franklin, the Supremes, the Jackson Five, Michael Jackson, and Marvin Gaye all made guest appearances. The show also featured cameos by Fred Williamson, Cicely Tyson, Lola Falana, Richard Pryor, Melvin Van Peebles, and Reverend Jesse Jackson, to name a few.[27] The relationship between *Soul Train* and black music was symbiotic, and the combination of these elements led to communal moments that had distinct political ramifications.

For example, during the 1972–73 season, James Brown made an appearance on the show. Brown, although representative of often-contradictory politics, was a model of black entrepreneurship and self-sufficiency.[28] Unlike the majority of guest appearances, in which the musicians lip-synched to the recorded track, Brown provided a live performance. During his rendition of his 1968 hit "Say It Loud, I'm Black and I'm Proud," he had a special shout out to the Soul Train audience, repeating the refrain "Soul Train . . . say it loud," to which they responded, "I'm black and I'm proud." In traditional call-and-response fashion, Brown, the Soul Train dancers, and the wider audience of the black viewing community presented a clear moment of black self-affirmation and self-pride, helping to transition national television into a highly visible black communal space.

As the decades progressed, in recognition of the inequities that continued to plague African Americans, Cornelius recognized the need for public recognition of black musical artists who were largely ignored by mainstream awards shows. In 1985 he established the Soul Train Music Awards and, in 1995, the Soul Train Lady of Soul Awards.

> There was not a legitimate avenue to recognize African-American music. . . . [Black music was] relegated to the status of an afterthought, within the context and framework of most award shows. . . . [Blacks] just don't get the kind of recognition anywhere else [that] they do here.[29]

In recent years, these musicians have received mainstream American recognition; however, they understand the importance of *Soul Train* as an essentially black space and have echoed Cornelius's sentiments. As multi-Grammy winner Luther Vandross stated,

> Oh, I love my Grammys, I really do. . . . But there's always been a question as to whether they were in the same rhythm as black folks. I mean, that year George Michael received a best R&B award at the American Music Awards—whew! I'm prepared for anything now with those shows.[30]

African American artist Anita Baker also recognized the importance of the show. She commented that she continued to participate because it was like a family reunion and "[b]ecause it's really for us. . . . On shows like this, we're just saying thanks to an institution that through the years has given us exposure first. One we can always depend on."[31]

Cornelius is quick to address why the show survived music videos when *American Bandstand* closed its doors in 1989. He argues that

MTV was a white medium at its inception; "no black face went on MTV for the first five or six years."[32] So, through the early 1980s, *Soul Train* continued to provide an outlet for black artists who could not find a space on mainstream television. The situation at MTV has ultimately changed because of commercial mandates and has become one of the primary outlets for black musicians. However, a quick survey of the artists who have appeared on *Soul Train* in the 1990s and today reveals that the show attempts to maintain a contemporary cultural currency. The show booked artists such as Ice Cube, Snoop Doggy Dogg, Lil' Kim, Foxy Brown, Nelly, Ginuwine, Floetry, and India.Arie with a shout out to the past with appearances by Chakka Khan, Stevie Wonder, and the Isley Brothers.[33]

Cornelius's work on *Soul Train* is never finished, and although he withdrew as the regular host in 1993, he still struggles to keep the show on the air, in as many markets as possible and at decent hours. He also remains candid about the difficulty of maintaining black shows on commercial television.

> The things we've had to overcome to get where I am today still have NOT been overcome. . . . It's still difficult to get certain aspects of the TV media to accept the concept of ethnic or black-oriented television. We still have to fight our way onto TV stations.[34]

Soul Train features both classic and contemporary artists, such as Stevie Wonder (center) and Don Cornelius (far right).

I might be inclined to accept it if you tell me, "Hey, we have another black show that is more relevant that we put on at a more decent hour." Or something of a higher quality. But in every instance that's the only black show we have there. And this is based on a music genre that is more powerful now than it has been in its history.[35]

Soul Train remains the longest running syndicated show on television.[36]

Soul Train's relevancy has been directly tied to the era of the 1970s and this watershed moment of black politics. The convergence of the conflicting Civil Rights and Black Power movements, the agenda of integration, and yet the continuing need for black spaces revealed the essential importance of shows such as *Soul Train*. Within this exact social and political climate, *The Flip Wilson Show* took the route of network televisual integration by securing a position in the fall 1970 schedule of NBC. NBC was certainly not an exclusively black space. But could Flip Wilson use this exposure, as Don Cornelius had, to address an African American audience specifically and to encourage a feeling of black community during a time of political and social upheaval?

Flip Wilson: Mediating Blackness on Network Television

I wasn't the first black to headline a variety show . . . but I was the first with a successful variety show. Nat Cole had one. Sammy Davis Jr. had one. The difference was theirs just didn't click. My show went on right after the assassinations of Martin Luther King and Robert Kennedy and racial turmoil was at its peak. And still my show clicked with people of all races.

Flip Wilson, in David Martindale, "Flip Wilson Clicked at the Right Time"

What made Flip Wilson's show "click" in the early 1970s? Approximately sixteen other variety shows were on the three networks when *The Flip Wilson Show* premiered.[37] Also, race relations were in turmoil, as evidenced by the uprisings in many major cites in the years preceding the show's premiere. The rise of the Black Power movement and the politics of Black Nationalism in the late 1960s led to an even more directly confrontational relationship between many of America's black and white citizens. Yet, Wilson's show, which aired from September 1970 to June 1974, was highly rated, placed second among all television programs during its first two seasons, and won two Emmys, one for Outstanding Writing Achievement for a Variety Show and the other for Best Variety Series. In 1971, Wilson even made the cover of the illustrious mainstream magazine *Time*.[38] His commercial spots in 1971 were among the most expensive on network television.[39] How did Wilson bridge this divide, and what was sacrificed in the transition to mainstream American acceptance and embrace?

The Personal and the Visual Politics of Flip Wilson

> Funny is not a color. . . . Being black is only good from the time you get from the curtain to the microphone. . . . my main point is to be funny. If I can slip a message in there, fine. . . . Things can be funny only when we are in fun. . . . When we're "dead earnest," humor is the only thing that is dead.
>
> **Flip Wilson, in Mel Watkins, "Flip Wilson, 64,**
> **Over-the-Top Comic and TV Host, Dies"**

Flip Wilson's death at the age of sixty-four in November 1998 was unexpected and came amid a revival of the show on Nick at Nite's TV Land and rumors of a possible comeback effort. Comedian Steve Allen's words to KCBS-TV in Los Angeles suggest the way that Wilson has been remembered in the American imagination: "Nobody ever sent him a postcard objecting to any of his humor. . . . There was no vulgarity, there was no sleaze, there were no shock jokes. It was just funny."[40] A particular letter to the op-ed column of the *Washington Post* reiterates this point.

> The most wonderful thing about Flip Wilson was that he had only one agenda and that was upfront: to be funny and to make others enjoy his brand of humor as much as he did.
>
> For those of us who grew up with him, his non-expletive, non-political, non-topical humor will surely be missed.
>
> J. N. VOROBEY
> Falls Church[41]

This was not an unusual response; indeed, it is representative of the sentiments expressed in many of the articles and letters that appeared in newspapers across the country upon Wilson's passing.

What is evident here is not only the notion of acceptability and embrace on many levels but also the public perception of the humor that Wilson brought with him to the small screen. It is clear to me after watching many of the episodes that Flip Wilson was primarily a storyteller and situational comic. As Redd Foxx describes,

> He was known for his ability to tell a story. But it was his antics, along with the storytelling, that the public enjoyed. . . . he doesn't rely on monologues laced with one-liners. When he's telling a story, his phrases are emphasized with body motion, facial expressions, and funny voices. He acts out the entire story, character by character.[42]

His humor was not threatening and rarely addressed the contemporary American social and political landscape. His humor was not made up of biting political satire, and Wilson generally did not show a disdain for the racist politics evident in American society. Indeed, he forwarded an all-American, individualist agenda; he was the "pulled himself up by the bootstraps" archetype, the image that continually purports the notion of the classless and raceless American society.[43] In comparison to Richard Pryor's humor, which was overtly critical of mainstream U.S. society, Flip Wilson appeared a mild-mannered, unthreatening, and congenial comedian. He was easily dismissed and condemned by many of the more militant groups within black America for his seeming lack of engagement with black political issues. But was his humor nonpolitical?

While *Black Journal* used television to expose a black and mainstream audience to political and social issues within the black community, *The Flip Wilson Show* essentially avoided using the genre of the comedic variety show as a forum for confrontational black politics. Traditionally, the variety show as a genre was a showcase for skit comedy with musical and dance numbers. Many African American stars have made appearances on these shows throughout television's history. Although other African Americans had hosted their own variety shows—Nat King Cole, Sammy Davis Jr., and Leslie Uggams—Flip Wilson was the first African American to maintain high ratings and thus keep his show on the air. However, although he rejected the militant rhetoric of the time period, his work still had a political impact.

The Flip Wilson Show introduced aspects of black and urban black culture to the mainstream venue of television. Wilson's engagement in Chitlin' Circuit humor was apparent and appreciated by black audiences raised on this type of comedy. He also brought this to a mainstream audience, thus expanding the knowledge of aspects of black culture within U.S. society. He did not disguise his blackness, and his routines were based in traditional African American comedy. *The Flip Wilson Show* also brought many known and unknown African American entertainers to the public forum of television. Wilson used his position to increase their access to mainstream venues. This is a political act.

His comedy and the characters that he created had a lot to do with Wilson's upbringing. Therefore, it is relevant to explore his roots briefly in order to understand the transition of his comedy to the mainstream and also his somewhat ambiguous position as an African American celebrity in the early 1970s.

Clerow Wilson was born in New Jersey on December 8, 1933, and had seventeen brothers and sisters. As Wilson describes, "We were so poor, even the poorest looked down on us."[44] When his mother left the family, Wilson, then seven, was put into foster care, ran away several times, ended up in reform school, and did not return to his father's care until he was thirteen. When he was sixteen, he lied about his age, saying he was older, in order to join the air force. There, he gained the nickname "Flip," because he often related stories in a multitude of dialects. This led his service buddies to say that he was "flipping out." The name stuck, and Flip kept it when he was discharged in 1954. He began his professional comedy career at the Manor Plaza Hotel in San Francisco, where he managed to convince the owner to allow him, then the bellhop, to perform a comedy act at the hotel's nightclub.

Like many of the black comedians before him, in the following years Wilson performed in many of the small black clubs on the West Coast and then across the country. He worked on his skills in front of black audiences and began to introduce the characters that would eventually appear on his variety show.

> I got a special feeling working before black audiences. . . . I worked at a higher energy level when I was working in those little black clubs where people came in at the end of the week with about $20 and wanted to have a good time. You gotta get their attention, hold their interest. And to do that it takes a certain talent—you gotta work hard, keep the energy up.[45]

In 1960 he managed to get on the Chitlin' Circuit and was exposed to larger audiences. He made regular appearances at the Apollo in Harlem and was often engaged as the emcee. Wilson was thrust into the spotlight after Redd Foxx's 1965 appearance on NBC's *Tonight Show* with Johnny Carson. When asked to name the funniest comedian at that time, Foxx immediately said Flip Wilson. Wilson was booked on *The Tonight Show* numerous times and reportedly was the guest host seventy times for Carson. He took this opportunity to introduce other African American entertainers to *The Tonight Show* audience, including the Four Tops, Nina Simone, and the Dells.[46] This led to Flip's appearances on *The Today Show, Mike Douglas, Merv Griffin,* and *Rowan and Martin's Laugh-In* and an eventual exclusive, five-year development deal with NBC. He recorded the comedy album *Flip Wilson, You Devil You,* which won the Grammy award for Best Comedy Recording in 1968. That year he also hosted a television special, and in September 1970 *The Flip Wilson Show* premiered on NBC.

The Flip Wilson Show was a variety show, based on comedic vignettes and stand-up, and was aired at 8 p.m., during the family hour. It was "comedy in the round"—the audience was seated around the stage and became a part of the show's setting. Usually a musical act was performed, either solo or with Wilson. For example, the first episode of the series begins with a monologue by Wilson describing what the show will encompass. In the next segment Big Bird sings about the alphabet and dances in circles with Wilson until he passes out. He wakes to say, "This equal opportunity is killing me." In the following skit Flip introduces Reverend Leroy and the Church of What's Happening Now. The show closes with David Frost interviewing Geraldine, who ends the segment with a song, "All of Me." Bob Henry, the white producer of *The Flip Wilson Show,* explains,

> When Flip was doing the show, every fiber of his being was going at full speed. . . . For four years, he did one hour of comedy every week, except for two musical numbers. At times, he would say to me, "I wish there could be a little less of me on the show," but I told him that was the appeal.[47]

African American historian Mel Watkins suggests that Wilson's comedy was able to appeal and cross over to the American audience because of the path carved out before him by comedians such as Bill Cosby and Godfrey Cambridge, whom America accepted because of their colorless everyman style.[48] Many cultural critics argue that the rise in visibility of black comics indicated that mainstream America had grown accustomed to their presence. However, it is also important to note that by 1970, the continuing efforts of the Civil Rights movement and the rising Black Power movement across the country mandated that America must eventually deal with its black citizens.

Popular culture has consistently been a means through which the United States has addressed and expressed its internal conflicts. *I Spy* and *Julia* were examples of television's early attempts in the Civil Rights and Black Power era to address the integrating presence of African Americans, at least within a middle-class discourse of blackness. Flip Wilson brought a little more of the working class and urban black with him.

Like Norman Mailer's "white Negro," 1970s white America could experiment with blackness, hipness, and cool within the safe constraints of television.[49] Flip Wilson became white America's vehicle for cultural catharsis, as he expressed a distinct black, urban vibe, but unlike the so-called angry inner-city mobs, more critical black comedians, and programs such as *Black Journal,* Wilson was contained, clean, and uplifting. Bob Henry summed up the situation:

> It just so happens that I was on The Nat "King" Cole Show in 1957 and what killed us was that black was not beautiful in those days and Madison Avenue wouldn't go out and sell us. . . . [Flip] comes along at a time when black is in. . . . White people love Flip because even though his early life was bittersweet, he seems to be able to tone down the bitter and retain the sweet—unlike many other black comedians.[50]

The mainstream critics at the time echoed this sentiment: John Leonard, a *Life* magazine critic, describes Flip's work: "What Flip Wilson has accomplished is almost incredible in a time of Black Panthers and savage rhetoric. . . . He has taken the threat out of the fact of blackness."[51] A *Time* magazine writer supported this idea and took it one step further in analyzing the U.S. political environment: "Mr. Wilson is not just a black comedian, any more than Jack Benny is just a Jewish comedian. . . . His humor is universal. He has the talent to make blacks laugh without anger and whites laugh without guilt."[52] This was Wilson's edge—his unthreatening appeal and his ability to quell any white angst over the state of blackness. Here, mainstream Americans could sit back and laugh with a black man who had clearly made it. Indeed, Flip Wilson was used as a token at a time when many African Americans struggled for basic rights. Wilson's success indicated that the problems of black society were the fault not of racism but of the individual's lack of effort.

Being used as a token cannot happen without the compliance of the artist at some level. In media interviews Wilson was very clear about his career and economic goals. Understandably, he did not want the life of poverty he had experienced in childhood. In magazines he often spoke of his twenty-year plan. He studied the lives and careers of many famous comedians, and he found that it took most famous comics fifteen years to learn their craft and five years for the public to realize their talent. Therefore, instead of staying with the air force and seeking retirement after twenty years, he explained, "I decided to bet 20 years on me. . . . I just didn't notice too many millionaire sergeants hangin' around."[53] To achieve this lifestyle he professed an integrationist agenda.

> I've always been aware that I'm Black, of course. . . . But I don't think it's a factor in my show. . . . I will succeed or fail on the merits of the show. . . . Humor is a deep emotion in people. Laughter can make them forget a lot of things. . . . My approach is based on pleasing myself and I'm difficult to please. There won't be any messages on my show. What I want to get across is that brotherhood can work.[54]

"Messages" had to be sacrificed in order to achieve this integration, yet the final sentence of the quotation entails a "race-blind message."

From the beginning of his comedy career, Wilson shaped his act so that a wide audience would accept him. Even on the Chitlin' Circuit, Wilson's act was typically devoid of profanity and overt sexual humor. He therefore changed little in his style to appear on network television.[55] Even Richard Pryor told him, "You're the only performer that I've seen who goes on the stage and the audience hopes that you like them."[56] Apparently, as his character Geraldine would express, with Flip Wilson "what you see is what you get."

So what, therefore, did Wilson bring to U.S. television? Did he forward any black agenda or resist mainstream co-optation? Flip Wilson brought distinctly African American characters to the mainstream and provided a space for black entertainers of the past and the present. While Wilson increased the mainstream knowledge of traditional African American comedy, the program also specifically addressed an African American community through the notion of "hidden transcripts."[57] A black audience familiar with the characters in many of the skits was able to understand these performances on a different level and recognize a different level of humor in them, and therefore the show served as a community-forming locus.

Wilson was clearly in his element when he presented the numerous African American characters he developed on the show. Regulars included Herbie; the Good Time ice cream man, who despised children; Freddie Johnson, the Mack, who wore the crushed-velvet suits recently resurrected by Austin Powers; and Charlie the chef. His most famous and lasting portrayals were the Reverend Leroy of the Church of What's Happening Now and Geraldine Jones. Wilson was occasionally accused of reincarnating the stereotypes of Steppin' Fetchit and *Amos 'n' Andy*. However, this critique was based on the tenets of uplift, the fear of what white America would think of the black characters that Wilson presented.

Wilson lampooned the black church with his character Reverend Leroy, who was based on his Washington Heights childhood preacher, Reverend Ike. In 1971 he told the New York *Daily News*, "I was very impressed with him, and I was always amazed that he wasn't well-educated. But, in his simple way, he was dynamic and exciting."[58] Wilson's act has a historical basis. The African American relationship with institutionalized religion is rooted in contention.[59] Stripped from their homeland and their own religious practices, Africans were forced into accepting Christianity, the same religion that provided the justification for slavery. The notion of suffering today for the benefits to be gained in the afterlife was indoctrinated into the slaves with the hopes of their developing acceptance of their circumstances. When the black church came into its own, it also began to reflect the class divisions in African American society.[60]

In the 1920s, Carter G. Woodson's seminal work, *The Miseducation of the Negro*, echoed these concerns; while acknowledging the important role that religion could have, Woodson warned, "It is very clear, then, that if Negroes got their conception of religion from slaveholders . . . there may be something wrong about it, and it would not hurt to investigate it."[61] However, these are concerns that many African Americans would prefer to keep within the black community and behind the closed doors of the black church.

When Wilson took this character to weekly television, there was an acknowledgment of the incongruities of the church. Reverend Leroy, while preaching the word of God, was unethical, and there were constant allusions to his spending church money inappropriately. He was also lecherous and made many sexual comments about the female members of the congregation. Reverend Leroy was introduced in the first episode of *The Flip Wilson Show* and begins the skit from the pulpit with church announcements, a segment of the service familiar to churchgoers. However, these announcements incorporate Wilson's distinctive humor. He informs the congregation, "The combination baptism and beach party scheduled for this Sunday, I am very sorry to tell you, we had to postpone it due to the oil slick." He also introduces a new trading stamp program to encourage church attendance. Trading stamps were redeemable at Mom's Barbecue Palace, located next to the church.

Later in the skit he attempts to guilt the congregation into giving money.

> REVEREND LEROY: For five years we've been planning Angels on Parade, and it hasn't gone on yet. Now this year we're gonna put it on, assuming we can solve our money problems. Yes, we got MON-EY problems. Friends, we don't have enough money for costumes, we in bad trouble. These, Brothers and Sisters— *(Three women in angel robes walk in, and Reverend Leroy puts his arm around one woman and looks her up and down.)* How you doing there, mama? These sisters need costumes. You know that these angels don't even have a harp to pluck on?
>
> FEMALE ANGEL: We got harps! *(He quickly covers her mouth with his hand to keep her quiet.)*
>
> REVEREND LEROY: Can I get an Amen?
>
> CONGREGATION: Amen.
>
> REVEREND LEROY: *(Under this breath)* Send the kid in. *(In full voice)* Brothers and Sisters, we got to make this a show we can be proud of. So it's got to be done right, got to be done right. *(Under his breath)* Send the kid in.
>
> *(A small angel arrives.)*
>
> REVEREND LEROY: Brother Edwin, how you doing? Brother Edwin. Can I get an Amen for Brother Edwin?
>
> CONGREGATION: Amen, Brother Edwin.
>
> REVEREND LEROY: Brothers and Sisters, we've gone as far as we can go. *(He turns Brother Edwin so that his back faces the audience, revealing that he has only one wing.)* Now, we need another wing, got to have another wing. We can't let this little angel come in on a wing and a prayer.

Reverend Leroy is a critique of the black church.

Unlike Flip Wilson's humor, that of other comedians is more easily cited with written examples, but placing Flip Wilson's comedy onto the page somewhat limits its impact because it was based so much on the performance. The physical moves, as he sashayed around the podium of his church and called out for an "Amen" from the crowd, were unique.[62] However, the skit above does address critical issues within the black church. Raising money from the congregation is a constant task. Reverend Leroy's use of a small boy as bait and the oppositional comments of the female angel, which indicate that the church may not need as much as the reverend suggests, question the honesty of the preacher. While a black audience viewing this could value the humor, the fear of what a white audience might think was certainly an issue for anyone concerned with portraying an uplifting view of the black community.

Wilson's most popular character by far was Geraldine Jones, who, he said, "carried me longer than my mother did."[63] Geraldine gained such prominence in the early 1970s that several of her expressions, "The devil made me do it," "What you see is what you get" (the phrase was captured in a 1971 popular R&B song by the Dramatics and used to describe the Apple computer system in the 1980s—WYSIWYG), and "When you're hot, you're hot; when you're not, you're not," entered the American lexicon. Wilson performed Geraldine's voice in his stand-up but was truly able to bring her to life in all her glory on his show.

> I noticed when comics spoke about women, they either knocked their wives or their mothers-in-law. They were always putting women down. So I said, well, I'm going to go the other way. I'm going to make a positive image of a female character. . . . When it came time to do the show I said, damn! Who am I going to get to play her? . . . I said, well, maybe I can get somebody to do it and I can ad-lib from offstage. Then a voice in the back of my mind said, "Are you kidding?" Anything that any great person has done has been a bold step. So I said, well, let me boldly step into my panty hose.[64]

Yet some critics said Geraldine was reminiscent of Sapphire from *Amos 'n' Andy*. Again, this was a knee-jerk reaction to the exploration of black characters on network television. Geraldine was strong, sharp, stylish, and had a cutting wit and a sense of self-assurance.

Flip Wilson created Geraldine to counteract negative female representations by other black comics.

The secret of my success with Geraldine is that she's not a put-down of women. . . . She's smart, she's trustful, she's loyal, she's sassy. Most drag impersonations are a drag. But women can like Geraldine, men can like Geraldine, everyone can like Geraldine.[65]

In one episode Geraldine takes on Muhammad Ali. She flirts with him endlessly and has the normally overpowering Ali wrapped around her finger. She interrupts the loquacious Ali constantly until he admits, "I thought I could talk, but I met my match." She persuades Ali to speak to Killer on a phone in her purse and then makes fun of him for believing that there were actually such things as "pocketbook telephones." In a day before cell phones, the joke works quite well.

When Ali discusses his upcoming fight with Joe Frazier, Geraldine pulls him aside and says, "Come over here; I don't want them to hear this, is between me and you." Geraldine encourages Ali to win his fight but says, "Don't hurt him, because he is one of us." Geraldine reiterates the point several times by repeating the line "He is one of *us*" (emphasis added). Through Geraldine, Wilson was allowed to acknowledge the importance of black unity within an African American community at that historical moment, a black community that was separate from the wider U.S. community that he entertained on a weekly basis.

Outside of character interpretations, Wilson also presented readings of key moments in history from a black perspective. The following is a sketch with Christopher Columbus and Queen Isabella.

> COLUMBUS: If I don't discover America, there's not gonna be a
> Benjamin Franklin, or a "Star-Spangled Banner," or a land of
> the free, or a home of the brave—and no Ray Charles.
> QUEEN ISABELLA: *(Responds screaming)* Chris, go on! Find Ray
> Charles! He goin' to America on that boat. What you say!

Wilson's endeavors to bring these aspects of black life to the small screen caused some embarrassment to the black middle-class sensibilities of a segment of the audience. However, this was familiar imagery to an African American audience, raised on the comedy of vaudeville and the Chitlin' Circuit.[66]

Flip Wilson presented a contradictory figure, especially as it pertained to African American notions of uplift. On the one hand, the characters that Wilson presented caused concern; some African American critics viewed these as demeaning and minstrelesque. On the other hand, as host of a popular network variety show, he was a symbol of African American success, middle- and upper-class respectability, and the tenets of integration and uplift. He performed as effortlessly with such African American celebrities as Bill Cosby, Ray Charles, Jim Brown, Aretha Franklin, Sammy Davis Jr., Ella Fitzgerald, and Lena Horne as he did with his many famous white guests, who included John Wayne, Cher, Bob Hope, Bing Crosby,

Johnny Cash, Lucille Ball, Dean Martin, Ed Sullivan, Burt Reynolds, and Raymond Burr. He did not appear intimidated to perform with any of these legends. As a matter of fact, Wilson's custom of never dressing in the drag costume of Geraldine during rehearsals threw off many of these actors when he appeared on stage in full regalia. They often hesitated, blew their lines, laughed, which, while adding to the humor of the sketch, also allowed Wilson by comparison to shine with confidence. In the end, the public image of Wilson as the American success story would seal his reputation and override any of the criticisms that were geared at the so-called negative representations.

These underlying aspects of uplift are evident in the responses of many African Americans upon hearing the news of his death. The Reverend Jesse Jackson told the *Washington Post* that "Flip was a breakthrough artist for African Americans. He led with a brand of comedy that was clean and decent and not vulgar. To the end, he was a man I held in high esteem—as a comedian and as a person."[67] Veteran African American actor Ossie Davis remembers, "He was a pioneer in a way. His show was a trend-setting show. And we felt proud and gratified to see someone from our community get so far up there."[68] The tone of these eulogies suggests that much emphasis was placed on what Flip Wilson represented. He was a black man who had achieved it all and did so in a "clean and decent and not vulgar" manner.

Wilson also followed through on this reputation of self-made man in other ways. When he signed his deal with NBC, he made sure that the show was produced through his company, Clerow Productions. This decision allowed him a much larger share in the profits, and he also maintained the rights to the show. Even today it is rare to see any person, much less a black man, own his or her own show.[69] Wilson was able to live off the earnings from *The Flip Wilson Show*, working rarely and enjoying a life of leisure. He also owned a recording label, Little David Records, which among other artists produced George Carlin's comedy albums.

Many black people felt affirmation, appreciation, humor, and pride in having Wilson at the top of the entertainment industry in the early 1970s. However, black people who felt that he should have used his position on television to create changes for blacks in the industry and in essence to represent the black struggle more decisively often called him to task. In *Jet* magazine he responded:

Geraldine's outfits and attitude often surprise guest performers, as with Cher (left) and Johnny Cash (right).

> When people pay to see me, I try to make them laugh, not deliver
> a sermon or become a spokesman for this or that; I guess I am in-
> volved in civil rights because I am a Negro. But if you're a come-
> dian, your first obligation is to be funny.[70]

When questioned about racism in television in 1971, he replied,
"It would be ridiculous for me to say anything negative regarding
blacks having an equal opportunity on TV. After all, I was Number
One in the ratings four times last year and twice this season."[71]
Again in rugged individualist fashion, Wilson was an advertisement
for the American Dream and was unable to make an assessment
that went beyond his personal experience. He did not perceive a
need to make any statement beyond what he embodied as a black
man who had succeeded in a racially hostile American society.
He became another model of classlessness if not racelessness in
American society.

What perhaps rings as ambivalence in this analysis of *The Flip
Wilson Show* and, indeed, in black America's reception of the show
has to do with the time frame: this was the 1970s, the offspring of
the politically charged '60s, when the black struggle was still of
critical importance. In the '90s, Cuba Gooding's mantra from the
film *Jerry Maguire*, "Show me the money," although not a laudable
change, became the new addition to the American lexicon. Black
and white entertainers who amass cash without any sense of political consciousness are common in contemporary society; indeed, it is
the rare few that give back to their community who stand out. Our
politicized image of the 1960s and the '70s implores us to imagine a
world of self-sacrifice for group achievement. This was not the case
with Flip Wilson, and certainly this was not the case with various
other African Americans in the '60s and '70s. However, Wilson
was in the spotlight, and his deficiencies were contrasted with other
more politicized entertainers in this very public forum.

The Veil of Double Consciousness

Although some TV accounts claim that *The Flip Wilson Show* was
dropped from NBC because of stiff competition from *The Waltons*,
producer Bob Henry insists that

> NBC wanted him to do more shows. But after four years of this
> tremendous adulation, he just wanted to have peace and quiet. He
> never had that drive that other performers have that you always had

to be out there all the time, in front of a crowd. . . . Flip's only problem was that he was a man who wanted to be left alone to sleep in
his Rolls if he wanted to.[72]

Wilson's version is consistent with Henry's. Wilson said that he received custody of his children and chose to leave the entertainment
industry.

[I wanted to] give my kids their chance. I went through five foster
homes when I was a kid and I knew my kids needed me. . . . Television made me a hero to other people's kids, but I knew I needed to
be a hero to my own kids. I had to do that. And I did.[73]

Wilson's reluctance to move beyond his character sketches and
incorporate direct political critique is one of the reasons that the
show has not held up through the years. Expectations of what a
show like Wilson's should have been, or could have been, play into
the contemporary reading of Flip Wilson. A *Washington Post* reporter highlights the core issues of a contemporary viewing of Flip
with an understanding of the historical moment:

"The Flip Wilson Show" was gentle, classy and soulful—the television equivalent of a Motown tune. By the time of its 1974 cancellation, America had embraced the coarser, more flamboyant rhythms
of funk and disco. Comedy was headed on a similarly edgy path.
Wilson failed to keep pace and lost his hep-cat reputation.[74]

The *Washington Post* reporter fails to acknowledge that many
earlier comedians such as Redd Foxx, Dick Gregory, and Richard
Pryor had previously headed up the edgy path, but his quotation
illustrates an awareness that *The Flip Wilson Show* was not keyed
to the changing social times. After *The Flip Wilson Show,* Wilson
withdrew from the public eye except for occasional appearances
on variety shows, an attempted revival of the quiz show *People
Are Funny* in 1984, and the short-lived situation comedy *Charlie
and Company* in 1985. He and the Reverend Leroy popped up
in a Spike Lee commercial for the Fox Network's coverage of the
Stanley Cup in 1998.

Perhaps the "veil" of W. E. B. Du Bois's *Soul of Black Folks,* the
constant existence in a state of double consciousness, was the ratio-
nale upon which Flip Wilson based his public career. Perhaps he
knew what he had to disguise in order to be successful and accepted

within mainstream U.S. society.[75] One incident related in an interview gives us a glimpse of this possibility.

Wilson kept a notebook with him at all times, and he would jot down ideas for future shows as they came to him. He recalled that on one occasion after having driven out to the Grand Canyon, something that he did several times a year, to relax and contemplate life, he began to think, "What color is the blues?" One of the thoughts he came up with was, "The Negroes didn't give the blues to America; America gave the blues to the Negroes." He scribbled this into his book, but, soon after, he scratched out the idea because he felt it was "too bitter."[76] The moment may have passed, but his recollection of it suggests that anger and frustration may have been below the surface and simply veiled for the mainstream.

Using two different political positions, *Soul Train* and *The Flip Wilson Show* succeeded in their own venues and opened doors within television. Many programs starring African Americans appeared throughout the 1970s. However, when given the spotlight, what would these African American performers do with their opportunity? Would they reach out to other black performers? Would the politics of integration, Black Nationalism, capitalism, and uplift impact the decisions about African American characters, story lines, and comedic performances? Flip Wilson had been given his opportunity by Redd Foxx's recommendation on *The Tonight Show*. Using his position as major network star, Flip Wilson in turn used his visibility to introduce *Sanford and Son* to the American television audience. In the weeks preceding the premiere, Redd Foxx appeared as a guest star on *The Flip Wilson Show*. As Wilson had used his own show, Redd Foxx used *Sanford and Son* to further explore the legacy of African American humor. However, Foxx's show did not always veil the emotions behind the humor.

4. This Ain't No Junk

Sanford and Son and
African American Humor

Of course I'm Redd Foxx. I was Redd Foxx before I was Sanford, and
I will be Redd Foxx after Sanford is dead gone and forgotten. Sanford
ain't never going to bury Redd Foxx!
Redd Foxx, in Joe X. Price, *Before Sanford*

In the late 1970s Redd Foxx visited Trinidad to give a performance
at the Jean Pierre Stadium. *Sanford and Son* (1972–77) was one of
the most popular shows on Trinidadian television, and Foxx was
a celebrated star. The day after the appearance the local papers reported that they were appalled at Foxx's performance. Apparently,
the audience expected the much-beloved Fred G. Sanford and was
unprepared for Redd Foxx's "blue" material. He later apologized
in the newspapers, saying that he did not realize that the audience
was unaware of his nightclub stand-up routine.

This is not an isolated cross-cultural example. When *Sanford and
Son* premiered on NBC in 1972, Redd Foxx was introduced to a
nationwide audience, many of whose members had never heard of
the veteran comedian. To many Americans, Redd Foxx would be
Fred Sanford. Indeed, Foxx addressed this issue in an episode called
"Fred Meets Redd" (1976), in which Fred wins a look-alike contest
hosted by Redd Fox at the NBC studios. There, the X-rated nightclub performer Redd Foxx confronts his television personality, Fred
Sanford. Sanford describes Foxx to his son Lamont as

> my idol, I love him, I love the way he spells his name with two *d*'s
> and two *x*'s. . . . I don't know why he uses two *d*'s, but I saw his
> nightclub act once and I know why they got all them *x*'s. . . . I heard
> he was so sharp and debonair and charming and good looking. . . .
> I happen to be the spittin' image of him. I have often been stopped
> on the street by people who thought I was him 'til they saw I was me.

Foxx publicly and vociferously denied the connection between his
television persona and role as stand-up comedian. While on the
nightclub stage he was a sharply dressed, acerbic, and blue stage
performer. Fred Sanford, on the other hand, usually dressed in sus-
penders, baggy pants, and a shirt that had not seen an iron in years.
Indeed, in the aforementioned episode, Foxx and Sanford are pictured opposite each other and, although the same person is clearly
playing both roles, the characters' dress, demeanor, and speech
are completely different. Foxx wanted to maintain his own stage
identity. However, there is perhaps some truth to the sentiment that
Redd Foxx and Fred Sanford were innately connected. What makes
Sanford and Son relevant and humorous was gleaned from Redd
Foxx's extended career as a black comedian on the Chitlin' Circuit
and from a long tradition of African American comedy.

Many African American political groups protested *Sanford and
Son,* dismissed it as the white world's beliefs about black people,
and discussed it as television's reinscription of stereotypes. This will
be discussed in greater detail later on, and analysis of the articles of
protest indicates that the ideology of uplift played a significant role
in the rejection of the program. *Sanford and Son* was considered an
antiprogressive text by various black political groups and politicized
individuals who were concerned about the impression the show
conveyed to an American public. *Sanford and Son* appeared particularly regressive because it was produced during the era of the Black
Revolution, when many in the black community, of varying political
beliefs, wanted to convey a sense of a progressive black society.
While acknowledging these concerns, I still argue that because of the
active role played by Redd Foxx and other black writers and performers, the show exhibited resistance to mainstream co-optation.
Foxx used mainstream network television and the format of the
situation comedy to bring traditional African American folklore and
comedy of black communal spaces aboveground. He also used his
valuable position within the network to create new opportunities
for African Americans in the typically exclusive industry.

Redd Foxx before Sanford: The Chitlin' Circuit, the Party Records, and Redd's Place

> I ain't gonna do no marching nonviolently. Ain't no way I'm gonna let
> a cracker go upside my head with a stick and do nothin' but hum "We
> Shall Overcome." I'm going to cut him. I'm from St. Louis, and we wake
> up buck-naked with our knife on.
>
> **Redd Foxx, in Redd Foxx and Norma Mailer,**
> ***The Redd Foxx Encyclopedia of Black Humor***

Born in St. Louis and raised there and in Chicago, Redd Foxx moved
to New York in 1939. He performed with a three-man washboard
band, worked as a dishwasher with a young Malcolm Little (X),
and practiced his comedy routines in local Harlem clubs and at the
Apollo. In the late 1940s and early '50s, he worked the Chitlin'
Circuit in a team act with Slappy White. Within this black-only
space, Foxx observed and learned from comedy legends such as
Moms Mabley and Pigmeat Markham. Foxx removed the rural
black dialect, molded the humor of these acts, and placed it within
a contemporary urban context. As Quincy Jones explains, "He
was the first of the *urban* black comics, and Dick Gregory and
Flip Wilson and all the others who came later took from *him*."[1]
However, the team of Foxx and White was never able to cross over
and break into white settings. Although their humor went over well
at the Apollo and in other communal black spaces, when the team
played the Palace on Broadway, they "died like dogs," to quote
Foxx. "[T]he whole act bombed. That was the first and last time
at the Palace."[2] His comedy was specifically created for black audiences and was not easily extricated from that context.

Foxx was not ready to censor his material. "I always say 'Fuck
convention.' My bag has always been to talk about things like sex
and everything that most people don't like to talk about in public."[3]
His style indeed harkened back to some of the African American
comedic traditions. His albums contained many instances of signifying and traditional African American toasts.[4] His gravelly voice
may have given him the down-home feel of Moms Mabley; however, he had the attitude of the "Bad Nigger" of African American
folklore.[5]

The nature of his material often brought into question the incongruities of American life. For example, within sexually explicit stories, he challenged white separatism and the fear of miscegenation.

In an era in which lynchings were far from rare, he reintroduced notions of black sexuality and questioned the so-called color barriers that were more about propriety than reality. "As far as my ancestry goes, just take a good look at my face; you got to know someone back there got integrated. See those lips? Thin, huh? Can't hardly taste bar-b-que."[6] Although taken from a 1960s party record, the following skit exemplifies this idea and brings it to the highest echelon of white American society—the White House.

> President Johnson and Carl Stokes, you know the brother, they were in the restroom in Washington, and President Johnson looked over at Carl to speak to him, and being a little bit taller than Carl he had to look down, and he happened to glance into Carl's bowl. And he said, "I'll be damned Carl, how'd you get that?" And Carl said, "Well just before I have sex I always beat it on the bedpost four times, just take it and beat it on the bedpost four times, that's all I did." Well President Johnson says, "You know I'm gonna try that when I get home." He got home, took a shower, and walked into the bedroom and beat it on the bedpost four times, and Ladybird woke up and said, "Is that you Carl?"[7]

For a black man to engage in open discussions about sex was considered problematic, if not threatening. This joke in particular spoke about the black man's prowess over the white man's. While the joke seemingly feeds into stereotypes of black men, one must consider its political and social context. At a time in which many mainstream Americans feared the integration of black Americans into their neighborhoods, here was a black man finding his way into the home and bedroom of the most important southerner at the time.

Foxx also provided sharp observations of contemporary American society and made direct reference to problems in the South, the casual way in which some white southerners regarded the lives of black people and the incompetent investigations into the continuing lynchings in the South.

> I don't even go down South. They found a Negro in Mississippi with six hundred pounds of chains wrapped around his body. Found him in the river. The sheriff viewed the remains and says, "Just like one of them niggers, steal more chains than he can carry."[8]

Foxx and White moved to Los Angeles in 1952 to work with Dinah Washington at the Cotton Club. When the act broke up a month later, Foxx stayed in Los Angeles and continued to work in local black theaters, but he often ran into trouble with nightclubs because he refused to curb either his language or the sexual innuendos in his material.

In 1955 he made a deal with Dootsie Williams and the Dooto Company to produce records of his comedy routines. He made at least fifty records for Williams and was underpaid, often receiving no royalties when his older albums were repackaged and resold.[9] These party records brought Redd Foxx to a much wider African American audience and confirmed his status as an underground comedian.

> The Redd Foxx albums, usually kept in the back of record collections, beyond sight of "polite" Negro company, were seldom mentioned at racially mixed gatherings. An underground source of uncensored black humor, these early recorded examples of comic routines and monologues popular in black cabarets and the black stage circuit were among the first of their kind to be made available to the general public. Although at the time of their release they were considered more contraband than mere race records, the albums were . . . essentially connected to the core or unassimilated black community.[10]

Because of the content of his material, as well as the rather conservative and segregated era of the 1950s, Foxx remained virtually unknown to the white American audience. Mainstream America in the 1950s and even the 1960s was simply not ready for Redd Foxx, and he was therefore prevented from performing in mainstream venues. Although to a contemporary audience Foxx's material may seem mild, to a mainstream white population weaned on *Leave It to Beaver* and *Father Knows Best,* Redd Foxx was antithetical to the postwar conservatism.

In 1959, Foxx began his transition into mainstream American venues. He was eventually booked into the Basin Street East in New York and in 1960 began to play smaller clubs and hotels in Vegas, such as the Castaways. He moved from there to the Aladdin and eventually to more prominent casinos, such as Caesar's Palace. Foxx appeared on *The Today Show* and *The Tonight Show* in 1964, and these opportunities led to regular television gigs and a contract to appear nightly at the Las Vegas Hilton.

Although he had mainstream opportunities, Foxx remained committed to the humor and context of all-black settings. In 1967, Foxx bought his own nightclub on La Cienega in Los Angeles, the Redd Foxx Club, more commonly referred to as Redd's Place. It was here that Foxx relaxed, because no one censored what he had to say. The club was small, what Bill Cosby would refer to as "an aisle."[11] Foxx's love of the club motivated him to invest most of his nightclub earnings from Vegas into Redd's Place.

> The atmosphere was always intimate, as the lights were kept low and the red carpeting . . . soft to the walk. The music was always mellow, too, piped in low whenever there was nothing live coming from the stage. And when you heard anything but a Dinah Washington record, it was rare.[12]

Redd's Place was known for hosting some of the best performers of the time. Jazz musicians Billy Eckstine, Dizzy Gillespie, and Sarah Vaughan and comedians Bill Cosby, Flip Wilson, and Richard Pryor were a few of the artists who performed at Redd's Place. Redd often stood out front of the club under the canopy, just rapping with anyone who passed by. For Foxx, the idea of the club was to provide a communal yet public space for comedians to try out their material. As Foxx reminded the entertainers, "Nobody's gonna fire you outa here, pal, at least not for just talking."[13]

As Richard Pryor, whose comedy album *Craps (After Hours* was recorded at Redd's Place, stated:

> I hung around there often. I loved it. I loved watching him. I loved getting on that stage and just tripping—ad-libbing new routines and so on. . . . Those sure were the fun days. There was never a club quite like it and probably never will be again.[14]

The audience was hip and well versed in the oral traditions. Comedians therefore had to expect hecklers if they did not get it right. Occasionally performers realized that the people taunting them were other comic greats such as Pryor and Wilson.

When the club got into financial trouble, Foxx made an appearance on the *Joey Bishop Show*. This performance brought some prominent African American stars to Redd's Place. Sammy Davis Jr. would drop by to do a few shows, and Bill Cosby, a well-respected and mainstream comedian, invested in the club. This in turn attracted not only the Hollywood crowd but also a more mainstream white audience to the club, which still maintained its censor-free policy. In this way, Foxx's club introduced undiluted private black comedy to an integrated audience. Although Redd's Place brought in the best artists and often did quite well financially, Foxx was not as shrewd a businessman as a comic. He often let his sympathetic nature get in the way of running the club. Knowing what it was like to be a comedian on the road, he often paid more than the going rate for the artists, even if the act did not draw in the crowds. As he was often in Las Vegas, he could not manage the day-to-day running of the club. He had untrustworthy people in some of the key positions and lost several bartenders and managers because of major cash extortion.[15] Bill Cosby eventually pulled out because of its chaotic management, and the club, on its last legs, literally burned to the ground in the early 1970s.

From *Steptoe and Son* to *Sanford and Son*

Considering the nature of Redd Foxx's humor, a sitcom on network television may have seemed improbable. However, Foxx came to the attention of the producers Norman Lear, Bud Yorkin, and Aaron Reuben with his performance of an older junkman in *Cotton Comes to Harlem* (1970). Lear was known as the creator of the controversial show *All in the Family* (1971–78), which debuted a mere six months after *The Flip Wilson Show* aired. Known for changing the face of the family-situation comedy by addressing social issues such as racism, politics, homosexuality, feminism, and abortion, *All in the Family* introduced bigot Archie Bunker and his dysfunctional family to the television audience.[16] One year later, in January 1972, NBC ran the first episode of *Sanford and Son* as a midseason replacement. Redd Foxx used television as a continuation of Redd's Place. He brought aspects of the black comedy performed in all-black settings to this mainstream forum and nuanced the format of the situation comedy. Through the use of vernacular black comedy, *Sanford and Son* thus specifically addressed a black audience familiar with the tropes of black comedy while crossing over to a wider mainstream white audience.

He was also able to insert some control over the shaping of the show. Some of the opportunities to keep the show within the confines of African American expression came from moments of clear ad-libbing, observed through many of the episodes. At these times Foxx was able to slip in lines, humor, or attitudes that he had garnered elsewhere during his stage career. At other times it was simply Foxx's persona, comments made, or vernacular used that brought African American specificity to light. Also, with Foxx's increasingly powerful position as a moneymaker for the network, he was able to use direct skills of confrontation to get what he needed from NBC. All of these issues will be discussed in further detail.

Sanford and Son was based on a British television comedy, *Steptoe and Son,* which had been on the air in Britain for the previous ten years. A Lee Tracy and Aldo Ray pilot was filmed, and another starring Barnard Hughes and Paul Sorvino was pulled together by Yorkin and Reuben. The producers wanted to "go the ethnic route" from the beginning.[17] The Sorvino-Hughes pilot created a tension between an Irish father and a son who favored his mother's Italian ways. However, it was not until Yorkin and Reuben decided to make the family black and suggested hiring Redd Foxx that NBC began to take notice. Thus, the white junkmen of England became Sanford and son of Watts, an enclave of Los Angeles made notorious by the aforementioned riots of 1965.

The series primarily involved the activities of Fred Sanford—taken from Redd Foxx's actual name, John Elroy Sanford—and his son, Lamont (played by Demond Wilson), a character named after one of Foxx's longtime friends. According to the script, Sanford's wife, Elizabeth, had passed away many years before, leaving the two to run the household and business. Other recurring characters included Fred's sister-in-law, Aunt Esther (LaWanda Page); Bubba (Don Bexley) and Grady (Whitman Mayo), Fred's best friends; Julio (Gregory Sierra), the Sanfords' Puerto Rican next-door neighbor; Rollo (Nathaniel Taylor), Lamont's best friend; Smitty (Hal Williams), as the black neighborhood police officer; and Hoppy (Howard T. Platt), as Smitty's white partner.[18] Hoppy was one of the few recurring white characters on the show and was used as a caricature of an African American perspective on white society. As African American characters were often used in stereotypical fashion to represent one specific characteristic, Hoppy is a case of flipping the script, using a character to encompass all of white society.

Sanford and Son is tied to notions of African American humor in several critical ways. First, Foxx as a black comedian embodied characteristics of traditional African American figures from the trickster to the Bad Nigger.[19] This is evident both in his performance and in the story lines. Foxx also showcased African American artists on the sitcom. He therefore brought comedians and performers from the underground clubs and stages to a mainstream forum. The show's story lines addressed social issues relevant to the African American population at the time. This is specifically apparent in the episodes written by Richard Pryor and other politicized African American screenwriters. Here it is evident that the comedians of two different generations combined style and voice to present a new, politically articulate sense of humor to mainstream American television. In these episodes, all facets of black underground comedy came aboveground in no uncertain terms.

Sanford and Son and the Roots of African American Comedy

The scripts of some early episodes of *Sanford and Son* were rewritten from story lines from the series *Steptoe and Son*. However, the contributions of Redd Foxx, African American screenwriters, and other cast members transformed this British program into a show reflective of African American experiences and African American humor. As discussed in the introduction, African American humor not only is based in notions of realism but also has the potential for satire and self-critique.[20] These three key elements of black humor are evident in *Sanford and Son*.

The choice of setting for *Sanford and Son*, Watts, Los Angeles, situated the comedy in the experience of African American everyday life and culture. Watts had come to represent a space of black uprising and was intimately connected to the ideas of contemporary black protest because of the urban revolt within the community. The show was definitely not escapist, although many perceived it as such. To accuse the show of escapism is to ignore the form of traditional African American comedy, which uses humor to deal with harsh realities.

Although related in a humorous vein, many of the problems that occurred were caused by the Sanfords' lack of money. There were repeated jokes about the meals that Fred concocted out of what the pair had left in the refrigerator, which, along with his Ripple mixes, were visible indicators of their lower-class existence. Although Sanford owned his own junkyard, it was clear that he and Lamont were usually one sale away from losing the business. Lamont's constant search for his identity and for his potential future in a variety of activities such as acting, Afrocentricity, and new jobs was rooted in the frustrations of working at the same job day after day and not getting anywhere—experiences that many working-class black Americans could and still can relate to.

Satire worked on many levels within the story lines of *Sanford and Son,* but perhaps no more significantly than in the representations of the LAPD. Two police officers had recurring roles in the show—one white (Hoppy) and one black (Smitty). Smitty was efficient and perceptive; Hoppy was always the butt of the joke. Hoppy's officious attitude and his attempts at "being down" with black culture were recurring jokes. Smitty repeatedly corrected him for his improper use of black vernacular. The episode "Tower Power" (November 27, 1974) presents a typical example when the two police officers try to solve an argument between Lamont and Fred.

> SMITTY: Fred, Lamont, look why don't we come back when you get this all settled?
> HOPPY: Yeah, you get together and you know *knock* to each other.
> SMITTY: No no. That's *rap* to each other.
> HOPPY: Oh yeah, rap to each other, just be honest, you know, let it *all hang off.*
> SMITTY: *Hang out.*
> HOPPY: Hang out, hang out, hang out. So long. It's so long, right?
> SMITTY: Just get in the car.

Considering the negative reputation of the LAPD, especially in relation to the events surrounding the Watts rebellion, it was a bold act to ridicule this organization on a national forum.

Another aspect of African American comedy found in *Sanford and Son* was the use of self-critique. The representation of Aunt Esther and her devout religious beliefs perhaps provided the sharpest arena for criticism. The tenuous historical position of religion in black life was discussed previously, in chapter 3. Aunt Esther is basically a caricature of the black church, and she continually calls Fred a heathen and prays to Jesus to save his soul. She is positioned in opposition to Fred, who as performed by Foxx can be seen as this secular black character who does not accept the incongruities of the church.

The roots of African American humor are again evident in one of the lasting legends of African American folklore, the trickster. In a 1970s context, Fred Sanford is the consummate trickster. The ma-

The character of the white police officer Hoppy suggests the incompetence of the LAPD. Left to right: Hoppy (Howard Platt), Smitty (Hal Williams), and Fred Sanford (Redd Foxx).

jority of *Sanford and Son* episodes hinge on this very premise. Fred and Lamont are continually at odds, because Fred is constantly devising plans so that he can avoid the work of "coordinating" the junkyard and can relax and watch television. He also has many grand schemes to get rich quick, from making deals at the junkyard to playing the numbers and gambling a hunch in Vegas. Some black activists saw this image as a problematic stereotype, because Hollywood has a legacy of representing black men as shiftless and lazy, out to make a quick dollar by any means necessary.[21] However,

Aunt Esther (LaWanda Page) is used to question Bible thumping in the black church.

to cast *Sanford and Son* into the category of stereotype is to ignore its positioning within traditional African American folklore.

"The Great Sanford Siege" (March 3, 1972) illustrates the workings of the trickster and also exemplifies another aspect of African American humor, the physical component.[22] Fred's constant complaints of heart attacks or his arthritis with his flailing arms and stumbling movements exemplify the ways in which the physical combines with the verbal to present the nuances of African American humor. The episode begins with Fred and Lamont discussing the numerous final notices from unpaid bills. According to Fred the "bills come in time but there has been a slight delay on the money." The lights and the gas in the house have been turned off, and the two are stuck at home avoiding a summons server. A collection agent from the Luau Layaway Furniture Company (Dick Van Patten) arrives to repossess his furniture, and he eventually brings the police. When Fred realizes that nothing will stop the repossession of the furniture and the television, he fakes a back injury. Lamont joins in the charade by helping his moaning father over to the couch, telling the repossessor, "All I know is that you threw an old man down the stairs." The repossessor continues to protest while Fred pulls out all the stops, "Hear that, Elizabeth, I'm coming to join you, honey, with a bad back." Van Patten looks to the police for help, saying to the black officer, "You know *your* people better than I do; what do you think that I should do?" The cop replies, "You want some real good advice? If I were you I'd get out of this neighborhood before it gets dark."

Van Patten decides to make a deal, and Lamont and Fred convince him to sign over a check for two hundred dollars. Lamont shows some regret at the end of the episode and wants to pay it back because it was "like stealing." Fred responds that he "worked for that money. Do you know how much Richard Burton gets paid for an acting job like that?" It is unclear at the episode's conclusion what they will do, but they now have the money to pay all of the bills.

Also, intricately tied to the character of the trickster is another "venerable black comic tradition—the tall tale or simply lying."[23] Sanford clearly took this to a new height in "A Visit from Lena" (January 1, 1973). While visiting the NBC studios for a tour, Fred sneaks into the dressing room of *The Tonight Show* to meet Lena Horne. When he sees her, he has another of his famous heart attacks

Fred Sanford is a contemporary trickster. At right is his son, Lamont (Demond Wilson).

but tells her what a big fan he is, mentioning that he saw *Stormy Weather* thirty-eight times. "Went in on a Saturday came out on a Wednesday evening." This is just the beginning of the joke or the lie. With each line, Fred elaborates on an unbelievable story. He tells her that he promised his son he would try to see her, that his son is a big fan, and his mother used to sing "Stormy Weather" to him when he was a baby. However, since she died, "Little Lamont" has not been the same, and he doesn't even go to school anymore. When Lena asks why Lamont feels connected to her, Fred says that she is the only one who can sing "Stormy Weather" like his mother. Fred says that Lamont looks to her as a substitute mother. When Lena asks why he did not bring Lamont and suggests that it might be that Lamont is lame, Fred readily agrees, "Lame, that's what he is—lame." He finally convinces her to visit "little lame Lamont" at their house.

Fred invites all of his poolroom friends to see Lena and bets each of them fifteen dollars that she will visit the house. When Lena finally shows up at the house, looking for Little Lamont, she discovers that Lamont is neither little nor lame. She is furious that she stopped by on a lie and that she is going to miss her plane to San Francisco, where she planned to raise money for Operation Headstart. When Fred's friends arrive and begin to pay off the bet, Lena explodes, calling him a "low down, jiving, conniving . . ." Fred cuts her off and turns the deteriorating situation around to his benefit. He tells her that he bet them only to raise money for Operation Headstart. Lena gives Fred a big kiss on the lips in gratitude, leaving him reeling.

Like the trickster of African folklore, Fred is unsuccessful with his plans in many instances. For example, in the episode "This Land Is Whose Land?" (1974), Fred is aggravated by his neighbor Julio, who is storing some of his junk on the Sanfords' land with Lamont's permission. Fred objects to Lamont's lenient ways.

SANFORD: I might accidentally sell some Puerto Rican junk. I might wind up selling it to the guy it was stolen from.
LAMONT: Hey Pop, Julio's junk is not stolen.
SANFORD: Then why is he hiding it over here in our yard? I want it out of here.
LAMONT: What for? We got plenty of room.
SANFORD: But we won't have if we don't stop it now. That's how

they move in. A tire here, a lamp there, then you have a big wide-rimmed hat in your living room and then cockroaches in your kitchen, and pretty soon your whole house is full of Puerto Ricans.

LAMONT: I knew the real reason would come out—you're prejudiced. You're never going to get used to the idea of Julio being our neighbor. Well Julio is our neighbor, and he is my friend, and he's not doing anything wrong.

The play on Sanford's prejudicial attitude continues when the surveyor shows up and has an obvious Latino accent. His name is Manuel Eduardo Estaban Gonzales y Rodriguez. Although Fred is concerned, the surveyor assures him that "the legal boundary comes from the county recorder; it cannot be changed." Fred realizes that he has overplayed his hand in this round when he is informed by the surveyor that Julio owns the majority of the land on which Fred's junkyard sits. The trickster is defeated by his own greed.

Another example of the trickster outdoing himself occurs in the episode entitled "Home Sweet Home" (1974). A Japanese investor offers the Sanfords and their neighbors money for their properties so that a brewery can be built. When the Japanese investor visits and offers twenty thousand dollars, Fred pretends to have sentimental attachment to the property. Although the company makes a counteroffer of over twenty-seven thousand dollars, Fred, sold on the idea that he can get the price up to thirty thousand dollars, refuses the offer. The Japanese family, so convinced of Fred's attachment to his home, withdraws the offer rather than uproot the Sanfords. This trickster, like Brer Rabbit in animal fables, often outfoxes himself.

Sanford and Son as Night-Club Stage

Redd Foxx took the atmosphere and training from the Chitlin' Circuit into the venue of mainstream American television. Although he made some concessions to network television—primarily the use of certain so-called coarse words—Foxx saw *Sanford and Son* as a continuation of Redd's Place. As then-coproducer Aaron Reuben reported,

> Foxx comes up with names like Tangerine Sublett and Leroy and Skillet, consummate performers he worked with in the $25-a-week nightclub days. The names befuddle the NBC casting department,

where they are totally unknown. But Redd finds brothers and sisters in obscure black bars and theaters all over the country and they go to work in the series in important supporting roles. . . . Redd also brings in great black performers who gave up in the segregation days of show business and now work in city or county government in Los Angeles. They moonlight for us on *Sanford and Son*.[24]

Foxx, for example, recommended the hiring of LaWanda Page, who played Sanford's sister-in-law. Page was a friend of Foxx's from St. Louis, and his comments about hiring her again address the connection between traditional African American humor and the sphere of television. According to Foxx, "You never heard of the lady, but the night that first show of LaWanda's goes on the air, there'll be dancing in the streets in every ghetto in the United States."[25] Page reportedly had a difficult time getting used to the format of a scripted show, and the directors were about to hire another performer. Foxx offered to work with her, and Page was hired on as a recurring character who would outlive Foxx on the show, continuing into *The Sanford Arms*.

Like Redd's Place, *Sanford and Son* also provided a stage for famous African Americans, some of whom were ignored or forgotten by mainstream white America. At these times the narrative is simply a backdrop for the performance. For example, the episode "The Stand-In" (January 7, 1975) featured Scatman Crothers and Billy Eckstine. Billy Eckstine, or Mr. B., was a famous bebop big band leader (1944–47) and vocalist. His band featured such jazz greats as Miles Davis, Dizzy Gillespie, Dexter Gordon, and Sarah Vaughan. Eckstine's career was at its height in the 1940s and '50s, when he continued as a balladeer after his band had broken up.

Crothers started his career in Dayton, Ohio, in the 1930s as a musician, singer, and comedian. He moved to the West Coast in 1944 and performed at many small clubs. He obtained a job at the segregated Club Oasis for about four years, and it was there that he met Redd Foxx and they began a lifetime friendship. Crothers had a starring role in the film *Meet Me at the Fair*, and he worked on television as the sidekick to Dick Lane on *Showboat*. Foxx eventually secured a permanent role for Crothers on *Chico and the Man*.

In "The Stand-In," much to Lamont's dismay, Fred's best friend Bowlegs (Scatman Crothers) and his partner Al (Al Williams) come to town to perform at a local nightclub. Within moments of the opening credits, Bowlegs takes out his guitar and asks Sanford to join him in a song. The two sing a duet of "All of Me." Foxx's raspy voice is reminiscent of Louis Armstrong. The camera maintains a two-shot of the performers, focusing on either Foxx or Crothers with only a momentary cut away to show Lamont's changing approval. The entire song is performed, presenting the moment as a close, proscenium view of a performance of the legendary artists. A moment after the duet, Lamont is asked to clear some "surface." He pulls back the rug for a tap dance routine by Al, who takes center stage and performs to the music of Crothers.

When Al later hurts his back, Fred steps in to help Bowlegs, who is under contract at a local nightclub. Reminiscent of a spot from the Chitlin' Circuit, the club is represented as a tough place with an unscrupulous owner who refuses to pay performers and threatens those who do not produce.

Billy Eckstine opens the next portion of the program with a ballad at the nightclub. The audience appreciates the piece, and the white club owner is shown as a buffoon when he tells Eckstine that he should give up his singing career. Scatman Crothers and Redd Foxx are given yet another opportunity to perform. The big finale at the club includes Foxx, this time playing an old wash tub instrument from his days at the Apollo and scatting in harmony to the strumming of Crothers. Lamont, although not quite a willing participant, presents a polished tap dance routine. They are a huge success.

In this situation, the narrative holding together the episode is very thin and basically provides an empty space to be filled by these black artists and their performances. While providing a critique of underhanded clubs that fleece black performers, Foxx primarily uses mainstream television to highlight the performance of Crothers and Eckstine. Eckstine was certainly not at the high point in his career at the time of this showing. However, Foxx shows recognition of the roots of black performance and, by recommending him for the role, pays a tribute to the artist. A definite camaraderie exists between Crothers and Foxx; they work off each other, both in the musical performances and in their bantering routines. It is easy to believe that they are truly enjoying themselves and at times seem to exist in an all-black space. Many parts of the program seem ad-libbed by the actors as they react to one another's performance. All of the cast members (excluding the white club owner) are black, and at times the jokes and relationships among the performers go beyond narrative containment and into the realm of African American communal humor.

Another episode that reflects the experience of African Americans in black-only communal spaces is "Fred Sings the Blues" (March 10, 1977). Lamont buys tickets for Fred to a B.B. King concert for Father's Day. Again, except for the officious white usher, everyone else in the club is black. When King starts his performance, Fred and others participate with him in a round of call-and-response. The camera focuses on King and cuts away to Fred, Lamont, and the others in the crowd, who cheer King on. Because both Fred/Redd and B.B. King are from St. Louis, Fred manages to encourage King to come over to his house for dinner. However, after reading B.B.'s book *Why I Sing the Blues,* Fred begins to think that King wants to kill him for marrying his wife, Elizabeth, King's true love. B.B., not an actor, seems to laugh spontaneously to the reactions of Foxx. The episode ends with yet another performance by King; however, this is a private performance for just the main characters. During the song, each character, from Bubba, to Aunt Esther, to Fred, improvises lines of the song.

Sanford and Son provides a showcase for a variety of black actors, comedians, and musicians, some well-known, such as B.B. King, Lena Horne, Della Reese, and others from his days on the Chitlin' Circuit. Foxx used the public space of mainstream television as he used Redd's Place—as a space for the expression of traditional black culture. The network then, as it is today, was concerned with the bottom dollar, and the show remained a crossover success. Either Foxx's ability to interject a specific African American address pleased the producers because the show gained a large African American following, or they were simply unaware of Foxx's actions.

Sanford and Son as Social Commentary

As *Sanford and Son* became entrenched on the NBC schedule, African American writers and script editors were also able to take a more active role in the production of the show. The effects of the changes were considerable and evident in the content and direction of several *Sanford and Son* scripts. Scripts reflected the issues not only of civil rights but also of the Black Power movement. Shows such as *Julia* and *I Spy* reflected integration inherent in the Civil Rights movement, and Flip Wilson managed to integrate himself into mainstream television. However, *Sanford and Son* was one of the first shows on network television to express the ideology of the urban black underclass and, indeed, that of the Black Power movement. The language of the scripts began to reflect a contemporary understanding of urban black America. There were everyday references to the concerns of living in inner-city communities, such as problems with the police, lack of job opportunities, and racism. One of the prominent writers who contributed to the scriptwriting process was Richard Pryor.[26] And it is significant to note how the shows for which he is credited differ sharply from the tone of the majority of the scripts.

Pryor's politics and sense of characterization are reflected in the portrayals of Fred and Lamont; the two share a camaraderie, and the scripts for which Pryor is credited demonstrate sharp, witty dialogue between the characters. Pryor's political agenda is also clear, as the episodes begin to challenge issues such as police harassment and the court system. In "Sanford and Son and Sister Make Three" (1973) Fred's old dance partner and girlfriend Juanita and her daughter Alice visit. Fred invites them to stay awhile, but they remember that their car is in need of repair. The following dialogue ensues:

> ALICE: Mother, I think we'd better get that light fixed, you know, because we're gonna get stopped tonight if we don't get that light fixed.
> JUANITA: Oh, yes, one of our headlights is out.
> SANFORD: Well, you better get it fixed, because they death on a nigger with one light. Yeah, if you got one light, you better be on a motorcycle. I'm not kidding—you go down to traffic court and you sit around and you see so many brothers and sisters you think you were at a NAACP rally.

Despite its humorous tone, this example works as incisively as formal political commentary. The frustration over police harassment and other forms of discrimination was graphically depicted in the 1960s and early '70s through the televisual representations of rebellions in many urban centers across the United States.

This critical mode of humor was evident in the comedy performed in African American nightclubs at the time. These were perhaps some of the few venues for the expressions of this frustration. In *Sanford and Son*, the traditional black humor of both Pryor and Foxx moves aboveground to the very public site of television. For example, Pryor and Foxx's use of the word *nigger* in this scene is evidence of a shift from the typically derogatory use of the term on television and in other media sources; here, the word is used as it would be in an all-black setting. Turning the word around and using it within a black context is the start of the public reclaiming of identity.[27]

This type of writing also becomes evident when the show began to rely on the scripts and editing of other politicized African American writers, such as Ilunga Adell. In 1973, the twenty-four-year-old black playwright was brought in by Reuben to be a script editor and eventually a writer on the series. Adell was one of the playwrights in Joseph Papp's Public Theater in New York and claimed to have never spoken to a white person for the first eighteen years of his life. He thus believed that he wrote the characters as they would exist in all-black settings, in which their relationships with whites would be "unsure and uncomfortable. . . . This is the norm in the heart of large black communities like Harlem and Watts."[28]

Ilunga Adell worked on "Fred Sanford, Legal Eagle" (1973–74), which tackles the issue of the police and the court system. Lamont receives a traffic ticket that he believes he does not deserve. As he explains, "You can [get a ticket] if the light is green, and you black, and the cop is white." Lamont is encouraged by Fred and his friend Grady to fight the ticket in court. When the judge asks for Lamont's counsel, Fred takes on the role.

> SANFORD: I've been counseling him his whole life. I want to ask the officer here a question.
> JUDGE: Very well, proceed.
> SANFORD: Now, here's the question: What do you have against black drivers?
> *(Cop gestures in denial, and the people in the courtroom cheer.)*
> JUDGE: Order. I will not tolerate these outbursts, and you will restrict your inquiry to the matter before the court.
> SANFORD: Well, that's what's wrong with the court, Judge—a black man ain't got a chance down here.
> JUDGE: I'm black.
> SANFORD: Well, you're the judge. That don't count. *(Turning back to the cop)* Listen, why don't you arrest some white drivers?
> COP: I do.
> SANFORD: You do? Well, where are they? Look at all these niggers in here. Look around here. There's enough niggers in here to make a Tarzan movie.
> [The camera cuts to the all-black courtroom, which cheers in response to Fred's comments.]

Although Lamont is found not guilty of the charges, Fred is held in contempt of court because of his behavior, and the trickster's actions seemingly work to his detriment. However, in this case he expresses outrage, and his interventions lead to a positive outcome for Lamont. Many of the other episodes that Adell wrote and edited allow Fred to critically address various issues topical within the black community at the time. For example, Lamont tackles Afrocentric thought in "Lamont Goes African" (1973), and "Rated X" (March 16, 1973) discusses the representations of African Americans in film.

The scripts also more closely reflect the inner workings of humor seen in traditional black communal settings such as barbershops and pool halls. For example, in "A House Is Not a Poolroom" (1973–74), Fred receives a pool table from Lamont and Donna for his birthday. All of Fred's cronies practically move into the house, which takes on the feel of a traditional poolroom. The atmosphere is unique, and the interactions among the older characters reverberate with the hilarity and familiarity of private black humor, where signifying is plentiful and one-upmanship is the rule.

Ad-libbing with his "cronies," Redd Foxx (center) mainstreams traditional black humor in his role as Fred Sanford. At the left in this frame is Grady (Whitman Mayo).

FRED: Hey fellas, get ready for some real pool shooting now.

LEROY: This is your table, Fred. We'll let you break 'em.

GRADY: Because it might be the last time you touch the balls tonight.

FRED: Listen, Grady, I'll whip you like I was your daddy.

GRADY: OK, y'all heard him. All right, I got him first. Get on down here and break some balls.

FRED: Donna, excuse me a minute, honey. I won't be but a minute. You can watch if you want to, because it won't take me long. . . . I just want to show the fellas a few trick shots that I learned from Minnesota Fats.

SKILLET: Hurry up, Fred. You can't talk the balls into the bucket.

FRED: Five dollars a bet . . .

[Later in the episode, at another game]

FRED: Skillet, Skillet, will you take your belly off the table? Do you want me to put a cue ball in your navel?

As noted, with the addition of black writers on the *Sanford and Son* staff, the comedy and politics inherent in black sites emerge in the public space of television. However, the show was not embraced by all segments of the black community.

Sanford and Son Is White to the Core: Answering the Critics

Considering the time in which the program was made, black leaders feared the mainstream white audience's perception of the black community, and the show received much criticism. Many believed that *Sanford and Son* resurrected the stereotypes of *Amos 'n' Andy,* while others accused it of portraying the black experience as perceived by white producers. Some critics argued that the show soothed white liberal angst, as it showed that blacks might be poor but happy.

Perhaps one of the most vitriolic of critiques came from Eugenia Collier, a writer at the *New York Times*. The title of her article suggests Collier's point of view, "Sanford and Son Is White to the Core." Collier argued that because the show was based on a British series, it automatically rendered a poor representation of the black American experience. She believed that the show used humor to destroy the black self-image and to perpetuate negative images, that it presented images of "child-men" rather than strong black men. Her article is worth quoting at length.

There is nothing here that has traditionally motivated black humor—no redemptive suffering, no strength, no tragedy behind the humor. . . . So "Sanford and Son," as far as I am concerned, is far from black. The show reflects the culture of contemporary white America rather than any intrinsic black values. And there is something extremely deceptive about encasing whiteness in a black skin. . . . Fred Sanford and his little boy Lamont, conceived by white minds and based upon a white value system, are not strong black men capable of achieving—or even understanding—liberation. . . . We—all of us—need to be surrounded by positive—and true—images of blackness based upon black realities, and not upon white aberrations.[29]

Collier's sentiment mirrors that of many critics of the show, as well as the political climate of the times, in which every image had pro found meanings. The very language she employs suggests the importance of the media in the construction of a public black self at a critical moment in the Civil Rights and Black Power movements.

The crux of these critiques rests upon the aforementioned notions of racial uplift evident in African American society since the late nineteenth century. Collier judges the program on the basis of this ideology. *Sanford and Son*, Collier argues, works against the ideals of black liberation in the 1970s. The Sanfords are not a patriarchal black family or black activists, nor do they promote bourgeois values. These characters are contrary to the racial uplift projects of the 1970s in their many forms.

Writers such as Ilunga Adell were well aware of the criticism of the show by critics such as Eugenia Collier. Adell responded:

Nine out of ten blacks love Sanford. The tenth is critical because Fred and Lamont aren't . . . in what they call the mainstream of the black revolution. In an answer to Ms. Collier, I said that in addition to money, property, political awareness and motivation, black people desperately need positive images of themselves. Because we've really been bombarded with negative ones via television, movies, literature and mass media in general.[30]

The essentially class-based critiques are reminiscent of the flurry of protests over *Amos 'n' Andy*. Some thirty years later, the concerns of significant black political organizations, such as integration and purporting a Black Nationalist image, were still of utmost concern. Fred Sanford, as a junkman with questionable morals, was an embarrassment to the middle-class image of blackness. He was not the politicized image of the black man desired by several nationalist strains of black politics at that time. A black junkman who did not always make so-called moral decisions, argued frequently with his son and sister-in-law, appeared racist toward neighbors, and was always out to make a buck was not the poster child for either a civil rights or a Black Nationalist agenda.

Indeed, the show is not unproblematic, and as *Sanford and Son* moved into the later seasons, although still popular, the use of innovative new material decreased and many of the scenarios were simply repeated. But the concerns of the critics are more palpable in the context of the times and of television, which limited the number and types of roles for African Americans and purposely reiterated caricatures and maintained a rigid system of exclusion. It was thus easy to overlook some of the more relevant qualities of *Sanford and Son*. Far from being irreconcilable to black life, *Sanford and Son* was ensconced in traditional African American humor usually seen in black communal sites.

Sanford and Son remained NBC's most popular show from 1972–73 through 1975–76.[31] The popularity of the show arguably spawned other black sitcoms, including *Roll Out* (1973–74), *That's My Mama* (1974–75), *Grady* (1975–76), and *What's Happening!!* (1976–79). However, except for *Good Times* (1974–79) and *The Jeffersons* (1975–85), none had equal longevity or popularity. Redd Foxx's background as an African American comedian schooled in the ways of traditional black humor brought to the show a legacy of style and purpose that went beyond the initial scripts. Foxx's dealings with NBC also symbolized the contentious relationship between black and white America. Because of what he perceived as a lack of respect from executives and producers at NBC, Foxx walked off the set in 1974 with six shows left to shoot for the year. Foxx had many demands. At that point he was making ten thousand dollars an episode. His demands were "whatever Carol O'Connor gets, plus a dollar."[32] He disliked the production approach of Bud Yorkin and Aaron Reuben and wanted to have more input in the casting and the scriptwriting. He also asked for a better rehearsal space, with a window and a private dressing room. When Foxx returned to the set

> he probably had the best contract of any half hour series star who doesn't produce his own show: $25,000 an episode for 24 episodes

a year, up to $5,000 for reruns, and 25 percent of the producer's net profits. Yorkin and Reuben were gone from the set.[33]

Although these conditions might seem like the workings of a star's ego, what they symbolized were Foxx's demands for the network's respect for black performers. In a year when NBC made a profit of over sixty-six million dollars and signed Bob Hope to a three-year eighteen-million-dollar contract, Foxx believed that NBC needed to recognize his significant role in the network's success.[34] Foxx's lengthy career made him very aware of the inequitable workings of a white-controlled industry, and he would not tolerate this on his own show. Clashes continued with the executives at NBC, with many arguments about royalties and working conditions, and Foxx also wanted the network to show some respect for the black performers who made its executives such profits. Foxx complained bitterly that the network refused to give him development deals and movie roles offered to other successful NBC performers, thus limiting the prospects for black performers. He noted that NBC never sent tokens of appreciation for the ratings or stopped by the set to congratulate the performers, a common practice with many other NBC shows. Indeed, Foxx reported that the network sent two bottles of whiskey as a wedding gift when they knew he was on the wagon.[35] Most important, when the black-oriented shows were winning Emmys for NBC, African Americans were rarely given opportunities in writing, directing, or producing roles. Therefore, although the show was still doing very well, Foxx left the network for ABC in 1977.

Sanford and Son allowed voices and opinions usually contained within the all-black settings to be expressed to a mainstream audience, albeit within the constraints of network television. Black people across the country who had not achieved the American promise of integration were able to identify with familiar aspects of their lives reflected in the show. Similarly, mainstream white audiences were confronted with the sentiments of a politicized black comedian and were presented a window into some aspects of traditional black humor. Foxx was also very aware of the entertainment industry's ability to use and dispose of the talents of African American entertainers. He would not allow either his show or himself to go that route.

5. Respect Yourself!

Black Women and Power
in *Julia* and *Good Times*

The conflictual relationship between Norman Lear's Tandem Production company and Redd Foxx indicates, among other factors, that with the changing times some African American television performers were becoming more politicized. This politicization was commensurate with the legacy of difficulties faced by African American entertainers as well as the changing political climate of America, evident in integration and the Civil Rights and Black Power movements. *Julia* (1968–71) and *Good Times* (1974–79) demonstrate how black women in particular used not only the television text but also popular magazines and journals as forums for black social and political concerns. These outlets were used to produce counternarratives to combat the co-optation of the television shows by a white-controlled industry. Both Diahann Carroll and Esther Rolle were empowered black women with very clear ideas about the role of television in the expression of black culture and politics. In order for us to understand their actions, it is important to place them within the continuum of black women whose images and actions came to represent the African American struggle in the 1960s and 1970s.

From Rosa Parks's 1955 refusal to give up her seat on the Montgomery bus, the image of the black woman was central, though often overlooked, in political movements of the Civil Rights era. Black women were involved in all aspects of the major political organizations, including the NAACP and SNCC. As Ella Baker stated, "The movement of the fifties and sixties was carried largely by women, since it came out of the church groups. . . . It's true that the number of women who carried the movement is larger than that of the men."[1]

This is exemplified by these select images that have become a part of our national memory: In 1964 America heard the impassioned and televised testimony of Fannie Lou Hamer as to the atrocities she faced in the Mississippi jails. By 1970 the United States was also well aware of the stand taken by Angela Davis, whose political beliefs had resulted in her removal from the UCLA faculty. While continuing her work for the rights of black prisoners, Davis was eventually placed on the FBI's most wanted list for her alleged involvement with an attempted escape of one of these prisoners. She was eventually arrested and acquitted of the charges. However, her image with clenched fist raised is a permanent part of African American visual history. Shirley Chisholm, a congresswoman from New York, was the first black woman elected to Congress, and she ran for the presidency in 1972. Although the campaign was unsuccessful, she became yet another image of black female determination.

In popular culture, the image of the black woman took on similar connotations of strength and empowerment. In the music industry, black women took center stage. For example, while dealing with marital problems advertised widely by a June 1968 cover of *Time* magazine, Aretha Franklin's music on the Atlantic label became the sound for black women in the 1960s. As music critic Nelson George describes,

> [T]he one voice that spoke most directly to the aroused black psyche of the 1960s . . . was a woman's. If anyone wondered what "soul" was, all they had to do was play any of Aretha Franklin's Atlantic albums. . . . [Listening to her music,] one discovers not one Aretha Franklin but a cast of hundreds of women. . . . Franklin expressed all a black woman could be.[2]

"Respect Yourself," "Natural Woman," and others became anthems for black women, songs that still have currency today.

Within the film industry, the Blaxploitation movement was at its height in the early 1970s, and two of the most popular stars were Tamara Dobson *(Cleopatra Jones)* and Pam Grier *(Coffy)*. These women, although caricatures, like most Blaxploitation stars, male or female, were as powerful as their male counterparts. They wielded guns and at times bazookas and were involved in hand-to-hand combat against oppressive white society.

This was the public discourse of black femininity that both Diahann Carroll and Esther Rolle became a part of with their entrance into mainstream popular culture. Perhaps because of the nature of the familial situation comedy, these women were also working against the image of the black woman proposed by the Moynihan report. With *Julia* and *Good Times* in particular, recuperating the image of the black family is of critical importance. The poor impression of the African American community disseminated by the Moynihan report motivated a desire to uplift the image of the black family, which played a role in Carroll's and Rolle's interventions in the industry and thus in the women's constructions of their television identities.

The legacy of the Moynihan report, its meanings for black women and the black family, is evident in the discourse surrounding the creation of the sitcoms as well as in battles over the progression of characters and story lines. The desire for uplift entails a constant awareness of seeing oneself through the eyes of white America. The public nature of television, a venue in which the majority of white Americans would see these representations, created a crucial situation, because repeated fictionalized representations could reinforce preconceived beliefs about the black family. These women therefore concluded that it was their responsibility to place a corrective lens over the representation of the black family, not only for the black audience, but also for the large white television audience.

Far from simply being disempowered cogs within the television machine, both actresses are examples of increasing black agency within the industry. Furthermore, what they were unable to produce within the television image, they counteracted loudly within other media contexts. The actions of these women helped in opening up the concept of the television text beyond what was on the screen.

Because of the inherent power of the white-controlled television industry, it is often easy to overlook avenues of black agency within the industry. Certainly, as I will describe, *Julia* and *Good Times* themselves at times seemed to contradict this presence of black agency; both shows expressed very gradualist, if not regressive, politics. However, it is important to acknowledge that the televisual discourse did not remain unanswered. A dialogue existed between the performers and the producers that was carried out in very public forums and that challenged the mainstream conceptions of black life. It is this dialogue that the following analysis addresses.

African Americans historically have improvised ways to obtain political agency within American society. Earlier in the book, the concept of hidden transcripts, as used by African American historian Robin D. G. Kelley, was discussed.[3] The use of mainstream publications as a method of political action was a more vociferous form of these hidden transcripts. The television shows themselves were unable to properly address the concerns of these women or, indeed, to create a well-rounded vision of the black community, so these women looked elsewhere to express their dissatisfaction. As Kelley suggests in *Race Rebels*, within subcultures one often has to look to other spaces, the hidden transcripts, to locate the complete story. In this case, mainstream magazines provide a deeper understanding of the politics of *Julia* and *Good Times*.

As the era of integration opened up some access to mainstream tools for African Americans, the politics previously expressed within black communal spaces were now articulated in these public forums. The United States became painfully aware of black dissatisfaction with mainstream actions. The actors' words in magazines sparked discussion and debate and challenged the American racial dictatorship.[4]

As cultural critic Lynn Spigel writes,

> We can thus explore media as a ground for cultural debate. . . . we should not forget that culture is a process that entails power struggles and negotiations among various social ideals. Thus although the debates do not reflect a "happy pluralism," they do suggest that cultural changes take place within a framework of unstable power hierarchies in which different social forces must constantly reinvent their authority through the methods of control at their disposal. Discourse and representation is one such mechanism of control.[5]

These black women sought various methods of control over their image through their screen representations and through their statements in mainstream magazines. By the 1960s, the power of the media was firmly established, and thus control over the methods of representation suggested a significant level of power within the hands of white television producers. However, the meanings of the historical moment and the role of blackness within American society were challenged by some black actors and black media watchdogs. Whereas the producers vacillated between the need to be topical and the need to provide profitable entertainment, the

actors and black media critics placed a greater emphasis on uplifting the image of the race and therefore on what each representation
suggested. The analysis of *Julia* and *Good Times* describes these
women's struggle for control over their images.

"I'm a Black Women with a White Image"

> At the moment, we're presenting the white Negro. And he has very little
> Negro-ness. I don't delude myself into thinking that I'm operating in
> the context of anything but a white society. . . . The white community
> has to assuage its own conscience. Julia, of course, is a product of
> that. The white society has put a television-show on the air about black
> people. Now don't you know what that's going to be all about?
>
> **Diahann Carroll, in Richard Warren Lewis,**
> **"The Importance of Being Julia"**

In 1968 a half-hour situation comedy called *Julia* was introduced
by NBC to a nation of television viewers.[6] The story line was mundane enough: "a beautiful woman, her bright eyed child and their
suburban apartment . . . registered nurse whose Army husband had
died a hero in Vietnam. Her search for a new life in a strange city."[7]
Yet the show was the focal point of much uproar and controversy;
Julia was black. Although television featured black characters in
minor or supporting roles, *Julia* was the first situation comedy
to place a black character in the sole starring role since *Amos 'n'*
Andy and *Beulah* had both been canceled in 1953. This was a
watershed moment in television history. The genesis of this show
proves instrumental to understanding the political agenda evident
in the program's inception and illustrates the discourse in which the
star, Diahann Carroll, attempted to intervene. On March 22, 1967,
director of the NAACP, Roy Wilkins, delivered a speech at a fund-
raiser in Los Angeles. He was invited by Jack Valenti, president of
the Motion Picture Association of America, to address some of the
most powerful executives in the film and television industry. Hal
Kanter, creator of *Julia,* stated that he wanted to do more than
donate money to the NAACP and that he felt compelled to write
the show after listening to Wilkins's words.[8] *TV Guide* reporter
Richard Lewis summarizes the event.[9]

> Wilkins spoke calmly yet firmly about solutions to the crisis in the
> cities, a sober contrast to the *demagoguery* of his more *militant con-*

The character of Julia (Diahann Carroll) was written to integrate smoothly into white society. Dr. Chegley (Lloyd Nolan) and Corey (Marc Copage) were also stars of the show.

temporaries. His simple eloquence, reflecting optimism rather than despair, visibly moved many of those present.[10] (emphasis added)

The description of Wilkins's demeanor reveals a less than subtle judgment of the "militant" organizations of the Black Power movement. There is an embrace by Lewis of Wilkins's words and the voice of the NAACP, which adopted a more gradualist way of addressing social conflict. This was representative of the mainstream media's approach to the Civil Rights movement, especially with the increased presence of the Black Power movement. In the late '60s, black demands for political and social gains were vocalized by the urgency of the Black Power movement, and the goals of the Civil Rights movement were questioned from within black society. In saying that Wilkins inspired him, Kanter aligned his personal politics with the NAACP and not with groups that asserted a black power agenda.

The acceptance of Julia's character by mainstream America (the show enjoyed a successful three-season run) was also the acceptance of the gradualist politics that Kanter and, in essence, Julia herself espoused.[11] The absolute mundane nature of Julia's life suggests that, if only one works hard enough, integrating into mainstream society is unproblematic. One may run into a racist or two, but generally the world is full of good people who support integration.

Kanter was heralded by the press as "indisputably one of the most original minds in the television-motion-picture-radio fields, a selfless citizen who had created the series from 'an idea born of one man's desire to serve humanity.'"[12] Although brimming with political compassion, Kanter was criticized on many fronts for the show's inability to translate the complexities of black life on television. By dealing with black subject matter, Kanter had indeed placed himself and the show within the realm of contemporary politics. Kanter said he discovered that he needed to defend the show on two levels: First, he had to handle the complaints that the show did not address contemporary black problems. Second, there was the concern that, because Julia was out of the contemporary political loop, it would not attract a black audience. Kanter stated, "This is not a civil rights show. . . . What we're driving at is escapist entertainment, not a sociological document. . . . I'm not writing for a Negro audience or a white audience, only the largest possible audience."[13] This statement indicates that while Kanter implied that he created Julia as a response to the pleas of Roy Wilkins, the bottom line was that he wanted to create a profitable show. Therefore, in Kanter's eyes, he could not afford for the program to reflect the urgency of the moment. Relying on the moderate politics of organizations such as the NAACP allowed Kanter to represent the successful integration of blacks into American society. While this was a worthy step in the right direction, Kanter believed that the incorporation of so-called radical black politics would not sell to a mainstream U.S. audience.

On the other hand, from its inception, Diahann Carroll acknowledged her differing views on the possibilities of the program. Herein lies the power of the black woman's voice to complicate the conciliatory imagery presented on the screen. Much more outspoken than her televisual counterpart, Carroll was an active supporter of the Civil Rights and Black Power movements. She not only participated in the March on Washington but also raised money for the more "militant" SNCC. She was hopeful, though not naive, about *Julia*'s presence on network television. If nothing else, she saw it as an opportunity to draw more African Americans into television production. She pushed for stories that would at least address some issues of race. In later seasons, she insisted that her character wear a natural so as to address the changing black views on black pride. To the wide audience reading popular magazines, Carroll's words presented an opposing dialogue to the discourse of the actual episode texts.

For example, when addressing one of the central points of contention over the program—the lack of a husband for Julia—which, as black critics suggested, "contributed to the castration theme prevalent in Hollywood's customary depiction of the American Negro male,"[14] Kanter responded:

> In every other TV situation comedy, Dad is a bumbling idiot . . . he can't change a light bulb without short-circuiting the traffic light on the corner. Is it better to have a stupid, fumbling father with a matriarch who really runs everything or to have, in absentia, a man of heroic proportions whom you can allude to and talk about?[15]

Diahann Carroll did not comply with Kanter's views and within the same article suggested, "To remove the father image, the strong center of the family, is a very damaging thing to do to black children." She also acknowledged that the writers tended to create, "the white Negro. And he has very little Negro-ness."[16] It is this oppositional dialogue that needs to be addressed when discussing *Julia* and other black-themed programs. It indicates that some black performers did not fear challenging a producer publicly. While this may not have changed the casting of this particular program, *TV Guide* relayed to the public that these issues were of concern to Diahann Carroll and others in the black community.

Julia was basic sitcom fare. When the show dealt with racism, Julia usually misconstrued a person's actions or intentions. If someone was racist, he or she was usually an obvious target, someone constructed by the program as small-minded, marked as out of the ordinary and not a part of the day-to-day lives of Julia or her son,

Julia and Corey: Diahann Carroll objected to the decision to make Julia a single mother.

Corey (Marc Copage). The show denied that racism was a serious problem in American society; it worked to undermine the contemporary political and social realities of African American existence. Julia was a safe black person whom America could embrace. Unlike Carroll, Julia did not acknowledge, espouse, or approve of Black Nationalism, so evident in contemporary late-'60s U.S. society.

In the pilot, "Mama's Man" (March 29, 1968), Julia copes with moving into a new apartment and looking for a job. Knowing no one in her neighborhood and being a single mother, Julia must leave her seven-year-old son, Corey, at home to go on an initial interview. It is strongly insinuated that the interviewer, Mr. Colton, will not pass her résumé on to Dr. Chegley (Lloyd Nolan), the head physician, because she is black.

When she returns home, she finds Corey at a neighbor's apartment. Earl J. Waggedorn (Michael Link), a neighbor whom Corey invited in to play, has accidentally cut himself with a knife. Marie (Betty Beaird), Earl's mother, who is initially angry, forgives Julia almost instantaneously, offering to baby-sit whenever Julia needs her to. Julia is accepted into the white neighborhood, although she is a single black mother who has apparently jeopardized the safety of the children. The boys' conversation summarizes the atmosphere of the situation.

> EARL: That's your mother? *(Corey nods.)* You know what?
> COREY: What?
> EARL: Your mother's colored.
> COREY: Of course—I'm colored too.
> EARL: You are?
> COREY: Yeah. *(Laughter between the boys)*
> EARL: Oh boy!

Thus, Julia makes an unproblematic transition into the integrated world. While the show opens with the issue of racist hiring practices, the gravity of the situation is undermined by Julia's acceptance into the neighborhood. The aforementioned scene places the question of race into the conversation of the children, while the issue is of no concern to the adult Marie, who embodies the attitudes of white America as accepting of integration. Considering that as late as 1974 there were riots as a result of bussing black students into white schools in the so-called liberal, northern city of Boston, the supposed nonissue of Julia's color is somewhat naive.

This theme of tolerance, if not embrace, is supported by a follow-up conversation between Dr. Chegley and Julia. Chegley, who is shorthanded at the clinic, demands that Colton provide him with Julia's contact information after viewing her résumé. At the end of the episode, Chegley offers her an interview over the phone.

> JULIA: But has Mr. Colton told you?
> CHEGLEY: Told me what?
> JULIA: I'm colored.
> CHEGLEY: What color are you?
> JULIA: I'm a Negro.
> CHEGLEY: Have you always been a Negro, or are you just trying to be fashionable?
> *(Julia laughs.)*
> CHEGLEY: Nine o'clock, try and be pretty.

Chegley is clearly a sexist, not a racist. As Aniko Bodroghkozy suggests in her discussion of *Julia,* race can be approached within this mainstream setting only if regressive gender roles are endorsed.[17]

"The Interview" (April 4, 1968), the second of a two-part episode, also operates to deflate the seriousness of racism. On this occasion, the show also manages to implicate Julia in "falsely accusing" someone of discrimination. During the interview, Hannah Yarby (Lurene Tuttle), the white head nurse at Dr. Chegley's office, questions Julia's credentials and asks her about the Glade Hill Hospital of Nursing, where Julia obtained her degree.

> HANNAH: Is it [the hospital] black?
> JULIA: No. It's a lovely old red brick.
> CHEGLEY: Good for you! *(To Yarby)* And what kind of arrogance would prompt an outrageous question like that?
> HANNAH: What I meant was—
> JULIA: I know what you meant, Miss Yarby.

Julia, seemingly justified in her anger, walks out of the interview. However, Hannah visits Julia at her apartment to explain her actions. It was not a case of racism. Hannah explains that Dr. Chegley disagrees with everything she says; therefore, she treated Julia in that manner so that Chegley would hire her. All is well, and Julia is hired. Yet, the way the show leaves it indicates that Julia prejudged the situation. Never is it questioned that Yarby could have taken another tack—other than the use of race—and achieved the same result.

When the show deals with racism, the transgression is assigned to a character who is an outsider to the peaceful environment in which Julia exists. "Am I, Pardon the Expression, Blacklisted?" (May 6, 1969) is one such example. Julia works in a clinic situated within a government agency building and discovers that she has failed the initial security check. She is restricted to the clinic because of her participation in a group called ANTI. Mr. Potts, the head of security, assumes that the group is a militant organization. When Julia confronts Potts, he states, "My job is to question everyone, and in these days of militant demonstrations—with divisive forces at work in our land—you people in particular." The man is overtly discriminatory, and Julia quits when she realizes that she has been targeted because of her race. Also, what seems to outrage Julia even more is that ANTI is actually the "American Negro Training Institute . . . a nonprofit group of volunteers who teach our profession to underprivileged children . . . *of all races!*" (emphasis added).

Unfortunately, Julia's stand against this type of discrimination is fleeting. She heads back to work once she passes the security clearance. Racism is boiled down to being a personal misunderstanding. Julia's battle is only with Mr. Potts. Everyone else who works with Julia is outraged at the problem. The program does not explore structural or institutional racism but instead centers it on an individual. This, in turn, reduces the problems of racism to just the few who are not progressing with the times. It also works to code Julia as the "safe Negro," someone who obviously would not be involved with any of the so-called militant organizations that were active in America at the time. This, in turn, codes these black militant groups as dangerous and does not acknowledge that the U.S. government had, indeed, started an all-out offensive against these "militant" groups.

The outcome of "Am I, Pardon the Expression, Blacklisted?" is a delicate negotiation with contemporary reality. The show is topical, as the viewer is aware of black political activists. The episode acknowledges the practice of investigation and infiltration yet elides the visceral effects. The show describes the effects on Julia's life but will not condemn government infiltration. Julia is not a militant Negro; ANTI works to serve the "underprivileged children of *all* races." She returns to work because her catalyst to quit was personal outrage, not political or community consciousness. Julia remains isolated from a black community, which is reflected in her level of consciousness.

This is further illustrated in an episode from the second season. In "The Doctor's Dilemma" (February 17, 1969), Julia confronts the notions of black separatism. This is perhaps the most insidious of all of the episodes discussed here, because it not only exonerates white Americans from the contemporary problems of race but also turns blame on African Americans for societal divisions. Julia asks a black woman, Mrs. Deering, to baby-sit Corey while she is at work. Julia discovers that Mrs. Deering refuses to let Corey play with Earl and instead brings along young relatives to keep Corey company. When confronted by Julia, she admits to keeping Corey in to play with the other black children, as the only friend he seems to have is Earl, who "don't even look high yeller." Julia defends her position:

> JULIA: Corey and Earl both have *other* friends—black, yellow, red and white—and that I am thankful of. They share friendships with *all* children—to *know* each other. Is there anything wrong with that? Certainly not!
>
> DEERING: Maybe. But there's so many people trying to drive folks apart. We got to be careful.
>
> JULIA: Being careful is one thing—over protective, another. Mothers can't suffocate their children Mrs. Deering, not in today's changing world.
>
> DEERING: Changing too fast for me!
>
> JULIA: It was too long coming. And I want my son to have every opportunity I had to stand up and fight for—but some people were afraid to even dream of.
>
> *(Stage directions: As the words sink in, Mrs. Deering's awakening is expressed by a wide-eyed, smiling admiration.)*[18]
>
> DEERING: Lo-o-r-rd-dee!

Julia is presented as someone who has reaped the benefits of integration and simply wants to provide her child with the best the integrated world can offer, while Mrs. Deering questions the overall embrace of integration.

The 1965–66 academic year at Howard University exemplifies the extent to which integration was questioned. As an academic institution, Howard strove to create a curriculum that replicated the best white universities in the country. Often called the Black Harvard, Howard confronted the black consciousness of its student body in the late '60s. This was exemplified by the victory of Robin Gregory as homecoming queen in the fall of 1966. Gregory based her campaign on issues of black pride and wore a natural, or an Afro, in contrast to previous homecoming queens, who were judged on their ability to imitate white standards of beauty—one of the cultural pitfalls of integration. Gregory's victory sparked protests in which students demonstrated against mandatory ROTC training imposed on incoming freshmen as well as discrepancies in the educational curriculum, which largely ignored black history. Students suspended attending class and eventually took over the administrative building until Howard administrators were willing to agree to many of their demands.

As discussed in chapter 1, this was a period in which many black political and social organizations discussed the ramifications of integration, selling out, losing one's identity, and the breakup of black communities with black professionals' exodus to the suburbs. In "The Doctor's Dilemma," all of these concerns, which were part of the rhetoric of Black Nationalism and black consciousness, are invalidated because they are embodied in a woman who is demonized and positioned as ignorant.

Even when Julia expresses a sense of consciousness, her words are easily diminished. In "Am I, Pardon the Expression, Blacklisted?" Julia comes home to discover that Corey and Earl have been shining shoes to earn money for a toy. Very upset about the incident, she explains to Marie why she will not allow Corey to continue.

> JULIA: Because there was a time when that was all our men could do—shine shoes, wait tables, menial jobs.
> MARIE: Times have changed, Julia. Today they're supreme court justices, senators, labor leaders, mayors—Thurgood Marshall, Philip Randolph, Edward Brooks, Carl Stokes. Oh Julia, come on! Maybe there used to be a stigma attached to manual labor, but today hod carriers and brick masons all earn as much as a lot of professionals.
> (Stage directions: Julia smiles, agreeing with and impressed by Marie's simple logic. Things are changing and we know that this is a better world because of the Marie Waggedorns.)

Julia's point is based on historical precedent. However, her concerns are invalidated or reduced by Marie's "simple logic." Mainstream U.S. society has traditionally used the success of the few to deflect the problems of the majority. The underlying implication: if these few can make it, it is not a case of institutional racism but a case of personal failure.

Julia and Corey were embraced by their neighbors the Waggedorns, Marie (Betty Baird) and Earl J. (Michael Link).

Carroll would not be deterred by her televisual representation and worked at countering this within the written media. In a 1970 issue of *TV Guide*, featuring her portrait on the cover, Carroll addressed the contemporary black political situation, the realities of the militant organizations, and the police attacks on the Panthers. Acknowledging the recent police raid on Panther headquarters in Los Angeles, Carroll spoke with vehemence to the reporter, and her analysis of the political moment is worth quoting at length.

> I can understand the police not liking the Panthers, even thinking that the Panthers are a threat to the Government, but to stamp them out in that way. . . . It's a funny thing about the Government . . . there'd be a beating or a lynching or a mutilation, the Government had such difficulty tracking them [members of the Ku Klux Klan] down, or gathering evidence about them, or taking their arms away. The police never could seem to find out who they were. But here come the Panthers . . . and all of a sudden the forces of law and order have no trouble at all finding headquarters in every city, going right in to look for arms, shooting everybody who either gives them any trouble, or looks as if they're going to. All of a sudden the Government is strong, plenty strong.[19]

Carroll's sarcasm and anger are clear, and the publication of her statements in such a mainstream periodical worked as an intervention in the televisual discourse, a way of jarring the American viewer out of the reality of *Julia* and into the American reality. Carroll referred to her character as a sellout in this article and questioned whether the United States would ever accept shows that are about black people who are neither stereotypes nor "superspades," programs that would show black people simply relating to each other. At this point, she considered the changes in television for blacks:

> Minuscule . . . pitiful . . . minute . . . it's a vogue. It started as a vogue. . . . I think the whole thing is going to be measured in dollars and cents. If it's to the advantage of the management, the sponsors, they'll keep us on. When the vogue ends, and when somebody starts counting up the profits, that's when we'll find out what's going to happen.[20]

While it is difficult to measure the effects of such statements, their words remain evidence of black resistance within mainstream spaces. These voices refused to comply with television's depictions. Without such active black response in producing counternarratives, the regressive politics suggested by *Julia* would have remained unchallenged. Future programming also would not have needed to address or attempt to explore black life beyond the confines of integrated and assimilated *Julia*.

Julia ended in 1971 after three seasons; both Kanter and Carroll reportedly wanted to work on different projects. Diahann Carroll continued to respond to the televisual image after *Julia*'s demise. In 1974, she starred in the film *Claudine*. As Claudine, Carroll played a character who was conversant with the representation of Julia. Although both are single mothers, Claudine lives in the inner city and has to deal with the harsh realities of the welfare system. Carroll's image was far from the highly made up and stylish Julia; she was often pictured in a housecoat, tired after a long day of work.

The film is very critical of the welfare system, and Claudine incisively points out the flaws. In a conversation with the welfare investigator, she questions her treatment by the worker, who is suspicious of her efforts to make a better life for her children. She also critiques the media and societal discourse, which suggest that the welfare system allows one to live a comfortable life. Furthermore, she reveals the ways in which the system actually works to keep black men and women apart. Carroll earned an Academy Award nomination for her performance.

The use of other media resources to question the televisual discourse carried over to other black-cast shows in the 1970s. This method of resistance, seen with the production of *Sanford and Son*, was even more evident in the conflicts surrounding the production of *Good Times*.

Good Times?

MICHAEL: There are a lot of good movies out there—*Black Belt Jones, Blacula, The Black Godfather, Six Black Men.*

FLORIDA: They all sound like violent pictures to me. I don't like violence.

THELMA: There is a comedy out with James Earl Jones and Diahann Carroll called *Claudine*. James Earl Jones is a garbage man, and she's on welfare.

FLORIDA: Julia on welfare—this I've got to see.

Good Times, "The Gang," 1974

I have to watch closely to see the show doesn't stray too far from the ideals in which it was conceived. Sometimes people go for a quickie— a cheap laugh. I don't mind not getting every laugh if we stick to the spine of what we started with. A good gutsy laugh comes out of a real situation, not from the surface. A laugh out of nothing is soon forgotten, but a laugh with a twist you remember for a long time.

Esther Rolle, in John Riley, "Esther Rolle the Fishin' Pole"

There was a level of intertextuality to the women's performances, a realization that each image was building on, or in conversation with, one from the past. While Carroll attempted to broaden the image of black women in the arena of film with *Claudine*, Esther Rolle stepped into television with *Good Times*. As the dialogue and quotation above indicate, Rolle and the writers were aware of televisual history and sought to create an oppositional dialogue.

Along with the individual performers, black organizations focused on television as a tool to raise the consciousness of the nation. There was an immense amount of public pressure placed on the industry for discriminatory practices within hiring and programming. In 1972, the Black Caucus, an organization of African American Democrats in the U.S. Congress, organized hearings entitled "The Mass Media and the Black Community." The caucus charged the white media organizations with racist news coverage and hiring practices. The chairman of the caucus, William L. Clay, stated,

> The fact that the black community, black community workers, black organizations and the black movement are variously excluded, distorted, mishandled, and exploited by the white-controlled mass media [is obvious] to the most casual observer. . . . [The media] have not communicated to whites a feeling for the difficulties and frustrations of being a Negro in the United States . . . [or] indicate[d] the black perspective on national and local issues.[21]

Waymon Wright of the Black Caucus's staff also indicated that "[t]he media, because of racism, see all blacks as interchangeable, undifferentiated. . . . This is the deepest kind of racism, that denies all individual differences."[22] The importance placed on the role the media play in conveying black life to a white audience again ties into the underlying dilemma of uplift, the concern with how the white world views the black world. This is expressed in the desire to see a positive black identity on national television. However, the fact that blacks in Congress debated television is also evidence that television became a site of struggle to change the U.S. racial dictatorship.

When Esther Rolle accepted the role of Florida on *Good Times,* this was the atmosphere that she entered—one in which the role of the black image was actively debated in public settings. She came to television from a long career in community theater and on- and off-Broadway productions. She also worked in sweatshops in the garment and luggage industry and in the city civil service to support her acting career. She was selected by Norman Lear for the role of a maid on the sitcom *Maude* (1972–78) after she was featured in Melvin Van Peebles's play *Don't Play Us Cheap.*[23] When offered the part, Rolle at first refused, saying, "No! I don't want to be no Hollywood maid. They don't want a *black* woman. They want something they cooked up in their heads."[24] Eventually, Lear convinced her that the role on *Maude* would be different from that of the stereotypical Hollywood representation of the domestic. In her acceptance of the character, Rolle acknowledged what she thought her position in television could do.

> I've always been very unhappy about the role of domestics. The black woman in America doesn't need to go to drama school to be a maid. The old actresses who played the black maid stereotypes are not villains—it's the ones who hired them. We have been stereotyped and unrecognized for too long. Anyone who digs in the earth or scrubs somebody's floor—I don't blame them for taking that job, I ache that they had to do it.[25]

Rolle sought to rewrite, challenge, and uplift the role of the stereotypical Hollywood maid in what she conceived of as a more positive image.

Norman Lear and Tandem Productions had already gained the reputation of dealing with contentious matters. With Lear's decision to create another spin-off with Rolle as the lead character, the controversial hook was evident, not only in the characters, but also in the setting of the show, which placed the characters in the Chicago projects known as Cabrini-Green. Even with renowned producers such as Norman Lear on board, it was clear to Rolle that she would have to monitor the program for the ways in which the black community was represented. She wanted the show to provide an uplifting view of the black family.

Uplift, within the trajectory of *Good Times,* works in terms of both image and pedagogy. This is apparent in the actors' concern with the image portrayed on the screen and with the ways in which the show attempts to work as a pedagogical tool—education being one of the implicit desires of an uplift project. As Rolle suggests in her comments on the types of roles that she chooses,

> I've always been selective about my roles . . . still am. First of all, I have to like me, and I couldn't like me if I depicted crap that made a black child hang its head. I feel an obligation to do something that will make him stick his little chest out and say, "Did you see that!?" My goal is [also] to give black women dignity.[26]

Rolle felt obligated to portray a character that uplifted the African American image and instilled black pride in a viewer.

To begin with, unlike any previous black-cast sitcom, the show had a nuclear black family. This was not a part of the visionary genius of Norman Lear but the result of the increased agency of black performers. It also shows the role that uplift played in the actors' demands. According to social historian Kevin Gaines,

> [o]ppression kept African Americans from fulfilling the majority society's normative gender conventions. . . . For educated blacks, the family, and patriarchal gender relations, became crucial signifiers of respectability. Bitter, divisive memories of the violence and humiliations of slavery and segregation were and remain at the heart of uplift ideology's romance of the patriarchal family, expressed by black men and women's too-often-frustrated aspirations to protect and be protected.[27]

When Rolle first read the script, she noted the absence of any black father and simply responded that if this was not rectified, they could get someone else to play the role.[28] The desire to embrace the notion of the nuclear family is an important part of uplift ideology and a key point in the discourse surrounding the production of *Julia.* Rolle's actions also represent a cognizance of the impact of the Moynihan report, which branded the black family dysfunctional. Rolle refused to participate in furthering this legacy by placing the image of the matriarchal black family into the media forum and instead presented what she believed to be an uplifting image of the black family.

The story became that of the Evans family: James Sr. (John Amos), the father, who works long hours for little pay or is out of work and looking for a job; Florida, the mother of the house, who is struggling to make ends meet and keep her family together; Thelma (BernNadette Stanis), the intelligent daughter, who is determined to succeed; J.J., or James Jr. (Jimmie Walker), the elder son, who is an artist and provides comic relief for the show; and Michael (Ralph Carter), the younger son, who is the voice of militancy, speaking the rhetoric of the revolution and often termed the militant midget by other characters. Their neighbor and Florida's best friend is a single workingwoman, Willona (Ja'Net DuBois). *Good Times* proposed to address the life of a black family living in Cabrini-Green, one of the most notorious housing projects in Chicago.

According to African American historians John Hope Franklin and Alfred A. Moss, between "1940 and 1970 the black population outside the old Confederacy increased from nearly 4 million to more than 11 million, representing almost 50 percent of the total black population."[29] The majority settled in large cities, such as New York, Chicago, Los Angeles, Oakland, Detroit, Boston, Washington DC, and Philadelphia. Chicago was representative of the large northern, urban, inner cities to which African Americans migrated. It was also a particularly politically charged and nationally known arena because of the vocal and publicized attempts of the SCLC to intervene in the poor living and working conditions of the black population there.

In the January 5, 1966, report, "A Proposal by the Southern Leadership Conference for the Development of a Nonviolent Movement for the Greater Chicago Area"—the Chicago Plan—the SCLC stated, "The Chicago Problem is simply a matter of economic exploitation. Every condition exists simply because someone profits by its existence. The economic exploitation is crystallized in the SLUM."[30]Among many other charges, the report specified that black families paid over twenty dollars more in rent per month than families in other neighborhoods, and they received fewer services. Slum landlords did not pay for the upkeep of the buildings, because properties that were more rundown cost less in taxes. The amount of money put into the education of black children in Chicago was from half to two-thirds less than what was spent on white children. The education system thus perpetuated the lack of job opportunities open to blacks in the community. Martin Luther King and the SCLC initially proposed a list of twenty-four demands to

The characters of *Good Times*: (from left to right) Michael (Ralph Carter), Thelma (BernNadette Stanis), Willona (Ja'Net DuBois), Florida (Esther Rolle), J.J. (Jimmie Walker), and (center front) James Sr. (John Amos). J.J.'s role as comic relief is visible.

Chicago mayor Richard J. Daley. However, a ten-point agreement that lacked any political recourse—no way of protesting injustices within the system—was signed in 1967, leaving the predicament of African American, inner-city residents of Chicago unchanged.

As previously mentioned, the Panther Party, under the leadership of Fred Hampton, became involved in Chicago to address the poverty and general malaise evident in the community; the group instituted free breakfast programs, educational programs, and job training. However, the FBI also targeted Hampton. The bureau conspired with the Chicago police to raid Panther headquarters, and the two organizations were involved in tactics to encourage gang warfare between a local black gang, the Blackstone Rangers, and the Panther Party. They plotted to destroy the free breakfast programs, school, and newspaper. This aggression culminated on December 4, 1969, with the planned assassination of Chicago Panther leader Fred Hampton in his apartment as he slept. Chicago was the archetype for urban black life. The placement of *Good Times* in Chicago, like the setting of *Sanford and Son* in the inner-city Los Angeles community of Watts, is again evidence of Lear's attempts to keep the shows topical. This created a direct link to aspects of African American contemporary social and political realities.

The series initially addresses realistic problems, such as the threat of eviction in "Getting Up the Rent" (February 22, 1974). "Junior the Senior" (March 7, 1974) discusses the aforementioned notoriously inferior school system, as J.J. was passed a grade without earning it. "The Gang" (October 24, 1974) confronts the problems of local street gangs. Even within these early shows, the gravity of the episode is balanced by the safeguard of J.J.'s humor, whose ritualistic yelling of "dy-no-mite" seems to allay the seriousness of most situations. The use of comic relief is to be expected in any sitcom format; however, as the seasons continued, the focus began to shift more toward J.J.'s clowning, which advanced from mere comic relief to disruption and a subversion of any political agenda.

Consequently, as with *Julia,* the actors used newspapers and magazines to counteract the images on television. As Rolle suggested in the second epigraph that opens this section, she indeed perceived her role as being the guardian over the process, to make sure that the show stayed within what she conceived of as its original goals. As the times allowed, these black television stars began to use their popularity and commercial viability to their advantage in order to gain agency within the industry. Esther Rolle and, to some extent, John Amos used their voices to impact the scripts and the direction of the show. When this did not work, they used their absence, as well as media resources, to protest. Rolle in particular used the press to create vocal counternarratives to the presentations on the screen when they did not meet her personal standards.

This is why, as a whole, *Good Times* is politically contested terrain in which contradictory meanings often occurred. *Good Times* vacillated between competing agendas. Some of the cast members desired changes in the script to provide uplifting images of the black community. These changes took on both representational and pedagogical qualities. There were also the needs of the market and producers and the necessity for the show to be commercially viable. Three types of episodes arose from these internal conflicts and became evident in viewing the series: pedagogical, political, and "pure sitcom."[31] Rolle reacted most vehemently toward some of the pure sitcoms.

Pedagogical Content

The pedagogical episode typically involves an overt attempt to teach the audience about a particular issue. Many episodes have a moral or message, and the manner of conversation within these episodes is quite pointed and didactic. Characters often engage in monologues about specific topical issues, such as health, education, and gang violence. These conversations encompass much screen time without furthering the plot line. These episodes are illustrative of uplift through education. They also satisfy the producers' needs to address complaints of groups such as the aforementioned Black Caucus by creating socially responsible shows.

In "IQ Test" (1974), Michael deliberately does poorly on the test because he believes IQ tests are biased. The school suggests that Michael enroll in a trade program rather than pursue an academic career. Michael, Florida, and James engage in long monologues, backed up by statistics, about the cultural biases of standardized examinations. As Michael explains,

> They don't know it, but that IQ exam was nothing but a white racist test. . . . This one was given by the white people, made up by white people, and even graded by white people. It don't tell you how smart you are, just how white you are. That's why the average black score is fifty points lower than the average white. . . . The black community is different, it has a different language and culture altogether. . . . They ask questions on the test like this: complete the following phrase, "cup and ___," and you have to choose from four words, *wall, saucer, table,* or *window.* . . . You know what my friend Eddy put down? *Cup* and *table,* because in his house he don't have no saucers to put under his cup.

The characters also directly refer to published books that explore the subjects, such as standardized tests, discussed in these pedagogical episodes. "Michael the Warlord" (October 13, 1976) addresses the younger son's involvement with a street gang. The parents call a building meeting to discuss the gang situation in the neighborhood. Statistics about urban youth are used to support the reality of their concerns.

One of the clearest examples of what I am describing as a pedagogical program is "The Checkup" (May 3, 1974). The Evans family is concerned that James's erratic behavior may be caused by hypertension. James has been coming home in a bad mood each day and is easily frustrated by the actions of his children. He yells frequently, smashes chairs, and kicks in doors. Michael conducts research on the possible causes and reads aloud to the family a long segment on the symptoms and causes of hypertension. He suggests that it is "the number-one killer of black people" and is "caused by the stress and frustration of ghetto life."

When Florida decides to cook James's favorite meal to cheer him up, the menu includes "fresh collard greens, chitlins, sweet potatoes, corn bread and butter, and pork chops." Thelma quickly chimes in, "Soul food is one of the big causes of hypertension. It's not really the soul food, but it is all the grease and salt we use when we cook it." Although it turns out that James does not have hypertension, his cholesterol is high, and the doctor warns him to stay away from fried foods and advises him to eat cottage cheese and to come in for a yearly physical.

This program has an educational dimension, which also provides an underlying cultural critique. "The Checkup" episode seeks to explain the problems of hypertension, seemingly to a black audience, and provides steps that one should take to alleviate the condition. When the family encourages James to go for a checkup, he worries about the cost:

MICHAEL: Daddy, the article said that most black people don't take enough physical examinations.

JAMES: I hope that article also said that most black people can't afford to pay for physical examinations. *(Audience applauds.)*

FLORIDA: Oh, but, James, you can get a free one at the clinic.

The episode is a guide for how to deal with hypertension and the routes that one can follow to alleviate the problem. In the early

1970s, the social conditions described by the SCLC were obviously still an issue in Chicago and many other urban centers. The programs recommended by the SCLC were not implemented, and free health care probably was not as easily accessed as on *Good Times*. The physician that James sees is clearly well qualified, and the clinic does not appear to be crowded or lacking any major supplies. Concluding the episode on such a positive note is misleading, projecting a false sense of hope that was not a contemporary reality. However, what the episode constructively illustrates in a striking manner is the underlying agenda of education and the use of television to deliver the message.

Political and Daily Life

Although the agendas or political projects of many of the *Good Times* episodes are veiled, many others assert themselves as overtly political. In "Michael Gets Suspended" (March 8, 1974), the child voices his complaints about the inaccuracies of American history lessons and is suspended because he calls George Washington a racist. "J.J. Becomes a Man" explores the prevalence of false arrests and blatant racism in the police department. "The Crosstown Bus Runs All Day, Doodah, Doodah" (October 1, 1974) is one of the clearest examples of an overtly political episode. It addresses the issue of busing—a result of the long battles for school desegregation and one of the central civil rights controversies. Here it is interesting to observe the ways in which television acknowledges a multifaceted black community with varying ideas on political issues. Within the episode, various family members actively debate many sides of this complicated issue.

Michael claims that his school is one of the worst in the country, a claim easily supported by the aforementioned SCLC report. He pickets the board of education with a sign that reads, If You Can Read This Sign You Did Not Go to Harding Elementary School. Mr. Pierson, Michael's principal, visits the Evans parents to discuss the voluntary busing program. Students will be bused to the Roger Park School in a white neighborhood. He says, "We've found students like Michael tend to learn a lot more when they are surrounded by other students who are also highly motivated to learn." The fact that Pierson is a black man is relevant, as it alleviates the racism in his comment, which implies that black people are generally not motivated to learn. This comment also ignores the disparity in the school system and the possibility that white children may benefit simply from better facilities.

Michael on the other hand, as the voice of black youth and possessing a sense of militancy, believes that "busing is just a way of buying us off." Florida and James believe that Michael should participate, but the family debates the pros and cons of busing. Thelma believes that Michael will lose all of his neighborhood friends and thus his connection to the community. Florida worries about the destruction of buses that transport black children to white schools. James replies,

> I wish y'all could hear yourselves. . . . I'd be worried about him too, but I worry less about him making his mark in the world if I know he got a chance to get a good education. . . . But two minutes ago y'all was talking just like white people do about bussing—the only reason they talk that way is because they trying to cover up the fact they don't want to go to school with us.

What James's voice represents is the traditional concern of uplift ideology—the notion that education is the key to moving yourself up into the middle class. However, James's role also serves another purpose: While acknowledging white society's role in disrupting school desegregation, he lessens the responsibility by shifting part of the blame onto the fears of black people. Further, when James claims that the busing assaults were the result of a "few sick people," he deflates the issue from an institutional level to an individual one. The issues against busing and the problems of the elementary school are primarily enunciated through Michael, the person who wields the revolutionary rhetoric but the least power in the household. This constructs militant ideology as childish.

The parents both agree that Michael should participate in busing and manipulate him into attending the school in the white neighborhood.

> JAMES: Florida, you heard the boy—he don't want to go to school.
> It's okay. Ain't nothing we can do if he's ashamed of being black.
> MICHAEL: What you mean—'shamed of being black?
> FLORIDA: Oh, that was just a mistake. Your father didn't mean it.
> MICHAEL: I ain't ashamed of nothing.
> FLORIDA: Of course you're not. Maybe you're just scared to sit

Good Times constructs militancy as childish: younger son, Michael, embodies black power ideology.

down in the middle of all those white kids and prove to 'em that you're just as smart as they are.

MICHAEL: That ain't it.

JAMES: That's all right, son. There's a lot of players in the minor leagues who'd rather stay there than try and face major league pitching.

MICHAEL: I could get just as good grades in that school as they do, if I wanted to.

FLORIDA: I guess we'll never know.

MICHAEL: You don't think I can.

FLORIDA: There's only one way to prove it—still got time to catch that bus.

MICHAEL: You think I'm afraid of them.

JAMES: Must be. I don't see you moving.

Within this dialogue, the dignity, strength, and issue of double consciousness implicit in uplift ideology—the notion of proving yourself to the white population—are all evident. Again, however, it places the responsibility of fighting racism solely on the shoulders of black folks.

Pure Sitcom

Numerous episodes of *Good Times* fall within the category of pure sitcom. As the seasons progressed, the frivolous episodes outnumbered the more relevant as J.J. became the focal point of the sitcom. As early as 1975, Esther Rolle and John Amos began to express their displeasure with the role that J.J. was taking on the show. John Amos had concerns about the writing and felt that the show began to concentrate too much on J.J.'s antics.[32] Amos's comments again reveal the importance placed on the medium of television and the role of the patriarchal black family within the notion of positive representation.

> The only regrets I would have about leaving Good Times is that it might mean the show would revert to the matriarchal thing—the fatherless black family. TV is the most powerful medium we have, and there just are not enough positive black male images.[33]

In a 1975 article in *Ebony* magazine, Rolle, who insisted that she was "more dedicated to doing a show of worth than to doing a funny show," stated:

He's [J.J.] 18 and he doesn't work. He can't read and write. He doesn't think. The show didn't start out to be that. Michael's role of a bright, thinking child has been subtly reduced. Little by little—with the help of the artist [Jimmy Walker], I suppose, because they couldn't do that to me—they have made him more stupid and enlarged the role. [Negative images] have been quietly slipped in on us through the character of the oldest child. I resent the imagery that says to black kids that you can make it by standing on the corner saying "Dy-no-mite!"[34]

Norman Lear released John Amos from his contract in September 1976. Rolle eventually quit the show before the 1977–78 season because of her displeasure with the character J.J. and the general direction the show was taking. Once Rolle was gone, J.J. became entrenched as the head of the household, and the category of pure sitcom is clearly evident.[35]

In the episode "Wheels" (September 9, 1977), J.J. and his friends purchase a used car from the building manager, Bookman. Although the suggestion that wealthier people who live in better neighborhoods pay less insurance is briefly introduced, the episode revolves primarily around the mishaps with the vehicle and provides time for J.J. to sing with his friends. In "J.J.'s Condition" (January 19,

Esther Rolle criticized the character J.J. in newspapers and magazines.

1978), J.J. becomes involved with a married woman. He develops stomach pains and, in a familiar routine, blames it on Thelma's cooking. He later discovers that it is not guilt that is causing his pain but a stomach ulcer.

One blatant example of the pure sitcom is "Blood Will Tell" (January 18, 1979). In this episode J.J. must decide whether he will donate his blood to Sweet Daddy, the neighborhood loan shark. The loan shark and his gang are dressed in slick suits, and the "audience" erupts with comments such as "Hey, Superfly" upon the group's entrance. Later we see Sweet Daddy dressed in red velvet pajamas, riding around in a matching wheelchair, and he has a red velvet bedspread with a heart on it.

When J.J. considers making the donation, Willona says, "Forgive my expression, but it really is a black day in the Evans family." The show was reduced to using the accoutrements of urban blackness without any sense of relevance. The basic pun or play on words replaces the realistic yet humorous exchanges of the early series.

The regressive politics of the series did not remain unanswered. Esther Rolle continued to scrutinize the developments, and her comments were published in various magazines. She criticized the ways in which the writers wrote her out of the series. The show explained that, because of illness, she had moved south after her second marriage. Rolle believed her departure made her appear to have deserted her growing children. "A mother just wouldn't do that. It's wrong, terribly wrong."[36] She was dismayed when Willona adopted a child, Penny, because the character whom Ja'Net DuBois portrayed was single and rarely home. Rolle's vigilance paid off, and Norman Lear pursued her to return to the show. CBS agreed to replace the producers and deemphasize the role of J.J. Rolle was also given a position as script consultant.

> There were a lot of things that I was dissatisfied with. Well, CBS fixed the things that were troubling me the most. They agreed to my terms. . . . They are supposed to make J.J. a more meaningful character. They say they'll take some of that junk off him and dress him a little differently. They say they'll try to make him more intelligent. Personally, I don't know how intelligent they can make him. After all, you can't get blood from a turnip. But we're sure gonna try. Basically, we hope to put the show back on the foundation it started on. . . . I just hope it isn't too late to make the show work.[37]

The episodes of the final season do indicate an attempt to engage in the issues and situations of the early series. "Where Have All the Doctors Gone?" (February 15, 1979) interrogates the flight of the professional class from inner-city communities. Everyone in the family is sick and particularly concerned about Penny. Florida tries to find a doctor to take care of her. The show describes internalized racism, as Dr. Kelley, a black woman, continually refers to the Evanses as "you people." She also blames them for their health problems and suggests that all they have to do is not purchase "fat back and pigs feet" and instead buy "lean meat, fresh fruit, and vegetables." Florida, of course, challenges her assumptions, points out to her that the items she recommends are too expensive, and gets her to realize how she has distanced herself from inner-city African Americans.

Unfortunately, it was too late for *Good Times* to recuperate in the ratings. Even the aforementioned "Blood Will Tell" appeared after Rolle had returned to the show, and the series was canceled in 1979. In the final episode all of the loose ends are tied up. Thelma's husband, Keith, who had quit football because of an injury and was informed that if he played again he could be crippled, accepts a sixty thousand dollar offer to play for the Chicago Bears. J.J. sells his cartoon, Dy-no-woman, and goes to college. Florida is invited to live with Thelma and Keith, and Willona gets the apartment in their new house.

African American cultural critic Henry Louis Gates once described *Good Times* as the television show that represented the greatest potential and yet was the greatest failure.[38] The unproblematic conclusion to the series is perhaps the clearest indication of the collapse of a show that had started off with such great promise. More significant, however, is the trace evidence of resistance that both *Good Times* and *Julia* leave behind—that of the strength of black women to challenge the white mainstream television venue using whatever means or resources at their disposal.

It is also clear how uplift ideology, in its contemporary form, informed the battle over the images of black televisual families. The emphasis was placed on the need for images of the patriarchal black family, and these women displayed an urgency regarding how their image was constructed and received by viewers, black and white. The women's interviews in major magazines targeted to black and white consumers are visible signs that challenges to mainstream imaginings of blackness were no longer hidden in the postintegration era. With political and social integration and the integration of television came the opportunity to openly express the concerns of black society and to resist the constructions of black people perpetuated by the media and the U.S. political machine.

6. That Nigger's Crazy

The Rise and Demise of
The Richard Pryor Show

The debut of *The Richard Pryor Show* on television in the fall of 1977 was a seemingly natural progression, considering the presence of increasingly outspoken African American television performers in the late 1970s. As seen on *Sanford and Son* and *Good Times*, for example, African American performers used their network visibility to express more directly black political concerns as well as issues with the industry's handling of black topics and characters. Within this climate, perhaps there was potential for a successful Richard Pryor series.

When NBC reached out to Richard Pryor in 1977, the network targeted a man whose popularity was established primarily within the black communal spaces of nightclubs and concert performances. Although Pryor had achieved mainstream attention through his films, in 1977 his primary venue of discourse remained critical stand-up comedy, either in live performances or on platinum-selling comedy albums. During the late 1970s, the opinions he expressed and the characters he performed defied mainstream co-optation. Yet NBC could not resist the potential for financial gain by making Pryor one of its family.

The results? *The Richard Pryor Show* lasted four episodes, a circumstance that elicits several questions. Why was network television unable to accommodate Pryor's comedy? Can this show be considered a black site of resistance against mainstream constructions of blackness? What does the show represent within the larger scope of African American social, political, and industry politics at the closing of the Black Revolution? To answer these questions, one has to delve into Pryor's personal history and engagement with mainstream and underground comedy.

Super Nigger: From the Streets to Las Vegas

In 1940 Richard Pryor was born in Peoria, Illinois, to former boxer LeRoy Pryor Jr. and prostitute Gertrude Thomas. His paternal grandmother, Marie Carter Pryor Bryant, ran a series of whorehouses in Peoria and was primarily responsible for Pryor's welfare. Drug dealers, pimps, prostitutes, winos, and junkies were all a part of his neighborhood. Kicked out of Catholic school because of his family's line of work, Pryor was unable to fit into the public school system; he was expelled from one high school and dropped out of another. From then on he took jobs here and there, and until he joined the army in 1958, he spent the majority of his time on the streets or hanging out in a bar and pool hall owned by his family. Pryor began performing comedy while enlisted in the army from 1958 to 1960, and when he returned to Peoria he worked at black venues, such as Harold's Club and Collins' Corner as an emcee and opening act. Like Redd Foxx and many other black comedians before him, he began traveling the Chitlin' Circuit and in 1963 moved to New York City. After he was rejected at the Apollo, Pryor performed at local clubs in Greenwich Village, including the Improv, the Bitter End, and Café Wha? It was at these Village clubs that Pryor gained a reputation as a performer and was subsequently offered stints at the uptown New York clubs. During this time in his career he was a self-described imitator of Bill Cosby's comedic style. In his autobiography Pryor discusses his reaction to seeing Bill Cosby perform at a club called the Cellar in the early 1960s:

> I decided that's who I was going to be from then on.
> Bill Cosby.
> Richard Cosby.
> If the material wasn't exactly Bill's, the delivery was. So much so I
>   should've informed people.
> But other comics caught on and asked, "What the fuck happened?"
> I said, "I'm going for the bucks."[1]

Early on, a white agent confirmed Pryor's beliefs by telling him that he needed to act like Bill Cosby, a black person that white people would accept into their homes.[2] Pryor continued to perform "color-less" material in major venues and in his TV debut on a variety show, *On Broadway Tonight,* on August 31, 1964. He followed this with television appearances on *The Tonight Show, Ed Sullivan, Merv Griffin,* and *Kraft Music Hall.*

In an interview with *Ebony* magazine in 1967, Pryor discussed his feelings about television. He said that while he enjoyed per-forming he was frustrated by the limits created by the sponsors. He believed that to be on television comedians had to compromise themselves.

> Be clean. They always say "be clean." . . . They want you to be something that really doesn't exist at all. . . . I do the shows, but I just get bugged. I don't know about the other cats, but it bothers me. . . . They would rather use the dirtiest ofay cat in the world, man, than use [the term] black cat.[3]

Later that year Pryor had what he considered a breakdown.[4] Comedic vignettes that are typically the most hilarious evolve from personal experiences. By imitating Bill Cosby, Pryor denied the ex-istence of the earlier years of his life. While Cosby was a storyteller of a middle-class and family lifestyle, Pryor's life experience was garnered from a much different perspective.

One night while appearing at the Aladdin Hotel in Las Vegas, he simply walked offstage muttering, "What the fuck am I doing here?" As Pryor states,

> I couldn't explain the transformation taking place. I don't under-stand it myself. I only know my days of pretending to be as slick and colorless as Cosby were numbered. There was a world of junkies and winos, pool hustlers and prostitutes, women and family scream-ing inside my head, trying to be heard. The longer I kept them bottled up, the harder they tried to escape. The pressure built till I went nuts.[5]

. . . *Is It Something I Said?* Understanding Pryor's Comedy

Police live in y'all's neighborhood. . . . "Hello, Officer Timson, going bowling tonight? Yes, ah, nice Pinto you have, ha-ha-ha." Niggers don't know 'em like that. See, white folks get a ticket they pull over. . . . "Hey, officer, yes, glad to be of help . . . cheerio!" Niggers got to be talkin' 'bout, "I am reaching into my pocket for my license, 'cause I don't want to be no motherfuckin' accident."

Richard Pryor, *That Nigger's Crazy*, 1974

Richard Pryor moved back to Los Angeles and sought to discover his own personal comedic style and to develop characters incorporating events from Peoria and the language of the streets. This is evident in his first album, self-titled *Richard Pryor* (1968), but in the mildest form. For example, he introduced "Super Nigger," or Clark Washington, a mild-mannered custodian, "faster than a bowl of chitlins," who has "x-ray vision that enables him to see through everything except whitey."[6] He performed in clubs such as New York's Village Gate and the Redd Foxx Club in Los Angeles. He discussed the importance of working in front of black audiences.

> It was the right place for me at the right time [The Redd Foxx Club]. With a black audience, I was free to experiment with material that was more natural. It was frightening, since I didn't know myself and had to learn who I was. . . . Yet it was also lovely, comfortable, I talked about the black man's struggle to make it in a white world, which was also my struggle. For the first time since I began to perform at Harold's Club, I saw black people laughing—and not just at cute shit. They laughed at the people I knew. The people they knew. It was enlightening.[7]

Redd Foxx not only gave him the opportunity to experiment with this new material but also initiated his political awakening. He told Pryor stories about Malcolm X, and Pryor began to feel an affinity to the slain leader. "Strangely, I hadn't been affected by Malcolm X's death when it occurred. However, after Redd introduced me to him as a person and what he stood for, I missed him terribly."[8] In 1969, Pryor moved north to Berkeley and went underground, making few public appearances. He read more of Malcolm X's writings and listened to Marvin Gaye's album *What's Going On* repeatedly. Berkeley was a hotbed of countercultural activity, including the women's, student, antiwar, and black movements, and Pryor immersed himself in this political environment. He was inspired by Angela Davis, Ishmael Reed, Claude Brown, and the Black Panther Party and began to look toward his roots to inspire his comedy.[9]

By the time he left Berkeley in 1971, Pryor was ready to introduce his revamped, edgy, confrontational style. Slowly but surely Pryor's voice began to attract younger African Americans who were also inspired by the Black Power movement. Bill Cosby attended a Pryor performance during this period and remembers,

> I was in the audience when Richard took on a whole new persona—his own. Richard killed the Bill Cosby in his act, made people hate it. Then he worked on them, doing pure Pryor, and it was the most astonishing metamorphosis I have ever seen. He was magnificent.[10]

Pryor released the album *Craps (After Hours)* (1971), which was recorded at Redd's Place and followed this up with *That Nigger's Crazy* (1974), . . . *Is It Something I Said?* (1975), and *Bicentennial Nigger* (1976).

Pryor's very imagistic material relies on the use of street language and characters and deals with social issues as diverse as politics, the prison system, police brutality, and sex. While many comics then and now depend on joke-and-punchline humor, Pryor's routines are based on character development and storytelling more akin to theatrical monologues. Many comics expect the audience to laugh at their facial gestures by revealing bugging eyes or shocked looks. Pryor is different; he uses facial expressions, body postures, movements, and gestures to embody the characters and tells humorous first-person stories or relays a conversation among characters, all of which have their own unique voices, looks, and expressions. He described the process of creating his routines:

> I couldn't do it just by doing the words of the person. . . . I have to be that person. I see that man in my mind and go with him. I think there's a thin line between being a Tom on them people and seeing them as human beings. When I do the people, I have to do it true. If I can't do it, I'll stop right in the middle rather than pervert it and turn it into Tomism. There's a thin line between to laugh with and to laugh at.[11]

Some of his most famous characters include Mudbone, a wise old black man from Tupelo, Mississippi; Oilwell, a "crazy shoot me nigger . . . 6 foot 5, 422 pounds of man";[12] a philosophical wino; and a junkie. While their stories are often hysterical, depending on the direction of the narrative, Pryor reveals poignant and critical issues about the lives of these black characters, which lead one as easily to laughter as to tears. In one routine from *That Nigger's*

Crazy, Pryor discusses how he used to hang out with the winos on Sunday mornings when he was avoiding church. He first describes the wino directing traffic and then goes into a conversation between the wino and a junkie.

WINO: Hey fool, you better slow that car down. God damn, don't come drivin' down through here like you crazy. This is a neighborhood, this ain't no residential district. . . . *(Singing)* Jesus on my mind. *(Talking to himself)* Damn, nigger, I know Jesus, I remember when the boy got kill't, that's for real, man. It was on a Friday down at the railroad depot. . . . *(Seeing the junkie)* Look at that nigger, look at him in the middle of the street, junkie motherfucker, look at that. Nigger used to be a genius! I ain't lying, booked the numbers, didn't need paper or pencil. Now that nigger can't remember who he is. *(Speaking to the junkie)* Say, nigger, get your ass out the street, boy. *(He whistles.)* Move out the way, boy.

JUNKIE: Wha's happenin'!!!! Wha's happenin'—shit, I know somethin' happenin' 'cause everything's movin'. . . . Hey pops, you got anything on you?

WINO: Yeah, nigger, I got something for you. . . . I got some advice. You better lay off that narcotic, nigger, that shit done made you null and void. I ain't lying, boy. What's wrong with you? Why you don't straighten up and get a job?

JUNKIE: Get a job? . . . I worked five years in a row when I was in the joint. Pressin' them motherfuckin' license plates. I'm a license-plate-pressin' motherfucker. . . . Shit, where a nigger gonna get a job out here pressin' license plates? . . . I went to the unemployment bureau, baby, bitch sittin' behind the desk, ugly motherfucker, come tell me, talkin' about "You have a criminal record." I said, "I know that, bitch. . . . I'm a criminal! Just tell me where I'm gonna get a job." Ugly bitch—I seen better faces on an iodine bottle. . . . Bitch made me mad, I vomited and shit on the floor. . . . I went home, m'dear called me a dog. You dig that? My father said he don't want to see me in the vicinity. Just 'cause I stole his television. That's the politics, baby. I'm sick, pops. Can you help me? My mind's thinkin' about shit I don't want to think about. . . . Tell me some ah them ole lies of yours, make me stop me thinkin' about the truth. Would you help me?

WINO: I'm gonna help you, boy, because I believe you got potential. That's right. You don't know how to deal with the white man—

that's your problem. I know how to deal with him. That's right.
That's why I'm in the position I'm in today.[13]

Pryor's use of intonation brings these words and characters to life in a way that is difficult to describe on paper. Indeed, the visual nature of his comedy is somewhat lost even on CD, leaving one to his or her memories or imagination. While the conversation is quite humorous, Pryor also skillfully elicits feelings of sympathy and understanding. We discover in a one-liner (which is not transcribed here) that the Wino is one of a number of veterans not cared for by the system. In his own drug-induced way, the junkie reveals the truth about the supposed system of incarceration and rehabilitation. U.S. society frequently discusses the high rates of recidivism, placing the blame on the inability of ex-convicts to make it upon release. But what is the system actually doing to help these people? What they are trained to do in prison is unmarketable on the outside, and even the unemployment offices offer no assistance.

By the mid-1970s the mainstream U.S. press also began to take note of Pryor's prominence and growth as a comedian. In April 1975, the *New York Times Magazine* interviewed and wrote an extensive article on Pryor, acknowledging that while he was "one of the most popular comedians of his generation . . . he is largely unknown to the broad American public."[14] Like the early career of Redd Foxx, Pryor was unable to cross over as easily in this second round of his career. Even segments of the black middle class rejected Pryor's comedy, as they believed it was not uplifting to African Americans and brought to mind aspects of the black community that were considered negative. In moving away from his Bill Cosby impersonations, infusing his comedy with underworld black characters and cutting social critique, Pryor gave up the opportunity to perform for a wider U.S. audience on television, the most powerful form of communication at the time. Although Pryor wrote for *The Flip Wilson Show,* two comedy specials for Lily Tomlin (he also appeared on the show), for which he won an Emmy Award, and *Sanford and Son,* he was rarely seen on network television except for occasional appearances. *New York Times Magazine* reporter James McPherson explains:

> Pryor cannot utilize television in search of a broader audience. The cause of his exclusion is Pryor's choice of materials . . . characters . . . who are an embarrassment to the black middle class and

stereotypes in the minds of most whites who fear them in general. . . . As a result, Pryor's audiences have been limited to those who
attend his night-club and concert engagements. These are mostly
black people. When he does appear on television, it is only as a
guest; and even then he is likely to say something considered offensive to a larger and more varied audience.[15]

Pryor's comedy, while enjoyed within black communal spaces, was
considered too offensive for the mainstream U.S. television audience.
This was exemplified when Pryor hosted the *Mike Douglas Show*
for the week of November 25–29, 1974, during which he even got
into an argument in one interview with "Mr. Television," Milton
Berle.[16]

Perhaps because of Pryor's controversial reputation, producer
Lorne Michaels invited him to guest host *Saturday Night Live*
(then called *NBC's Saturday Night*) early in the show's first season.
Pryor met with writers and producers to give them his ideas for the
show, many of which were rejected as inappropriate for television.
Pryor was again reminded of the limitations of performing within
this venue. Although Pryor was not told ahead of time, on December 13, 1975, NBC aired the "live" episode on a five-second delay
so that his words could be censored. Pryor later indicated that had
he known of Michaels's plan, he would have refused to do the
show.[17] The episode was aired without a problem and produced
what is one of the classic moments in *Saturday Night Live* history.
In the skit, Chevy Chase interviews Pryor for a job, and they begin
an exercise of word association. Although the skit begins with benign words, the interview escalates:

CHASE: White
PRYOR: Black
CHASE: Bean
PRYOR: Pod
CHASE: Negro
PRYOR: White
CHASE: Tarbaby
PRYOR: What'd you say?
CHASE: Tarbaby
PRYOR: Ofay
CHASE: Colored
PRYOR: Redneck

A rare 1970s TV appearance of Richard Pryor, with McLean Stevenson and Flip Wilson.

CHASE: Jungle bunny
PRYOR: Peckerwood
CHASE: Burrhead
PRYOR: Cracker

CHASE: Spear-chucker
PRYOR: White trash
CHASE: Jungle bunny
PRYOR: Honkey
CHASE: Spade
PRYOR: Honkey-honkey
CHASE: Nigger!
PRYOR: Deeeeeead honkey![18]

Despite Pryor's success on *Saturday Night Live,* he was still considered unsuitable for network television. However, he continued to find success with his comedy albums and increasing opportunities in supporting roles in film. Still, his primary venue continued to be stand-up comedy. *That Nigger's Crazy* (1974) went gold, . . . *Is It Something I Said?* (1975) was a platinum record with excellent reviews, and *Bicentennial Nigger* (1976) was also a gold album. Pryor won Grammy Awards for all three albums, and his concerts were very profitable.[19]

Pryor had many small roles in a variety of films. For example, his stand-up was featured in the concert film *Wattstax* (1973), and he had a supporting role opposite Max Julien in the Blaxploitation film *The Mack* (1973). However, his performance as Billie Holiday's piano player opposite Diana Ross in *Lady Sings the Blues* (1972) and as private detective Sharp Eye Washington in the Bill Cosby and Sidney Poitier film, *Uptown Saturday Night* (1974), brought him to the attention of mainstream U.S. critics and audiences. Then in 1976, three films featuring Pryor, *The Bingo Long Traveling All-Stars and Motor Kings, Car Wash,* and *Silver Streak,* were released and became box office hits.

As discussed, many African American artists found ways to use popular culture as a site of resistance to discuss issues of importance to the African American community and to create community across a nation of black viewers. Much of this resistance was evidenced within hidden transcripts—themes, humor, and ideas that could be understood in ways unique to an African American audience. However, as the era progressed, black critical thought within popular culture became more vocalized. When Richard Pryor's success brought him an NBC television contract, he initially believed that he was allowed to make all creative choices. It quickly became apparent that this was not the case, and the adjustments that NBC

Pryor's stand-up comedy garnered Grammy and mainstream attention.

required would have reversed the process of change that Pryor put himself through during his career as a comedian.

Possibilities and Censorship: *The Richard Pryor Show*

It could be such an informative medium. One week of truth on TV could just straighten out everything. One hundred and twenty-seven million people watch television every night; that's why they use it to sell stuff.

The problem with the censors is that they don't like for people to communicate. I think it is on purpose and very political. I don't think they

Pryor as Sharp Eye Washington in *Uptown Saturday Night*. His film career was on the rise when NBC offered him the weekly series.

> are naive enough to believe they're protecting what people see. I think it has to do with anybody and anything that communicates a reality and might disturb or wake up people or relate; I think they try to stop that any way they can.
>
> **Richard Pryor, in Louie Robinson, "Richard Pryor Talks," 1978**

It is this disparity, between the politically vocal Richard Pryor of the 1970s and the limitations imposed by the NBC censors, that brought *The Richard Pryor Show* to its early demise. Initially, Pryor attempted to renege on NBC's offer, but at the end of negotiations he agreed to make four episodes of his ten-episode contract. The conflict between the network and Pryor again symbolizes (as Redd Foxx's problems did with NBC) the friction created when an African American performer who is unwilling to negotiate his beliefs confronts the narrow confines of acceptability in network television.

Pryor's increasing mainstream profile, his box office success, and album sales once again caught the eye of NBC. Network executives pursued the performer to host his own prime-time television series. Pryor was understandably skeptical; he had dealt with NBC censors during the taping of *Saturday Night Live*, and since his personal and political transformation in the early 1970s he had no desire to curb his comedy. However, Pryor saw the use of television, with its potential as a social and political tool, as a way to confront mainstream society and create change. With his realization that TV is primarily a commercial venture, Pryor believed that he could use the medium to sell a different agenda. He agreed to host one show, and on May 5, 1977, NBC aired *The Richard Pryor Special?*

The special included guest stars LaWanda Page from *Sanford and Son, Saturday Night Live*'s John Belushi, African American poet and author Maya Angelou, and a musical performance by the Pips. As his later series revealed, Pryor used both his comedic and dramatic skills when putting together the special. In one skit he plays the "Devine" James L. White, a television evangelist whose phone lines remain quiet until he makes the announcement that he is collecting donations for a "Back to Africa" campaign. In another scene he plays a drunk, Willie; similar to Pryor's Wino, Willie elicits laughter. However, the scene takes on a dramatic turn when he returns home to his wife, played by Maya Angelou. The special was a critical success, and this only further encouraged NBC in its pursuit of a Richard Pryor weekly show. Pryor finally broke down and agreed to a ten-episode contract.

During the summer of 1977, Pryor met with his team of comedy writers to conceive of skits for the first show. From the beginning, he expressed hesitancy and grave ambivalence about the project. He explained to *Newsweek* magazine:

> I don't feel this in my heart. It just stops here (pointing to his head). . . . Two years ago there was great shit on TV. Now people walk around without being outraged, numb from the shock. You know something? I don't want to be on TV. I'm in a trap. I can't do this—there ain't no art.[20]

Pryor believed the network's financial offer was so good that he accepted without thinking through all of the potential problems. As he explained to *Newsweek,* he feared that to continue with a weekly show, he would betray the audience and himself, which would send him into a personal spiral of drugs and alcohol.[21] At the encouragement of friends who believed that he should concentrate on his film career, Pryor attempted to break his contract with NBC, but the network refused. In addition to the four shows he agreed to follow through on, he agreed to do six specials for NBC, two per year over the following three years. Even so, like black television performers before him, Pryor employed the strategy of counternarratives and used mainstream magazines to rail against the censors at NBC.

> I think they hire people, about 6,000 of them, to do nothing but mess with people . . . for somebody to tell us that ain't right and they weren't with us and didn't feel our energies and are not working with us, that's just asinine. I think that after they got me, they did not want me when they realized that I was not going for that oke-doke pressure thing. [Comedy] should be related that way—from my point of view of Black awareness and where I come from and what I see. They couldn't see that. I don't believe they really wanted to.[22]

However, whenever he was able to do so, he used his control over the show not only to openly criticize NBC but also to expose the U.S. audience to vernacular black humor. Pryor created skits that ranged from silly, to experimental, to pieces critical of mainstream politics and U.S. stereotypical views of black people. He introduced unknown talent to the mainstream audience and experimented with both comedy and drama as art forms.

The Richard Pryor Show aired from September 13 to October 20, 1977, and, like *Saturday Night Live,* the show featured a regular cast of supporting actors, some of whom gained in profile in later years. Cast members were Paul Mooney, a long-time friend and collaborator of Pryor's, Tim Reid, Marsha Warfield, Argus Hamilton, Sandra Bernhardt, Victor DeLapp, "Detroit" John Witherspoon, Alegra Allison, Jimmy Martinez, and a young Robin Williams. From the beginning, the network proved problematic. Although promised that his show would be scheduled no earlier than 9 p.m., the show aired on Tuesdays at 8 p.m., during the family hour and opposite ABC's *Happy Days* and *Laverne and Shirley,* shows which were number one and number two in the ratings.[23]

With the show scheduled opposite the most popular programs in America, the audience was not encouraged to find *The Richard Pryor Show.* Pryor also made certain creative decisions that may have had a negative impact on viewership. He decided that the show shouldn't feature famous guest stars, who potentially could have attracted a wider audience. The show did not receive the attention it deserved. *The Richard Pryor Show*'s low ratings indicate not that it failed to reach a black audience but that it did not cross over to a white audience at the level necessary to create high ratings. However, the four surviving episodes reveal a truly significant legacy. True to form, Richard Pryor resisted the confines of television, expressed his feelings, and created both entertaining and insightful material for the U.S. audience while targeting issues of concern for the African American community.

During the taping of the first show, Pryor appears on camera and states directly to the audience, "There's been a lot of things written about me. People ask, 'How can you have a show? You'll have to compromise.'" As the camera pulls out to a wide shot, Pryor stands there wearing nothing but a flesh-colored body suit with his genitals hidden/missing. He then says, "Well, look at me. I've given up absolutely nothing."[24] Needless to say, the joke did not make it past the NBC censors. They believed that the image was inappropriate for television, especially during the family-viewing hour. In the end, the shot did not open the show; a Star Wars bar skit did, with Pryor featured as the bartender. An image of Pryor naked from the waist up was shown after the opening skit under the credits for it. However, the image had no commentary, seemingly silencing the comedian. Yet, the fact that Pryor shot the material at all eventually proved that it could not be completely suppressed by NBC; his commentary on network censorship was seen on ABC, CBS, and NBC when the evening news on all three networks covered the controversy and showed the clip.

Outside of this often-mentioned controversy, Pryor produced slapstick and silly, yet insightful and critical, programming, even within NBC's constraints. *The Richard Pryor Show* accomplished several important tasks through the show's structure, which included both the comedic and the dramatic. While the show provided a space for critical black comedy on network television, Richard Pryor also developed dramatic skits that humanized black life for a mainstream audience and allowed a black audience to see themselves in genres outside of comedy. Pryor improvised to exhibit his frustrations in new ways that the network could not legitimately censor. *The Richard Pryor Show* was a living critique of network television's attempt to shape black life. This was exemplified in each of the four episodes.

The first episode, as mentioned, begins with the seemingly benign skit of Pryor as a bartender in the Star Wars bar. However, Pryor immediately establishes the show and the bar as his own; he has a look of comfort on the set, and he strides around as he did during live performances. He clearly improvises many of his interactions with the patrons, and at one point when he sees a hooded alien, he exclaims, "You look just like a nigger from Detroit I know." His cadence, gestures, and walk remind the audience immediately that, although they are on NBC, they are on Pryor's stage. Numerous skits are presented in this episode: Western shootouts, a singing number in which a construction worker left alone on his lunch break strips to a bikini and sings "I Gotta Be Me," and one in which Pryor plays an old-time healer. However, in this first episode two particular skits come foremost to mind—one critical and the other poignant, which exemplifies the breadth of his talent as well as the possibilities of television to create a space for black expression.

The third skit in episode one sets up Pryor as the fortieth president of the United States entering the White House pressroom. As president, Pryor is asked numerous questions about world events, from the Middle East to the creation of new arms for the United States. In a spoof of politicians both then and now, Pryor continually spins the questions and his responses, and therefore avoids answering the reporters in a coherent manner. For example, he calls a new military development a neopacifist weapon. A white reporter asks Pryor whether his administration will lower the unemployment rate, which, the reporter states, stands at 5 percent. Pryor notes that the unemployment rate is actually 45 percent in the black community but indicates that in the upcoming fiscal year his administration plans to bring the black unemployment rate to 20 percent and the white community's "of course" lower to make it a "United States." The interview continues:

> REPORTER: Mr. President, Roberta Davies, *Jet* magazine.
> *(Pryor salutes her.)*
> REPORTER: Mr. President, on your list of candidates for director of the FBI, are you including the name of Huey Newton?
> PRYOR: Yes, I figure that Huey Newton is best qualified. He knows the ins and outs of the FBI if anyone does, and he would be an excellent director.

REPORTER: Brother Bell from *Ebony* magazine. As-Salaam-Alaikum, Brother.

PRYOR: Wa-Alaikum-Salaam.

(A white female reporter looks at the Ebony *reporter.)*

REPORTER: What you looking at, Snow White?! Brother, about blacks in the labor force, I wanna know what you going to do about having more black brothers as quarterbacks in the National Football League.

PRYOR: I plan not only to have lots of black quarterbacks, but we gonna have black coaches and black owners of teams as long there going to be football, gonna be some black in it some-where—you know what I'm talkin' about? I'm on the case now.

(A white reporter puts up his hand.)

PRYOR: *(In a dismissive manner)* Yes, what, what is it?

REPORTER: Mr. President.

PRYOR: *(Staring angrily at him)* Yeah, what?!

REPORTER: Mr. Bigby, *Mississippi Herald.*

PRYOR: Sit down.

(A white female reporter raises her hand.)

PRYOR: Yeah, what is it?

REPORTER: Mrs. Fenton Carlton Macker, *Christian Women's News.* Mr. President, since you have become president, you've been seen and photographed on the arms of white women. *(Audience oohs.)* Quite frankly, sir, you have been courting an awful lot of white women. Will this continue?

PRYOR: *(Looking around nervously)* As long as I can keep it up. I mean, why you think they call it the White House?

The session eventually breaks up when a white reporter starts a "your mamma" confrontation with Pryor. The room breaks into mayhem as Pryor leaps off the stage at the reporter and is carried out of the pressroom.

In this skit Pryor is able to comment on several issues relevant to black social and political life. His first comment on the unemployment rate immediately indicates the discrepancy of statistics based on race and the ways in which politicians' promises end up benefiting the white community more than the minority community. In 1977, the country was in the midst of an economic recession, which only worsened in the upcoming years. A connection can be made between this comment and the results of affirmative action, which in the end secured jobs for white women more than any other minority.

The presence of reporters from black publications such as *Jet* and *Ebony* at the news conference, with the president favoring their questions, assures that the discussion stays on black issues. The nomination of Huey P. Newton for the director of the FBI is an acknowledgment of J. Edgar Hoover's role in targeting the Black Panther Party for extinction. The idea of having Newton in Hoover's position is particularly humorous for a black audience cognizant of the FBI's tactics to repress black political speech. Today's continued lack of black ownership and coaches in the National Football League and the majority of other national sports is ironic in light of the president's promise to correct that situation. Pryor's dismissal of the reporter from Mississippi further emphasizes that, if there were a liberal black president, the black community would have a greater chance of getting its issues in front of the highest office in the land. For a black viewing audience, this was a pleasant fantasy, especially in light of the black community's suffering under Richard Nixon and Gerald Ford, whose presidencies immediately preceded *The Richard Pryor Show*. Nixon was successful in his overt attempt to reverse the progress made during the Civil Rights era. In his attempt to clean up widespread "lawlessness" caused by the antiwar and black power movements, Nixon, through the FBI, used repressive tactics to squelch African American protest.

Finally the white female reporter's question targets both the reality of Pryor and the fears of a nation, exemplified in the D. W. Griffith epic *Birth of a Nation* (1915). By having the black president, now in the ultimate position of power, engage in interracial relationships, the skit realizes the fears and expectations of Griffith and a segment of the U.S. viewing audience: that given the opportunity, black men will take advantage of the "virginal white woman."[25] While Pryor's skit can be seen as perpetuating a myth of black rape and black masculinity, he addresses the racism implicit in the idea through the look of disgust on the reporter's face. He flaunts his ability to make his own sexual decisions. Pryor also winks at the issue to a black audience. His personal life and his relationships with numerous women, both white and black, were a long-standing topic of discussion within black circles, driven by the idea that dating a white woman was selling out the black community. Pryor converses with the members of the black community who disagree with his lifestyle.

The next scene exemplifies a unique quality of *The Richard Pryor Show*: the shift from hilarity to poignancy, which was derived from his stand-up comedy. Unlike *Saturday Night Live*, which was based purely on comedic vignettes, Pryor's show exhibited his skills as a multifaceted actor and brought black drama to mainstream television, which historically has avoided casting black characters outside comedic roles. During each episode, at least one dramatic skit was presented. In the first episode, Pryor and a World War II buddy go to Club Harlem. Pryor's character wants to propose to Satin Doll, a performer at the club. Pryor states that Satin Doll, whose real name is Betty, is the world's greatest ballerina but could not make it because she is black.

The high production values of *The Richard Pryor Show* are evident in the set of this skit, which features a softly lit club with a live jazz band playing. Like other African American performers discussed previously, Pryor, from the first episode, used his position within the television industry to introduce black talent to the U.S. audience. A stellar emcee performs the voices of Ella Fitzgerald and Billie Holiday, and the scene becomes a showcase for black artists and talent as the dancers take the floor. Pryor appears honestly entertained by the performances, and interestingly enough the camera does not focus on him alone but on several black audience members, who are equally enthralled by the performances. When Pryor finally gets the opportunity to talk to Betty, he discovers that she is already engaged. His internal struggle is evident, as is his disappointment when leaving the club. Knowing Pryor as a comic, an audience watches the scene and waits for the punch line, which never appears. Instead, the audience is reminded that Pryor—and, in essence, black performers in general on television—can participate in dramatic pieces as well, an opportunity denied the majority of black television performers in the 1970s.

Exhibited through each episode, these qualities of comedy, drama, and critique portray different visions of blackness within television. In episode two, Pryor again produces a broad variety of sketches. In one, he flips the casting by placing himself in the role of Big Ed Garvey, a white prosecutor of a black man in 1926 Mississippi. A white man reports on the trial as if it were a sporting event, and the judge cools himself with a fan from Sam's Funeral Parlor. Robin Williams plays the northern defense attorney for the black man, accused of raping a white woman. The black man is never given the opportunity to tell his side of the story. When the defendant is asked by the judge if he has anything to say for himself, the sheriff holds a gun to his head and he is unable to speak. The judge says he is glad to see that the man is taking the Fifth Amendment.

Even Williams, from the liberal North, shows his implicit racism in his closing arguments. He says that the word *Negro,* a "wonderful word," comes from a Latin word that means "to tote," and he reminds the jury of what the Negro has done for whites, asking, "Who picked your cotton?" and "Who tied their hair up in neat little bandanas?" in reference to the Negroes who took care of the white children. He says, if you can't find this man not guilty, then let him hang. The viewer discovers that the accused man was in jail on the night the crime was committed, and the white woman is clearly "loose"; she is caught making out with a random man during the trial, and it is discovered that she slept with at least five men, including the prosecutor, on the night of the supposed crime.[26] However, the jury finds the defendant not guilty but decides that Williams, "this carpet-bagging communist pinko," is guilty for getting the black man off, and the crowd carries him away to be hanged.

Although the skit does not have an unhappy ending for the black man, the audience is allowed to see the ridiculous way in which African American men are treated by the court system. The accused clearly could not have committed the crime, yet he goes to trial for it; the prosecutors and judges manipulate the facts to fit their accusations. The judge's use of a Sam's Funeral Parlor fan signifies that the trial is but a formality. Finally, even the liberal lawyer is not to be trusted, as he carries antiquated views of blackness and has an inflated sense of self. He sees himself as sacrificing so much to defend black people and expects gratitude. Although the skit is set within the South in 1926 and presented within a humorous context, its themes are not so exaggerated when one considers the numerous false accusations and trials against black radicals and the black community in general in the 1970s. Also, in light of the Rampart scandals, the exposure of many incidents of police brutality and of planting false evidence on suspects in Los Angeles in 2000, Pryor's skit is relevant in a contemporary context as well as in the 1970s.

Looking to interpretations of history as a source of humor is a repeated theme in this episode. In another skit, Pryor plays an explorer traveling through 1909 Egypt with three white explorers. In one of the pyramids, they discover the ancient "Book of Life," which reveals that black people first walked the earth and started modern life as we know it. Pryor exclaims, "There ain't nothin' in here about whitey." Pryor wants to take the book out and tell the world. The white explorers quickly desert Pryor, who is engrossed in the book, barricade the pyramid, and call for the bulldozers.[27]

The extended segment that follows discusses the importance of African roots. It showcases performers of traditional African dance and music, acknowledging black people's African roots in a celebratory manner, roots that mainstream America dismissed as savage for generations. The interest in discovering one's origins increased after the January 1977 premiere of Alex Haley's *Roots* on ABC. However, Pryor does not embrace the notion of looking toward Africa uncritically. Instead, in the skit that follows, he plays Come-from-Man in a "Find Your Roots Village." As Pryor says, "I tell you where you come from, and for this you pay me a whole bunch of money. Okay. In some cases I tell you where you going. You going to the bank to get my money." The tourists include both white and black participants, and the white characters are particularly interested in purchasing the African artifacts to take back to the United States. Pryor creates ludicrous stories to explain the origins of the items for sale, which the tourists accept in a gullible manner. Pryor is able to poke fun at the commercialization of searching for one's original identity, which evolved in the post-*Roots* climate.

Next, a noncomedic piece provides another showcase for black talent. A group of young, black, street corner singers perform for the enjoyment of an older neighborhood woman. An older man attempts to quiet them until the woman intervenes, yells at him, and tells him not to come back. She encourages the boys to continue practicing as she explains that no black group has made it yet without starting this way. The image of the younger boys dissolves into that of the O' Jays on stage performing "Work on Me," from their album *Travellin' at the Speed of Thought* (1977). This piece also relates to specific black community issues. At a time of integration, the skit places the emphasis of developing and supporting talent within these communal black spaces, something that Pryor is able to do within the black structure that he created on *The Richard Pryor Show*.

Episode three more clearly reveals Pryor's continued struggles and frustration with NBC, even within this short four-episode contract. Looking at the results of his first effort to address network censorship, with the infamous body-stocking scene, Pryor chooses the most direct strategy of discussing his disgust within network limits. The episode begins with him speaking directly into the camera: "Good evening, ladies and gentlemen. My name is Richard Pryor . . ." His voice fades and is replaced by another official-sounding man, who states:

> Due to technical difficulties we cannot continue to bring you the audio portion of *The Richard Pryor Show*; however, I'm an NBC spokesman, and I will be happy to tell you what Mr. Pryor is saying. I will now read from tonight's network-approved script. Gosh, I'm just pleased as punch to be continuing on as part of the NBC family. They truly understand me, and they have been oh so fair. After all, I am only here to please. They only hired me to do what I do best, be humble. Later I will share my recipe with you for good old American pie. Meanwhile, I just hope to heck I haven't offended anyone. By the way I don't mind the fact that NBC never aired the opening of my first show. I know they were just thinking of me. They always put me first, and that is why for me they will always be number one. And now that they have finally let me say what I had to say, let's go on with the show.

Pryor remains on screen and angrily, but silently, yells at the camera. He takes off his jacket in frustration and pantomimes choking and punching someone. At the culmination of his speech, he makes the black power fist and the image is synched with the audio portion in which the NBC spokesman says, "That is why for me [NBC] will always be number one." In this spoof of his contentious relationship with NBC, Pryor goes far enough to get his critique of the network through to an audience, yet creates an opening skit that the censors cannot touch. Through the "NBC-approved script," he is able to address directly the censorship of the first episode and the thwarting of black speech and creativity. He also lets the viewing audience know about the problematic attitudes of NBC executives toward assertive black men such as himself. His suggestion that he was hired to be humble illuminates the racist notion that black people should be grateful for what they have and not complain about anything.

At this point it is clear that Pryor intends to finish his contract in any way that he pleases. Episodes three and four both contain a wide range of skits that vary from slapstick to experimental, and each episode reveals his varying skills as a performer. Pryor plays a Buster Keaton–like character, who makes everything he touches worse in "Mr. Fix It." In "Ward 8" the audience meets several off-beat patients in a mental health facility. One of the group is a white cop who mimics reading a person his rights and then shoots him.

In an even more experimental sketch, a Pryor musical sequence in which he imitates Little Richard dissolves into a white woman's censored sexual revelations to her therapist. It is a very voyeuristic moment, because the audience feels as if they are accidentally getting a restricted television feed that allows them to peep in on this private conversation. The woman describes several different scenarios of her lesbian affair: one that is a consensual encounter; one in which she is helpless and the other woman an aggressor. She also concedes that none of it may have actually happened. A CENSORED sign cuts off segments of her conversation, as if to hide its sexual nature. As mysteriously as it has arrived, the scene dissolves again, back into Pryor's performance of Little Richard.

In a particularly moving skit, Pryor plays a ringmaster in the ghetto circus. Considering his life, one can read this skit as the imaginings of Pryor as a child or as his empathy for black children who still grow up in ghettoes. In a smoky and low-lit tent, he mimes interactions with animals and performs a variety of circus acts; he is the clown, the high-wire artist, and tames lions to the delight of the children. When the parents call the kids in for the evening, the lights go up, revealing that it is just a junkyard, and the scene perhaps in the kids' imaginations.[28]

Pryor also performs the only stand-up comedy of the series in this episode. He appears in front of a primarily black audience and explains that he is doing stand-up because NBC believes that he is not a well-enough-known figure in the United States. He does his imitations of kids in trouble and reveals that, when his father beat him, his mother said to him, "It hurts me more than it hurts you." He replied, "Well let him beat your ass." Clearly unexpected, Pryor's mouth is literally covered with the word *censored,* and the sound is bleeped out. The camera cuts to a black woman showing a shocked expression and laughing, presumably because of his use of language within the television context. He talks about hillbillies and the difference between black people and white people at a funeral. Although the comedy is pretty mild compared with his most recent albums, it is definitely not Cosby.

Knowing that the show has but one episode left, Pryor takes the opportunity at the end of the program to introduce the cast of the show one at a time and involves them in a few improvisational acts. Pryor is able to showcase the artists and possibly provide them with opportunities in the future. The episode ends as it started, with further commentary on NBC. Pryor stands against the wall at the studio and says, "Well by the looks of things, I'll be seeing you next time. NBC made sure of that. I'm not going anywhere." The camera pans down to a lion that is guarding him.

Episode four contains equally funny and innovative skits, but there are some key moments of closure in the show. His very popular stage character the Wino makes his first television appearance on *The Richard Pryor Show,* when he meets Dr. Jeckell outside his home in England. In this sketch, the Wino, holding a bottle and singing, enters a darkened street and sees Dr. Jeckell.

> Hey boy, you know where Piccadilly Square is? . . . I am over here for the World War I convention. The Black soldiers of 1914. . . . *(Dr. Jeckell grunts and gestures throughout the conversation, and the Wino responds to him.)* I went down that way, man, and didn't see it. . . . Yeah, do all the people in England look like you? Well, I don't know nothing 'bout that. I lost my woman too. She left me for an Englishman. . . . Don't put your hands on me now. Excuse me, why don't you do something about your breath before you speak? And you can't see either, can you? Because if you could see, you would know you was too ugly to be out here on the streets at night. Watch out, you knock over this wine outta my hand, I'm gonna kick you ass.

"Wino Dealing with Dracula" was a popular comedy concert piece at the time.[29] The Wino's appearance is transitional in the final episode of the TV series, when Pryor was leaving television for his preferred arena of the concert circuit. In a more dramatic skit in the final episode, Pryor enters a gun store to purchase a weapon. As he picks up the different firearms, each gun reveals its personality and discusses who it has killed and why. Pryor, spooked, leaves the store without purchasing one.[30] Also in the final episode, he takes the time to introduce Mr. Charlie Hill—an Iroquois stand-up comedian, who certainly would have had little opportunity for mainstream exposure otherwise. However, the centerpiece of the final episode is a roast of Pryor given by the cast of the show.

Clearly, from the beginning the cast knew that working on *The Richard Pryor Show* was going to be a short-lived experience, and during the roast they acknowledge the challenges of working on the show, the ratings, and what it means to work with Pryor. Paul Mooney introduces the cast and explains that they are there to pay their respects to Pryor and to clear up public misconceptions about the show. Mooney sets the jovial tone for the roast, giving some interesting biographical information about Pryor, such as his birthplace, Peoria, where "half the children call him a superstar and the other half call him daddy." He also makes fun of Pryor's early career as a Cosby imitator. Each regular performer is given the opportunity to address Pryor. Tim Reid and Alegra Allison read supposed telegrams sent to the show. Allison says that she is going to read the nicer ones, of which there are only two. The first is from President Carter: "Just wanted to tell you that Miss Lillian [Carter's mother] loves your show. We are putting her in a home in the morning." The other says, "Dear Richard, thank you for canceling your dates in South Africa, especially the one with my daughter. Signed Ian Smith." Smith, a white supremacist and supporter of apartheid was the prime minister of Rhodesia in the previous decade.[31] Tim Reid reads another telegram and does so, as he explains, in the manner in which it was meant to be delivered:

> Dear Richard,
> Is about time that these honkeys heard the truth, brother. See, you're a man who stood up, got down, and told it like it was. Yeah. You know you refused to lick the boots and stuck to your roots. We know where you're coming from, because you see you haven't forgot where you came from. Right on, brother!
> Signed Miss Anita Bryant

Anita Bryant was an American icon and Grammy-winning vocalist as well as a notorious antigay crusader in 1977.[32] Reid's allusion to her support referred to Pryor's recent exhibition at a gay rights rally. In Pryor's autobiography, he states that, on Lily Tomlin's request, he agreed to perform at a gay liberation benefit at the Hollywood Bowl. However, when he arrived he was angered at the racism he perceived toward one group of black singers; he also admits to being drunk and stoned at the time.[33] When he went out onstage, he criticized the audience for "'cruising' Hollywood Boulevard 'when the niggers was burnin' down Watts.' Then he bade them farewell: 'Kiss my happy rich, black ass.'"[34] As complimentary as the telegram first appeared, Bryant was not an advocate to have in 1977. However, Reid takes the opportunity to go on and express how he feels about Pryor. In closing, Reid acknowledges that the ratings were so low that their show lost to one on PBS called *The Armadillo, Nature's Little Tank.*

When Robin Williams takes the podium, he calls Pryor a genius and, in addressing Pryor's wide range as a comedian, he says, "Now, who else can take all the forms of comedy, slapstick, satire, mime, stand-up, and turn them into something that will offend everyone?" The other cast members discuss various parts of Pryor's life, from his altercations with the law to his drug use and notorious sex life. Several skits follow, and Pryor eventually closes the episode and series from the scene of the roast and simply thanks everyone.

One can consider the two variety shows discussed within this book, *The Flip Wilson Show* and *The Richard Pryor Show,* and see them as the polar opposite bookends of a black television era. *The Flip Wilson Show* was entrenched in the ideals of integration. Although striving for the inclusion of black performers and opening up television to some levels of vernacular black humor, Wilson generally kept confrontational black political attitudes under wraps and enjoyed a successful television career. Pryor, on the other hand, was primarily about confrontation with mainstream U.S. politics as well as with the ideals of a black middle class that would rather conceal the presence of underclass blackness. On either the stage or the television screen, Pryor did not mask his sarcasm toward the U.S. political system and the continued oppression that African Americans faced on a daily basis. He thus brought to light and humanized the black underclass, the victims of racism who were still not allowed to benefit from the so-called gains that integration offered. As much as NBC executives said they wanted Richard Pryor, they were more interested in the Bill Cosby type, which they would obtain in the following decade.

Pryor understood the business of television but was still angry about the situation of his show. He believed that while television had great potential, over time it had lost its impact. He discussed his feelings with *Ebony* magazine after the last episode.

> They've misused it [television] a long time so now it's just a business, that's all. It's just a place where you sell products and they sell their kind of information the way they want to sell it to perpetuate their businesses. They're not going to write shows about how to revolutionize America. The top-rated shows are for retarded people.[35]

Pryor's lack of long-term success on television is symbolic and fitting within television's changing constructions of blackness in the late 1970s. Whereas Pryor's characters, like those of *Sanford and Son* and *Good Times*, were identifiably black and often underclass, television shows dealing with African Americans began to promote notions of successful integration. Popular television families such as the Jeffersons, on their self-titled show (1975–85), were "moving on up" into the mainstream U.S. social and, more important, economic life.[36] Pryor's experiences led him to less optimistic views of contemporary U.S. society, which, by the late 1970s, revealed signs of the reversal of civil rights within many forums, regressions initiated by the Nixon and Ford presidencies. The early 1980s and the presidency of Ronald Reagan permanently established this regressive pattern. Television followed the changing and conservative political times, often hindering and at times denying the politicized viewpoints established by African American television performers throughout the 1970s. What, therefore, became of black voices within mainstream television?

Conclusion: Movin' On Up

Contemporary Television as
a Site of Resistance

White Like Them. None of the fall's twenty-six new network shows stars
a minority. And one of them is *Roots: The Series*.
Jim Mullen, "Hot Sheet"

The nationally published magazine *Entertainment Weekly* has a
segment titled "Hot Sheet," which briefly and often sarcastically
informs the reader "what the country is talking about this week."
The opening epigraph was number nine on the list for July 23,
1999. This was not the first article in this magazine to target the
lack of minority representation on network television; indeed, from
the late 1990s, the approach of the fall television season signaled
an increase of articles in a variety of publications that attempted to
make sense of the continuing whitening of network television.

African American images on network television proliferated
throughout the 1970s in prime-time sitcoms, "dramas," made-for-
television movies, and miniseries. "Dramatic" television series included *Shaft* (1973–74), *Tenafly* (1973–74), and *Get Christie Love!*
(1974–75), police and detective shows based on the spirit of the
Blaxploitation film movement. Richard Roundtree, who played the
leading role in the film *Shaft,* played the lead in the TV version as
well, although the TV character is bland compared with his sexually charged image in the film. Teresa Graves played Christie Love, a
visual sister of Pam Grier and Tamara Dobson, the primary female

stars of Blaxploitation; the series was also the first police drama to star an African American woman.

One of the most successful programs of the mid- to late 1970s was Norman Lear's *The Jeffersons,* a spin-off of *All in the Family.* The show indicates the integrating face of African American representation at the end of the decade. The program follows the lives of George Jefferson (Sherman Hemsley) and Louisie (Weesie) Jefferson (Isabel Sanford) as they move on up to "a deluxe apartment in the sky."[1] George has a successful dry cleaning business, which has given him financial security and social mobility. George's sarcasm and obvious disdain for elements of white society give the program an edge, although many critics complained of George's buffoonery. The inclusion of a recurring, successful, married, interracial couple, Tom and Helen Willis (Franklin Cover and Roxie Roker), as neighbors of the Jeffersons was also a first on network television.

Other shows followed the integrationist theme, including *Diff'rent Strokes* (1978–86), *The White Shadow* (1978–81), and *Benson* (1979–86). *Diff'rent Strokes* places two black orphans, Arnold (Gary Coleman) and Willis (Todd Bridges), in the millionaire home of Phillip Drummond (Conrad Bain) and his daughter, Kimberley (Dana Plato).[2] *The White Shadow* deals with an integrated high school basketball team and their white coach, Ken Reeves (Ken Howard).[3] Benson (Robert Guillaume) worked as hired help around the governor's mansion and, in an unprecedented rise in status, becomes the state budget director and then the lieutenant governor.[4]

African Americans also became a focal point in many successful made-for-television films, including *My Sweet Charlie* (1970), starring Al Freeman Jr.; *Brian's Song* (1970), with Billy Dee Williams and James Caan playing the real-life football stars Gale Sayers and Brian Piccolo; and *The Autobiography of Miss Jane Pitman* (1974), with Cicely Tyson, a film that won nine Emmys. The miniseries whose impact is still discussed today is *Roots* (1977). Produced by David Wolper and based on Alex Haley's book, this series ran for eight consecutive nights on ABC. At twelve hours, *Roots* is the epic tale of African Kunta Kinte (LeVar Burton played young Kinte and John Amos, the adult), tracing his life in Africa and the United States, through capture and slavery. The film later follows his descendents through the Civil War and eventual freedom. Seen by 130 million viewers, approximately half of the population of the United

States at the time, the series was nominated for thirty-seven Emmy Awards and won nine.[5] The success of *Roots* led to the production of *Roots: The Next Generations* (1979), which takes Alex Haley's ancestors to the Civil Rights movement.

With the arrival of the 1980s, the theme of successful black integration was played out within weekly series, without the edginess of the working-class perspective seen in *The Jeffersons*. *The Cosby Show* is the prime example of this integrationist theme, and it was the most successful African American series of the 1980s. During a period of comparative African American invisibility in television that followed in the 1980s, *The Cosby Show* was one of the few African American–cast shows.[6] Television programming in the 1980s was complicated by the Reagan presidency, which sought to undermine any gains made by African Americans in the 1960s and 1970s. The coding of federal programs such as affirmative action as "reverse racism," combined with Reagan's appeal to the so-called disenfranchised white man, created an oppressive state for many working-class African Americans. This atmosphere was reflected on television in the networks' failure to produce African American subject matter outside of very narrow confines, such as the upper-middle-class Huxtables.[7]

A study funded by comedian Bill Cosby and published as *Enlightened Racism: The Cosby Show, Audiences, and the Myth of the American Dream* indicates the ways in which *The Cosby Show* became a part of the regressive national dialogue. As the authors, Sut Jhally and Justin Lewis, argue, although *The Cosby Show* promoted "an attitude of racial tolerance among white viewers and generat[ed] a feeling of intense pride among black viewers," there were negative ramifications.

> Among white people, the admission of black characters to television's upwardly mobile world gives credence to the idea that racial divisions . . . do not exist. Most white people are extremely receptive to such a message. Like Ronald Reagan's folksy feel good patriotism, the idea allows them to feel good about themselves and about the society that they are part of. The Cosby-Huxtable persona . . . tells the viewers that, as one respondent put it, "there really is room in the United States for minorities to get ahead, without affirmative action." *The Cosby Show*, our study showed, is an integral part of this process of public disenlightenment. . . .[8]

In the early 1990s, black presence on the small screen increased commensurately with the increasing visibility of African Americans in other fields of popular culture. The 1990s signaled the continuing rise in the popularity of hip-hop, which spread to the suburbs and altered the musical tastes of white suburban youth, as well as their clothing, language, attitudes, and icons. In professional sports, basketball, with its primarily African American NBA league, sought to overthrow baseball as America's favorite pastime, and Michael Jordan became a central icon of Americana. Yet, at the end of the decade the media again began to report the disappearance of the black image from network television, a situation that continues into the new millennium. Why did this occur? This is a complicated question, and a thorough analysis of the contemporary television landscape is beyond the scope of this book.

However, using the methodology proposed in this study of television during the Black Revolution allows one to answer questions about contemporary African American representation. For example: Does television still hold the potential as a site of resistance for African Americans? Is contemporary television a space that allows for the presence of vernacular black popular culture? How do contemporary social and political factors within black society influence the reading of contemporary African American television texts? Many of the concerns with contemporary television mirror those of 1960s and 1970s television and of every other decade since the inception of television. The conversations converge around two central issues: the lack and the quality of black images. In this new century, African Americans still debate these two core issues.

Political groups that push for the end of federally supported programs such as affirmative action base many of their arguments on the supposedly now irrelevant nature of these interventions. Apparently, full integration has occurred, and such programs are unnecessary. On a more fundamentalist level, the widespread proliferation of white supremacist web sites on the Internet and the violent acts of white militia groups indicate that various U.S. factions believe that the white man is losing the country to the minorities.[9] Minority groups have apparently achieved so many gains that they are literally, and unfairly, taking opportunities away from whites. Yet, the nation's most powerful tool of communication does not reflect this so-called integration, equality, and diversity of the American public, far less the diversity of the African American community.

Indeed, contemporary struggles over media representations are a microcosm of society's contestation over the changing American racial landscape.

While these challenges to the rights of minority groups are now coded into politically correct language—the end of "preferences"—this indeed makes the current political situation, although more veiled, as threatening to African Americans as the racial dictatorship was prior to the Civil Rights era. This situation indicates that perhaps now more than ever African Americans need to use all possible means, including the significant power of television, to challenge the mainstream constructions of black life and to instigate change. Using cable television and specifically Chris Rock's comedy specials *Bring the Pain* (1996), *Bigger and Blacker* (1999), and *The Chris Rock Show* (1997–2000), I explore the possibilities and problems of contemporary television as a black site of resistance and a forum for community.

Network Television: Hyperblackness Ghettoes and Invisibility

In his book *Watching Race: Television and the Struggle for "Blackness,"* Herman Gray describes the representation of African Americans in the 1990s as follows:

> [G]iven the level of saturation of the media with representations of blackness, the mediascape can no longer be characterized accurately by using terms such as invisibility. Rather, we might well describe ours as a moment of "hyperblackness."[10]

For the first time since the 1970s, many African American–cast programs appeared on television, although primarily within the genre of the situation comedy. Hyperblackness on television describes what was happening on the fledgling stations more than on the three major networks. Unlike the majority of television programs analyzed in this book, which appeared on mainstream U.S. television (*Soul Train* being the exception), these 1990s black-cast shows were primarily concentrated on the new networks. Warner Brothers (WB) and the United Paramount Network (UPN) followed in the footsteps of the Fox Network, whose strategy targeted the black audience with such shows as *In Living Color* (1990–93). By the 1990s this seemed to create a type of television network ghetto, in which one could locate the majority of black representations. By the fall of 1995, when it was difficult to find one weekly show dealing with African American subject matter on the three major networks, even within situation comedy, the most commonly used genre, shows of this nature flourished on the WB and UPN. These nascent networks absorbed African American–cast sitcoms rejected by the major networks. For example, *Sister Sister* (1994–99), an ABC sitcom for two years, became a mainstay of WB; *Minor Adjustments* (1995–96) lasted two months on NBC before it moved to UPN in 1996; and *The Hughleys* (1998–2002), which began on ABC, finished its run on UPN.

What ghettoized many of these programs was not only their placement on these minor networks but also the quality of the programs. While this is obviously subjective, I challenge anyone to find something redeeming about *Homeboyz from Outer Space* (UPN, 1997). While calling UPN the UnPopular Negro Network, Bill Cosby once said that African Americans should not be angry with those shows but strive for the inclusion of different programs.[11] On some level, it is difficult to argue with this sentiment, especially with the realization that even some of these shows are disappearing, seemingly along with the need of newer networks generally to target a black audience after they are established as a profitable business. In the late 1990s, WB became the network of dramas driven by white teen angst, such as *Dawson's Creek* (1997–2003) and *Buffy* (WB, 1997–2001; UPN, 2001–3), while UPN, still considered the sixth network, is likely to have at least one "black night" of television programming.

In the late 1990s and into the new decade, the expanding six-network television system has provided some space for black voices. Robert Townsend's *Parent 'Hood* (WB, 1995–99) and *The Bernie Mac Show* (Fox, 2001–) are examples of the attempt of individual black performers and producers to control their images on television. Still, white producers have a stronghold on the network system, and the lack of African American programming outside the situation comedy reveals that the networks remain unwilling to deal with black material outside this genre.

Cable Television: HBO, Black to the Future

People think the difference between HBO and regular TV is that on regular TV you can't curse. No. You can't think on regular TV. It is against the law to have an original idea. That's not like HBO.

Chris Rock, in Tom Shales, "Chris Rock: In a Very Soft Place Indeed"

Cerebral and black—that's hard to get. . . . That's like an impossible concept for a white studio executive to get. "Black and cerebral? Get the hell out of here! Black has to be over the top! Has to be slapstick!" But that's one thing I like about my show—it's actually dry every now and then.

Chris Rock, in Lloyd Grove, "Chris Rock: Stone Cold Funny"

The installation and pervasive reach of cable opened up the field of television to numerous representational possibilities. Cable perhaps holds the greatest potential as a black site of resistance within the context of television. This proposal has some limitations: cable is not as accessible to a national audience as essentially free network television is; it is not a public but a pay format. However, black viewership of cable programming has increased over the years, and cable is a forum in which blackness has not been erased.[12] In this section I focus on HBO as an example of cable's intervention in television's discourse on blackness.

A simple survey of made-for-television movies produced by HBO over the past years reveals the network's engagement with blackness. In 1997, HBO produced *Miss Evers' Boys,* chronicling the lives of the black men used in the Tuskegee experiment. The film won five Emmy Awards, including Outstanding Made for Television Movie and Outstanding Lead Actress in a Miniseries or Special for Alfre Woodard. The 1998 Emmy for Outstanding Made for Television Movie was *Don King: Only in America,* which also won the award for Outstanding Writing for a Miniseries or Movie. The HBO film *A Lesson before Dying* won the Emmy for Outstanding Writing for a Miniseries or Movie and the Outstanding Made for Television Movie in 1999. *Introducing Dorothy Dandridge* (1999) earned four Emmy Awards, including an Outstanding Lead Actress in a Miniseries or Special for Halle Berry. That year Berry also earned the Golden Globe Award for Best Actress in a Miniseries or Made for TV Movie.[13] Although awards are not necessarily the most useful gauge of a performer's ability or a film's merits, they are signifiers of a type of public recognition. Considering network television's limitations with regard to African American dramatic story lines, the developing space of cable television in the media landscape proves to be a fruitful area for interrogation.[14]

Because sponsors do not directly impact cable with the potential of advertising dollars or the threat of their loss, some cable channels take more risks and include topical material in their original films and programming.[15] The increased black viewership of these cable networks has correlated with the rise in films dealing with African American subject matter. These films play a role in recuperating lost African American stories within wider U.S. historical memory. Many of these stories are disregarded in official accounts of American history.

Three films relevant as examples of little-recognized stories finding a space on television are the *Tuskegee Airmen* (HBO, 1996), *Miss Evers' Boys* (HBO, 1997), and *Boycott* (2001). *The Tuskegee Airmen* relays the story of the fight for the black airborne to fly air combat in World War II; *Miss Evers' Boys,* as previously mentioned, discusses the victims of the Tuskegee experiment; and *Boycott* deals with the early days of Martin Luther King Jr. and his participation in the Montgomery bus boycott.

In American film and television, history is recuperated in two distinct ways. Hollywood revisions of black history include films such as *Mississippi Burning* (1988) and *Ghosts of Mississippi* (1996), and they use white protagonists as docents of black history.[16] For instance, Rob Reiner's *Ghosts of Mississippi* begins with the assassination of Civil Rights leader Medgar Evers and tells the story of a white lawyer's fight to prosecute Evers's murderer in 1989. The story focuses on the lawyer and his victimization by the white racists in Mississippi. The audience is barely given any information about Medgar Evers, and therefore the film does little to increase the public's knowledge of the fallen leader. Indeed, the construction of the narrative leads the audience to care less about the story of a racist prosecuted for a heinous crime than about the lawyer and whether he or his family will be hurt because he went, as the advertisement for the film indicated, "beyond the call of duty."

Although cable participates in this type of historical recuperation, it has at times created a forum to temper the process typical of films such as *Ghosts of Mississippi. Miss Evers' Boys* unquestioningly places the blame for the syphilis experiments on the shoulders of the U.S. government, which conceived of the plan and carried it out. The story is heard from the perspective of Miss Evers through her first-person voice-over and portrays her interactions with the men who went untreated for the curable disease. The *Tuskegee Airmen* clearly establishes the role of black men in World War II. African Americans have played a significant role in every U.S. war, and this film recognizes the black effort in the interest of U.S. freedom, even when African Americans faced unspeakable oppression on the home front. Although *Boycott* tells a familiar story of Martin Luther King Jr. and the bus boycott, the film offers different perspectives on and interpretations of King's motivations and emotions as well as conflicts over the boycott decisions. These films are important strides in acknowledging a lost history.

However, these representations reveal certain problematic trends. The majority of the films are set in the pre-integration era. The recurring image in such films as *Miss Evers' Boys* and *A Lesson before Dying* is that of the beaten-down African American exhibiting a sense of dignity in impossible situations. The narrative trajectory inevitably leads the viewer to the image of the stoic African American who stands up against all odds and confronts the problems of legalized segregation. While these are uplifting narratives, they do not reveal the complexity of emotions or motivations of the African American characters. For example, the *Tuskegee Airmen,* unquestioning of the potential conflicts, concentrates on the battle these black men waged for the right to fly and die for a country that despised them.

The proliferation of HBO films about the past prior to the Civil Rights era overlooks the narratives present in contemporary American society. Many current incidents beg for visualization, a way to come to terms with the contemporary U.S. social and political environment. Racism, while at times more covert, still plays an active role in the lives of all minority groups. The stories that have made their appearance on HBO in the late 1990s and into the early 2000s should have been told two to three decades ago. Again, these are important stories that need an outlet. However, over time, it appears that within this genre HBO is unwilling to tackle the present racial climate.

These HBO television movie images are in stark contrast to those created by black comedians such as Chris Rock, who use HBO as a forum for their specific brand of African American humor. Far from downtrodden, Chris Rock, in his comedy specials and weekly HBO series, presents an assertive and politically charged black man. Rock also brings us directly back to the present-day lives of African Americans.[17] What happens when Rock uses HBO to openly discuss African American existence within the United States? At times these programs create an oppositional image to mainstream constructions of blackness and present a textured vision of African American society.

Chris Rock: Televising the Politics of Black Communal Spaces

Who's more racist, black people or white people? Black people. You know why? Because we hate black people too. . . . There's, like, a civil war going on with black people. And there's two sides: there's black people, and there's niggas. And the niggas have got to go. Every time black people want to have a good time, ign'ant ass niggas fuck it up! . . . Can't keep a disco open more than three weeks. . . . Can't go to a movie the first week it come out! Why? 'Cause niggas are shooting at the screen! . . . "Hey, this is a good movie—this so good, I gotta bust a cap in here." I love black people, but I hate niggas. . . . Niggas always want some credit for some shit they supposed to do. . . . "I take care of my kids." You're supposed to, you dumb motherfucker. . . . "I ain't never been to jail." What you want—a cookie? You're not supposed to go to jail, you low-expectation motherfucker. . . . Some black people looking at me, "Man, why you got say that? . . . It ain't us, its the media. . . . The media has distorted our image to make us look bad." . . . Please cut the fucking shit. When I go to the money machine tonight, I ain't looking over my back for the media; I'm looking for niggas. Shit, Ted Koppel ain't never took shit from me. Niggas have. You think I got three guns in my house 'cause the media outside. Oh shit, Mike Wallace—run!

Chris Rock, *Bring the Pain*, 1996

In his 1963 speech at the Northern Negro Grass Roots Leadership Conference, "A Message to the Grassroots," Malcolm X said:

> Instead of airing our differences in public, we have to realize we're all the same family. And when you have a family squabble, you don't get out on the sidewalk. If you do, everybody calls you uncouth, unrefined, uncivilized, savage. If you don't make it at home, you settle it at home; you get in the closet, argue it out behind closed doors, and then when you come out on the street, you pose a common front, a united front. And this is what we need to do in the community, and in the city, and in the state. We need to stop airing our differences in front of the white man.[18]

This is a riff on the common adage "Don't air your dirty laundry in public." But this concept has a particular meaning to black society under the constant surveillance of white America. This was especially relevant in the midst of the Civil Rights and Black Power movements, because any rift evident in the black community was seen as a possible means of divide and conquer. Martin Luther King Jr. versus Malcolm X, one of the most discussed divisions in African American political history, was used to symbolize an opposition between the moderates and the so-called radicals, a split that some argued undermined a unified black political force.

As discussed, the prospect of a discrete political and social black community becomes less plausible in the era of legal desegregation and within the increasingly media-saturated U.S. society. Yet, this philosophy remains prevalent in the discourse of contemporary blackness, the notion that there are things better left behind closed doors. Along with the direct political ramifications, the notions of uplift and Du Boisian double consciousness run rampant throughout this ideal. How is the "black community" perceived by the white public when conversations usually maintained within the black communal spaces become the grist for national public entertainment?

In recent television history, one clear example of this debate occurred with the release of Chris Rock's HBO special *Bring the Pain*. It was one of the most significant moments in black popular culture of the late 1990s to test the bounds of Malcolm X's philosophy. The sentiments expressed in the monologue transcribed in this section's opening epigraph were debated among both black and white Americans. Should it have been part of the U.S. dialogue on race or kept within African American conversations? Questions of this nature again surfaced with *The Chris Rock Show* and his second HBO effort, *Bigger and Blacker*. Chris Rock's comedy hit a nerve, and the reverberations are still evident throughout both black and white society in this country.

Bring the Pain, shot at Washington DC's Takoma Theater, and *Bigger and Blacker*, shot at the Apollo in New York, place his comedy within spaces marked as centers of African American existence. Washington DC has one of the largest black populations in the country, and the Apollo, as previously mentioned, has historical linkages to black cultural and social life in Harlem. In *Bring the Pain*, Rock situates his humor within the trajectory of black performance and African American comedy. As the announcer introduces Rock, the camera focuses on his feet while he walks toward the stage.

Various album covers are superimposed over the image—those of Bill Cosby, Dick Gregory, Flip Wilson, Richard Pryor, Steve Martin, Pigmeat Markham, Woody Allen, and Eddie Murphy. As Rock explains,

> Those are my albums—I didn't have to go out and find them. I've got a big Pigmeat Markham collection, Moms Mabley. . . . I really study comedy in general, and I'm still learning from the old masters. . . . I meet a lot of the comics that have come up in the "Def Jam" generation and, frankly, the reason a lot of those young comics suck is that they don't study comedy. They look at Richard Pryor and Eddie Murphy and that's it. There's a much broader spectrum to get into. I'm still studying.[19]

Pigmeat Markham and Moms Mabley are not typical references. Rock has studied both African American and white comedians and has taken the time to understand the art form and its African American roots from the Chitlin' Circuit to today.

His comic presence and vocal cadence reflect an understanding of this history, as his approach to the audience echoes that of a country preacher. Yet he purports a contemporary urban aura as he paces ceaselessly back and forth on the stage. His topics for the night are varied, including the Million Man March, which "had all the positive black leaders there: Farrakhan, Jesse Jackson, Marion Barry. Marion Barry! You know what that means? That even in our finest hour, we had a crackhead onstage." In his observational style he pulls apart some of the core issues surrounding African American life: religion, relationships between the sexes, beliefs about education, jail, O.J. Simpson, and politics. What moves Rock on to another level is the purpose of this observational style. Other performers such as Jerry Seinfeld are considered observational comedians, because they target the everyday as a comedic source. However, Rock's comedy is on a different plane, as he addresses social and political issues. "I just talk about what is happening. If racism is happening, that's what I talk about. I'm the newspaper."[20]

Rock expresses a distinctive point of view about issues significant to African American life and is far from passive in his barbs regarding mainstream society and its views of African Americans. For example, his bit on Colin Powell addresses the external and inferential racist constraints placed on Powell and at the same time acknowledges the internal need for a black leader.

You know how I can tell Colin Powell can't be president? Whenever Colin Powell on the news, white people always give him the same compliments. How do you feel about Colin Powell? "He speaks so well." "He's so well spoken." Like that's a compliment. "Speaks so well" is not a compliment, okay? "Speaks so well" is some shit you say about retarded people that can talk. What—did he have a stroke the other day? He's a fucking educated man. How the fuck you expect him to sound, you dirty motherfucker?

What became more of an issue within black circles was Rock's pointed critique of problems within African American society. In the epigraph that opens this section, Rock describes a division in African American society between black people and "niggas." He went on to criticize this segment of society for various problems, such as not wanting an education and having more pride in a jail sentence than a master's degree. Internal critique, as explored in earlier chapters, has always been a part of the African American comedic tradition, as well as an everyday part of communal conversations among family and friends. What makes this a more critical issue is airing these problems in a mainstream forum such as HBO. These are problems to be handled behind the proverbial closed doors. Rock acknowledged this concern in an interview after the special aired.

> They've [African Americans] been thinking it and saying it for years. My mother's been saying it. It's not real news. My brother's house got broken into and he said, "Where do I sign up for the Ku Klux Klan?" and I like using that line. The people that get upset with that—the black people that get in my face—are angry mainly because I'm saying it in front of white people.[21]

The forum is no longer the black communal sites of the Chitlin' Circuit or the privacy of one's own home; it is the very mainstream venue of U.S. cable television.[22] The venue can change the meaning. No longer are you speaking to an audience that has a shared historical understanding underlying the humor. Once the material is released, the potential occurs for any number of interpretations by a multifaceted audience.[23] As Rock himself noted,

> That's the only thing I hated about all the press I got in the last couple of years about the niggers and Black people thing. They act

like I'm part of a minority of Black folks that want to do the right
thing. . . . No, I'm in the majority. . . . I'm no freak of nature.[24]

Rock's monologue actually indicates quite the opposite of the press's
interpretations and targets a black audience very aware of the numerous class divisions within African American society. In Rock's
perception, the press continues to view the black community as a
single uniform entity and interprets his critique as targeted at an
entire community of underachievers. The black comic's words are
turned against African American society and used to support preconceived notions of race. Should this prevent a comic or any other
African American public figure from expressing core concerns of his
or her community because of the possibilities of misinterpretation
by a white audience? Segments of the white mainstream American
society—politicians, policy makers, film and television producers—
represent the needs, desires, and goals of African Americans; thus,
black people are often spoken for by white society. Rock's performance is an act of black self-representation, and televised black
popular culture is in dire need of this type of articulation.

The ramifications of this performance were still being gauged
when *The Chris Rock Show* debuted on HBO in 1997. The half-
hour show was shot live to tape and typically began with a stand-
up routine focusing on contemporary news stories, followed by an
interview and a musical guest. The show was interspersed with
comedy skits or on-the-street interviews. Grandmaster Flash, of the
1970s and '80s hip-hop group Grandmaster Flash and the Furious
Five, provided the house music. *The Chris Rock Show* was a significant outlet for black social and political thought and, like *The Flip
Wilson Show* and *Soul Train,* a venue for black performance.[25]

Rock conducted interviews with political figures such as Rever-
end Jesse Jackson, Kweise Mufume, Marion Barry, and Reverend
Al Sharpton. He also invited guests such as Cornel West, Spike Lee,
Don King, Stanley Crouch, Wynton Marsalis, and Johnnie Cochran.
Musical performers included a wide variety of artists, such as Jill
Scott, Dr. Dre and Snoop Dogg, Sade, Jay Z, Rakim, Outkast, and
Saul Williams.

While allowing the guests to express their points of view, Rock,
when he does not agree, is quick to question their ideas and point
out the flaws he perceives in their arguments. In one particularly interesting episode, Rock invited University of California regent Ward

Connerly to speak on the show. Rock describes Connerly as one of "the leading forces in the national effort to dismantle affirmative action." Connerly, an African American, played a significant role in the cancellation of affirmative action in the University of California public education system.[26] He was also the key figure in the passage of Proposition 209, which made the consideration of race in public education, contracting, and hiring illegal.[27] The policy has had a significant negative impact on the number of African Americans, Latinos, Chicanos, and Native Americans enrolled in a university system that is supposed to serve a state with one of the largest multiracial populations.

In this interview Rock consistently questions Connerly's simplistic viewpoints on race. He begins by asking Connerly why he is so against affirmative action.

> CONNERLY: Treating people differently on the basis of skin color . . . in this nation, that's just fundamentally wrong. . . . We want to try to treat people equally.
>
> ROCK: Don't people get treated differently because of skin color anyway? Isn't there racism?
>
> CONNERLY: But I think our government shouldn't be legalized, sanctioned to do that.
>
> ROCK: But the government started it!

While Connerly is unyielding in his belief that the government should treat all people equally, which is his way of claiming that affirmative action is reverse racism, Rock reminds him that, while black men were created equal, nothing ensures equal treatment, so laws are necessary. As an example, Rock indicates the importance of minimum wage laws that guarantee people are paid for their labor. As Rock states, without that law, many workers would be abused and paid with "Spam or toilet paper."

Connerly still argues that the laws need to protect poor Asian and white youth and that these groups should have the same opportunities as poor and middle-class blacks.

> ROCK: I live in New York City, and I have been all over this country. When is the last time you saw a homeless Asian man?
>
> CONNERLY: Chris, you know where they are? They're in the library studying.

By following up on Rock's race-based joke, Connerly plays into the myth of Asian Americans as the model minority. The myth is based on claims that Asian Americans have had an easier time assimilating into American society, suggesting that Asians are more hardworking and therefore more successful than other minority groups. This has created resentment between Asians and other minority groups, although Asians are still impacted by many forms of discrimination.[28] Connerly problematically implies that the poverty within other racial and ethnic groups is a result of their lack of a work ethic.

Rock appears to try to understand how Connerly could have "dedicated [his] life to making sure the white man has a fair shake." But the way in which he leads Connerly into the following series of questions suggests that he may already know their answers. He asks Connerly his age (fifty-nine at the time of the interview), then continues:

ROCK: I've never met an old black man who didn't hate white people, 'cause old black men went through real racism. Young black men talk about not getting a cab; the black man *was* the cab. A white man jumped on his back and said, "Take me to Main Street."

CONNERLY: An old black man ought to know that race is not an appropriate factor to be discriminating against somebody for.

ROCK: What were you doing when black people were getting hosed down, beat up, dogs sicced on them? Where were you at? What was going on in your life?

CONNERLY: I was in California getting discriminated against *in getting apartments* [emphasis added].

ROCK: Yeah?

Rock sets Connerly up to reveal his lack of first-hand experience with overt racism. Thus, in the audience's eyes, the call to end affirmative action is voiced by a man who has not had to face more visceral types of discrimination. Connerly is a product of an affirmative action education system, yet he is unable to connect with the hardships African Americans still face in this contemporary and racially divisive society. Rock definitely wins the debate, and in his final diatribe he is able to use humor to expose the lack of depth of Connerly's argument. In this and many other interviews, Rock used

HBO to discuss social issues and political policies that have a real impact on black society.

As in *Bring the Pain*, in his weekly show Rock also used comedy sketches and his man-on-the-street interviews to critique African American society and to locate continued, but often more covert, forms of racism within American society. In one comedy sketch called "The Progress Report," Rock analyzes African American successes and failures by reading a Chutes and Ladders–type chart provided by the fictional "American Black Progress Association." A cardboard black man is attached by Velcro and can be moved up and down the ladder. The highest step on the ladder is labeled "There." Rock explains that African Americans often talk about other blacks who have set the black community back so many "steps" from the goal of being "There." He then describes several of these moments throughout African American history.

> In 1960 SNCC and CORE staged sit-ins. It was a great time for black people, putting us ahead four steps. But in 1988 the Crips and Bloods staged shoot-outs, putting black people six steps back and six feet under. . . . In 1984 Jesse Jackson hits the campaign trail, stressing, "Keep hope alive!" Seven steps ahead. But in 1990 Marion Barry hits the pipe in a hotel room, stressing, "Bitch set me up!" Twelve steps back.

Chris Rock charts the progress of black people.

Rock notes that whites have had an impact on the ability to make it "There." Rock discusses Susan Smith, the South Carolina woman convicted of drowning her two children. By blaming a black man she initially put black people back seven steps, but when the truth came out, black people moved forward two hundred steps. Generally, throughout the sketch he spends much of the time pointing out both the positives and negatives of black society, from Venus and Serena Williams to Daryl Strawberry. He even ends the skit by noting that black society had almost made it and was just ten steps away until the night of the infamous 2000 Source Hip-Hop Awards, which were cancelled because several fights broke out and chaos ensued at the Pasadena Civic Auditorium, in California. He places the responsibility on black people to check themselves and see their role in reinforcing beliefs about black people.

Rock's on-the-street interviews are a fascinating look at contemporary race relations. He goes to South Carolina "the heart of Dixie" to talk to people about the fact that the state still flies the Confederate flag over its Capitol dome. Rock interviews both white and black citizens of South Carolina. One older white man says the flag is flown because they are southerners and it should stay there forever. One white woman claims that the Confederate flag is a symbol of family and pride. She does not understand why Rock does not see her viewpoint. When Rock asks her if she thinks black people would feel better if they could put up their own flags, she says no, as if unable to acknowledge the flag's symbolic tie to racism and slavery. On an unnerving note, when Rock asks a black man if he thinks the police would be upset with the man if he tore the flag off the Capitol, the black man responds that the police "would handcuff me, take me to some woods, and beat me up."

Rock in turn proposes several alternate flags, which include one of O.J. and a white woman and one that states, "South Carolina is OKKK." As a matter of fact, when Rock riffs on the theme of the flag and asks the older white man if he is familiar with the Klan, the man pauses to think in a way that makes him look as if he may be quite intimately aware of the organization. Rock also suggests a combination of the Malcolm X symbol and the Confederate flag and a flag with a large white saltine (i.e., a "cracker"). The flag that is finally chosen is a version of the Confederate flag whose stars have been replaced by the stars of the WB network. While some of the interviewees are humored, others show increasingly horrified expressions at Rock's flag suggestions and take him quite seriously, showing their investment in maintaining a symbol of racism.

In another episode, Rock, noting that in white neighborhoods none of the streets are named after slain black icons, goes to the notorious Howard Beach neighborhood to see if he can get people to sign a petition to change Cross Bay Boulevard to Tupac Shakur Boulevard. Cross Bay Boulevard was the initial site of a 1986 assault on three black men by a gang of white teenagers armed with baseball bats and tree limbs. The racially based assault left one of the black men, twenty-three-year-old Michael Griffith, dead and another of them, Cedric Sandiford, badly beaten.

One white man driving a van at Cross Bay Boulevard tells Rock, "Tupac stinks, his music stinks, and I am not interested in having this boulevard's name changed to a piece of dirt like him." As the segment continues the man also claims that Tupac should have "died before he was born" and says that Chris Rock must have "some pair of balls to come around a neighborhood" like Howard Beach with such a petition. He agrees that Frank Sinatra Boulevard would be acceptable.

Rock and his cameraman drive around the neighborhood in a van with signs that read Keep Your Head Up: Support Tupac Shakur Boulevard. The quotation "Strictly for My Niggaz" appears on the back window. A white fireman tries to make them pull over and pushes the camera away. Rock refuses to pull over. One white woman runs away from him, and another man tells him he should go back to Jersey. Another, more pleasant woman suggests that a change to Olivia Newton Boulevard would be better. Rock does get several white residents to sign the petition, but the images of the resentful whites of Howard Beach at the turn of the last century cannot be ignored.

Not every member of this show's audience appreciated Rock's sketches and stand-up. The show was taped before a live audience, and television viewers can hear the comments of the audience members, many of them black women, who disagree with Rock's position. For example, in one fake advertisement for a product called Niggatrol, Rock claims that black men's lives are very stressful. He is seen standing in the street while various white people shout "Nigger!" at him. Niggatrol works on the headaches caused by being a black man. Niggatrol Plus was recommended for black

Rock encourages residents of Howard Beach to support Tupac Shakur Boulevard.

men married to white women and Niggatrol Maximum Strength for black men married to black women. The groans in the audience are palpable, and the looks on the faces of the black women leave little to the imagination.[29]

Like many comedians before him, Rock uses the ridiculous stereotypical beliefs about black people for humor. For example, within the preceding joke, Niggatrol tablets are shaped like drumsticks and are coated with hot sauce. To a black audience with insider knowledge of practices within the black community, these jokes take on their own site-specific meaning. However, some African Americans still believe, as they did during the 1970s, that these ideas allow a white audience to laugh at and confirm their stereotypical beliefs about black people.

Even with the early success of *The Chris Rock Show,* the black and mainstream press still questioned his popularity within the black community. Tired of constantly being asked about the black response to his comedy, Rock taped *Bigger and Blacker* at the Apollo Theater in Harlem. The show was edited together from three live shows and premiered on HBO in July 1999. Similar to the opening sequence of *Bring the Pain,* the show's beginning credit montage establishes Rock as a part of the pantheon of African American comedians, this time by using the symbol of the Apollo, a cornerstone of black cultural life. There is an aerial shot of Harlem and the Apollo Theater at night. As the credits come up, we see a

Niggatrol: to combat a black man's headaches.

split screen of famous markers that identify the streets as Harlem: the subway stop that is marked as Uptown and 125th Street, the sign at the corner of Lennox Avenue and Malcolm X Boulevard, the marquee advertising Chris Rock, and the African American audience waiting in line for the performance.

Beginning with comments about the Columbine tragedy, Rock shows that he is not afraid to tackle the controversial and at the same time provides a release from this seemingly untouchable topic.[30]

> I got on the elevator—and these two high school white boys tried to get on with me, and I just dove off. Y'all ain't killing me! I am scared of young white boys. If you white and under twenty-one, I am running for the hills. What the hell is wrong with these white kids? Shooting up the school! They don't even wait till three o'clock either.

In addressing this issue, he also challenges the assaults on the media that have resulted from the country's desire to reach a solution over the tragedy.

> Everybody want to know what the kids was listening to, what kind of music was they listening to, what kind of movies was they watching. Who give a fuck what they was watching? Whatever happened to crazy? You can't be crazy no more? Did we eliminate *crazy* from the dictionary? Fuck the record, fuck the movie—Crazy! The world is coming to an end. You're going to have little white kids saying, "I want to go to a black school where it's safe."

He then brings this around to the issue of gun control. Rock says he loves guns, and instead of recommending the control of them, he proposes another solution that seemingly targets the problem: "We don't need gun control. We need bullet control. If every bullet cost five thousand dollars, there'd be no more innocent bystanders."

Rock is concerned with three particular issues in this comedy special: race, politics, and black gender and family relationships. He addresses race through varied topics, such as the persecution of Bill Clinton, taxes, the Macy's parade, the police, and the media attention given to the white backlash against racial advancement.[31]

> Who's the maddest people? White people. White people pissed off. The white man thinks he's losing the country. If you watch the news, "We're losing everything, we're fucking losing. Affirmative action and illegal aliens, and we're fucking losing the country." Losing?

> Shut the fuck up! White people ain't losing shit. If y'all losing, who's winning? It ain't us. Have you driven around this motherfucker? Shit, there ain't a white man in this room that would change places with me—and I'm rich! That's how good it is to be white. There is a white one-legged busboy in here right now that won't change places with my black ass. He's going, "No, man, I don't want to switch. I want to ride this white thing out. See where it takes me."

While quick to note the problems inherent in U.S. society at the turn of the millennium, Rock insists that black people need to know where to draw the line when critiquing mainstream society. He explains this with an anecdote based on the reaction to the deaths of two significant hip-hop figures.

> I'm watching the news: Tupac Shakur was assassinated. Biggie Smalls was assassinated. Struck down by assassins bullets. No they wasn't. Martin Luther King was assassinated. Malcolm X was assassinated. John F. Kennedy was assassinated. Them two niggas got shot.

Again, when Rock focuses his observations on black society, the public forum becomes an issue for a television audience. The live and primarily black audience at the Apollo can have a different engagement with the comedian. As on *The Chris Rock Show,* they use call-and-response to agree or disagree with his statements throughout the show, and Rock clearly engages with them. The loudest audience reactions occur during Rock's discussion of relationships between black men and women and within the black family. External to this process of engagement between Rock and the black audience is the mainstream audience's response and interpretation. The comedian again is unconcerned with the white audience's opinions on the subject matter, and this again places him in the position of revealing issues that reside behind black walls.[32]

Rock has a clear agenda to recuperate the image of the black father.[33] He believes that while the mother has a tough job, at least she receives recognition for it. As he says,

> Think about everything that the real daddy does—pay the bills, buy the food, put a fucking roof over your head, everything you could ask for. Make your world a better, safer place, and what does daddy get? The big piece of chicken. That's all daddy gets is the big piece of chicken. And some women don't want to give up the big piece of chicken.

In this recuperation Rock envisions a generally patriarchal relationship, with each gender having its assigned duties and responsibilities. Whereas his societal critiques are sharp, his observations about black mothers, either single or married, are uneven. He blames these women for their children's illiteracy and delinquency. He places the man in the position of provider, yet he seems to forget the male role in the child's upbringing, and he overlooks the notoriously poor education system in urban neighborhoods. His comedy addresses some problems apparent within African American society. "If the kid call his grandmama Mommy and his mama Pam, he going to jail." However, this critique seems limited by a perception of black womanhood framed within the context of images presented on programs such as *The Ricki Lake Show* (1993–).

Rock left HBO and, to a large extent, stand-up comedy in 2000 to concentrate on a career in feature films. However, he has not been able to bring his prior level of insightful critique to the big screen. The disappointing *Head of State* (2003), in which Rock plays a Washington DC alderman who runs for presidential office, showed some potential but fell far below the wit of *The Chris Rock Show*. Chris Rock made a welcome return to the comedy stage with the Black Ambition Tour in 2004.[34]

As with any other African American public figure, an intense and unfair responsibility has been placed on Rock to be a spokesperson for the race. What this continues to suggest is the U.S. notion of a monolithic black society, in which one person represents all class and social backgrounds that compose African American society. The issue of uplifting the race is a constant concern, because what Rock says is inevitably interpreted by a mainstream audience as representing the entire race, not the specific segment of the society that he focuses his observations on. As discussed, this is the common concern of any mediated image of blackness, and this situation will continue as long as the present U.S. racial climate persists.

There is a need for an increased awareness of the influence of the ideology of uplift and the changing forums for black popular culture. The question, What will white America think? has been the basis of criticism throughout African American television history. This is a constricting situation for media critics that improves by changing the methodology of interpretation, understanding historical meaning, discussing the multiple meanings, and discovering underlying political agendas of artists and producers. I am not saying every black popular cultural text has a progressive political agenda; however, many representations resist the mainstream co-optation of blackness and are thus affirming. The access of these artists continues to crack the white wall of public culture. For example, Rock finances the *Illtop Journal*. Produced at Howard University, the magazine is based on the concept of the *Harvard Lampoon* and is used to develop the writing of African American comics.

This was the goal of many 1960s and 1970s television figures—to accept TV roles and open up the space for additional African American voices. The larger platform of cable television allows Rock and other African American performers to critique the society around them. This critique encompasses both the United States at large and the inner working of African American society. It is important that one not quell these voices because of fears of public perception. While certainly uneven in its representations of African Americans, television continues to have potential as a site of resistance for the black population.

Notes

Introduction

1. The first chapter discusses two books in particular, J. Fred MacDonald's *Blacks and White TV* and Donald Bogle's *Prime Time Blues*. These are the major single-author texts that deal with black television as a whole and 1960s and 1970s television in particular.

2. The first chapter discusses the history of *Amos 'n' Andy*, revealing the numerous political arguments about the merits of the show and the impact of the cancellation on the representation of African Americans on television.

3. See Michael Curtin, *Redeeming the Wasteland: Television Documentary and Cold War Politics*.

4. Gray argues that television of the 1970s attempted to locate "authentic" representations of blackness; however, the "urban ghetto sitcoms" replicated the white middle-class family structure. While this is certainly the case in the ghetto sitcoms, the scope of Gray's book does not focus on this era in particular and therefore does not explore the decade any further. I argue that the images and programs of this time are far more complex.

5. Michael Dyson, *Making Malcolm: The Myth and Meaning of Malcolm X*; bell hooks, *Black Looks: Race and Representation* and *Reel to Real: Race, Sex, and Class at the Movies*; Michelle Wallace and Gina Dent, *Black Popular Culture*.

1. Reading the Roots of Resistance

1. Gray, *Watching Race*, 148. Gray argues that in the 1990s, certain factors, including the rise in popularity of black youth style, led to a situation in which African Americans were no longer considered invisible

within U.S. popular culture; instead, there was media saturation of black images, "hyperblackness." I argue that the first case of hyperblackness on television occurred in the 1970s. Gray's cultural studies approach to the examination of 1980s and 1990s television is a useful framework, as he considers technologies, industrial organization, and the political economy in order to address the issues that shape commercial culture, representations of blackness, power, inequality, domination, and difference.

2. J. Fred MacDonald's *Blacks and White TV* is deeply entrenched in the positive/negative dichotomy of analysis. For example, the second chapter of his book is entitled "Blacks in TV: Nonstereotypes versus Stereotypes." The chapter does not address the basis for categorization; thus, what is positive or negative is assumed to be the same to any viewing audience. While the book includes important historical material, throughout it the analysis of television programs is framed by this assumption of uniform reading. By the end of the book MacDonald shows a complete lack of class consciousness when dealing with contemporary television. In chapter 21, "The Cultural Debate," he criticizes *The Cosby Show* for dealing with teenage sex and condoms through the character of cousin Pam. The introduction of Pam actually addressed the class difference in black society previously ignored on the show. MacDonald states that the show thus lost its "stately demeanor" (293). He considers cable television a problematic venue because black comics are allowed to express profanity heard only in locker rooms. He also suggests that cable stations, especially MTV, and shows such as *Yo! MTV Raps* have allowed urban underclass youth to "[mount] a forceful assault on middle-class norms"(294). MacDonald states that *Yo! MTV Raps* was "a hip-hop showcase replete with the full range of rap's verbal transgressions—from grammatical inexactitude and sexual boasting to crude sexist ideas—plus the stifling of melodic song by the repetitive rhythm and unsophisticated chant that are the hallmarks of the musical phenomenon" (294). While he admits they are spokesmen for racial problems, he states that "angry young black men" create hostility, and thus rap artists should make their acts milder (297). Although the chapter includes many examples of this lack of class consciousness, one can analyze this critique as emblematic of the chapter. MacDonald does not discuss the problems that black artists had in getting MTV to incorporate black images. As MTV became one of the best routes to publicizing and selling music, their exclusion put black artists at a disadvantage. Second, his description of hip-hop indicates an "old school" interpretation of music; hip-hop certainly does not qualify as being mainstream melodic. However, experimental jazz created by some of the most famous musicians, such as John Coltrane and Miles Davis, often did not fit into mainstream views of music. His critique of sexual boasting also does not acknowledge that toasting and signifying are part of a long

tradition of oral culture in the black community. Overall he indicates that middle-class images or uplifting images of the urban underclass are the only ones acceptable for mainstream television. Considering his analysis of 1990s television, one should question the validity of the assessment of the history of black TV that he presents.

3. Similar to his book on African American film, *Toms, Coons, Mulattoes, Mammies & Bucks*, Bogle's *Prime Time Blues*, while useful as a historical framework, focuses on biographical information about the actors during various historical decades. The book also tends to focus on the positive or negative aspects of black television shows.

4. Marlon Riggs, "Tongues Retied," in *Resolutions: Contemporary Video Practices*, 185–88. This chapter was written in response to the negative and homophobic feedback to his film about black gay men in the United States, *Tongues Untied* (1989). In the article Riggs responds to the arguments that his film should not have been supported with public funds or shown on public television because it does not comply with community standards. Riggs questions this idea of community standards and censorship by asking the questions, whose standards and whose community? He argues that the term *community standards* suggests one central community. This community is patriarchal, heterosexual, and white. Compliance with these standards will determine that any cultural product not within the majority will not be able to find a place in public television. If we use this idea of community standards within African American society, the community can be described as black, middle-class, and heterosexual. Thus, cultural products that do not meet this particular set of standards are similarly rejected.

5. I refer to the term *vast wasteland* as used by Newton Minow. Then chairman of the FCC, Minow responded to issues such as the quiz show scandals by describing television as a vast wasteland. Although television in the 1970s was often heralded as producing more socially progressive programming, black television programs were often considered as reveling in "regressive images."

6. *Cops* also reinforces ideas about the criminality of other minority groups and the white underclass as well. It is interesting to note that *Cops* thus far has not appeared on Wall Street to deal with the upper-class criminality such as the Enron, WorldCom, or Martha Stewart scandals of 2002.

7. A racial project, as defined by Michael Omi and Howard Winant, is "simultaneously an interpretation, representation, or explanation of racial dynamics, and an effort to reorganize and redistribute resources along particular racial lines." Michael Omi and Howard Winant, *Racial Formation in the United States: From the 1960s to the 1990s*, 56.

8. Bogle, *Toms, Coons, Mulattoes, Mammies & Bucks*; Ed Guerrero, *Framing Blackness: The African American Image in Film*. Both Bogle and

Guerrero discuss Sidney Poitier's loss of most cultural signifiers in order to achieve acceptance in Hollywood film and with the mainstream American audience.

9. Kevin K. Gaines, *Uplifting the Race: Black Leadership, Politics, and Culture in the Twentieth Century*, 14.

10. Ibid., 2.

11. Ibid., 3.

12. W. E. B. Du Bois, *The Souls of Black Folk*, 3.

13. Gaines, *Uplifting the Race*, 3.

14. Robin D. G. Kelley, *Race Rebels: Culture, Politics and the Black Working Class*, 8.

15. Omi and Winant, *Racial Formation in the United States*, 13.

16. John Hope Franklin and Alfred A. Moss, *From Slavery to Freedom: A History of African Americans*, 225.

17. Ibid., 247–63.

18. Kelley, *Race Rebels*, 36.

19. The need for black-only spaces is still discussed within African American critical circles. On a more personal note, my primarily black class at the University of California–Davis debated whether or not African American actors or comedians (such as Chris Rock in his HBO special *Bring the Pain*) should discuss issues pertaining to the black community on television. While some argued that it was appropriate to use the venue to speak to a wider black television audience, others felt that it was acceptable only if it was a black-only audience, something that cannot be controlled on television.

20. Du Bois, *The Souls of Black Folk*, 3.

21. Mel Watkins, *On the Real Side: Laughing, Lying and Signifying*, 35.

22. Henry Louis Gates, *The Signifying Monkey: A Theory of African-American Literary Criticism.*

23. Watkins, *On the Real Side*, 72.

24. Ibid., 52.

25. Eugene D. Genovese, *Roll Jordan Roll: The World the Slaves Made.*

26. This type of acknowledgment does not mean that every African American accepted minstrelsy. Indeed, segments of the black community refused to attend these performances.

27. Watkins, *On the Real Side*, 367.

28. Ibid., 367.

29. Call-and-response is a practice that can be traced back to the tradition of oral culture that existed in many African nations. This practice has been found in such cultural forms as storytelling and music. Call-and-response as well as other forms of oral culture transitioned with slaves to America. Ripped from their own environments, slaves used oral culture

to pass on their histories, stories, myths, and religion. Call-and-response was witnessed on the plantations when a person sang the lead and the group responded. Unbeknownst to the plantation owners, this form of call-and-response often contained messages of resistance, routes, and times of escape. Call-and-response made the transition to many areas of African American social and cultural life, such as the church and music, but can also be seen in more casual settings and in the black audience's response to popular culture. For example, attending a movie at a traditional black theater includes the expectancy of many people talking back to the screen. For more information, see Ben Sidran, *Black Talk*; and LeRoi Jones, *Blues People*.

30. These theaters' ownership by white businessmen, many of whom were racists, did place some limitations on the ability of African Americans to create black sites of resistance. Nonetheless, many white-owned venues were used for these purposes.

31. Redd Foxx and Norma Miller, *The Redd Foxx Encyclopedia of Black Humor*, 98.

32. Watkins, *On the Real Side*, 363–99.

33. For further information on this issue, see Nathan Huggins, *Harlem Renaissance*.

34. Watkins, *On the Real Side*, 388–89.

35. Kelley, *Race Rebels*, 56.

36. Ibid., 58.

37. Ibid., 66–67.

38. Ibid., 68.

39. Watkins, *On the Real Side*, 488.

40. See ibid., 364–99.

41. Ibid., 497.

42. Ibid., 497.

43. The trickster of African and African American folklore was located in slave stories and jokes as the character who outsmarts the slave owners and disrupts the working of the plantation by resisting work. As previously mentioned, he also conceives of ways to gain rewards and privileges for himself. The trickster remains a popular character in African American storytelling in such tales as Brer Rabbit. During the Black Revolution, Melvin Van Peebles created a 1970s trickster in the main character of Sweetback in his groundbreaking, avant-garde film *Sweet Sweetback's Baadasssss Song* (1971). For more information on the history of this figure, see Gates, *The Signifying Monkey*.

44. Gregory quoted in Watkins, *On the Real Side*, 502.

45. *Ebony*, June 1950, 22.

46. MacDonald, *Blacks and White TV*, 13.

47. Thomas Cripps, "Amos 'n' Andy and the Debate over Racial Integration," 41.

48. Ibid., 42.

49. Ibid., 50.

2. Was the Revolution Televised?

1. For a detailed history of the Civil Rights and Black Power movements, see Steven F. Lawson, *Running for Freedom: Civil Rights and Black Politics in America since 1941*; Franklin and Moss, *From Slavery to Freedom*; and Clayborne Carson et al., eds., *The Eyes on the Prize: A Civil Rights Reader*.

2. Quoted in Robert J. Donovan and Ray Scherer, *Unsilent Revolution: Television News and American Public Life: 1948–1991*, 4.

3. Quoted ibid., 4.

4. For a thorough analysis of these documentary series, see Curtin, *Redeeming the Wasteland*.

5. An analysis of the series as a whole could be an individual chapter in a book on 1990s television. Its exploration of civil rights issues, the student movement, Black Power movement, and Vietnam bordered on being right wing, and generally the miniseries proved more a vehicle for the music than for any social analysis. However, for our purposes here, I want to draw attention to a specific scene and the process it involved.

6. Herman Gray, "Remembering Civil Rights: Television, Memory and the 60's," 353.

7. Donovan and Scherer, *Unsilent Revolution*, 8.

8. Ibid., 16.

9. For more details on the SCLS news strategy, see Sasha Torres, *Black. White. And in Color: Television and Black Civil Rights*.

10. Ibid., 17.

11. Robert Kennedy Jr., *In His Own Words: The Unpublished Recollections of the Kennedy Years*, 171–72. Birmingham Alabama Police commissioner Eugene T. Bull Conner was notorious for his assaults on the nonviolent protesters, often using dogs and fire hoses.

12. Donovan and Scherer, *Unsilent Revolution*, 74.

13. Curtin, *Redeeming the Wasteland*. The Golden Age of Television Documentary differs from television's Golden Age, which is typically associated with the anthology dramas of the mid-1950s. Despite this, for my purpose here, I will refer to this period of documentary production in brief as the Golden Age.

14. Ibid., 32–33.

15. Ibid., 3.

16. MacDonald, *Blacks and White TV*, 95–98.

17. Curtin, *Redeeming the Wasteland*, 261–66.

18. Quoted ibid., 146.

19. Donovan and Scherer, *Unsilent Revolution*, 75–77.

20. Bill Nichols, *Representing Reality*, 141–49.

21. Mike Davis, *City of Quartz*, 296.

22. Raphael J. Sonenshein, *Politics in Black and White: Race and Power in Los Angeles*, 69.

23. Davis, *City of Quartz*, 296.

24. Ibid., 271, 294.

25. Sonenshein, *Politics in Black and White*, 76.

26. Lee Rainwater and William L. Yancey, *The Moynihan Report and the Politics of Controversy*.

27. Ibid., 24.

28. Ibid., 16.

29. Paula Giddings, *When and Where I Enter: The Impact of Black Women on Race and Sex in America*, 329.

30. Sophia Spalding, "The Constable Blunders: Police Abuse in Los Angeles' Black and Latino Communities, 1945–1965," 7.

31. Nichols, *Representing Reality*, 141.

32. Ibid., 143.

33. Donovan and Scherer, *Unsilent Revolution*, 77.

34. *Report of the National Advisory Commission on Civil Disorders*, 11.

35. Ibid., 3, 27, quotation from 48.

36. "TV's Black Journal Lacks Funds—May Close," 4.

37. Tommie Lee Lott, "Documenting Social Issues: Black Journal 1968–1970," 77.

38. William Greaves, "100 Madison Avenue Will Be of No Help," 13.

39. There were local talk and variety shows such as *Like It Is* on WABC-TV and *Positively Black* on WNBC-TV in New York. While certainly not denying their relevance, I choose to concentrate on *Black Journal* because of its national audience. In the fiction vein, shows like the groundbreaking *East Side/West Side* did tackle issues dealing with African Americans but did not sustain in the ratings and were quickly canceled.

40. As noted within the introduction, the positing of class differences also complicated uplift. However, when I refer to popular notions of uplift, I am implying the group struggles for advancement.

41. Among its many recommendations, the Kerner Commission's report suggested that the media needed to increase its coverage of issues within the black community.

42. Carson et al., eds., *The Eyes on the Prize*, 501.

43. Ibid., 529.

44. Huey Newton was eventually convicted of manslaughter.

45. Black Panther 10 Point Program:

1. We want freedom. We want power to determine the destiny of our Black Community.
2. We want the full employment for our people.
3. We want an end to robbery by the capitalists of our Black Community.
4. We want decent housing, fit for shelter of human beings.
5. We want education for our people that exposes the true nature of this decadent American society. We want education that teaches us our true history and our role in the present-day society.
6. We want all Black men to be exempt from military service.
7. We want an immediate end to police brutality and murder of Black people.
8. We want freedom for all Black men held in federal, state, county and city prisons and jails.
9. We want all Black people when brought to trial to be tried in a court by a jury of their peer group or people from their Black communities, as defined by the Constitution of the United States.
10. We want land, bread, housing, education, clothing, justice and peace. And as our major political objective, a United Nations–supervised plebiscite to be held throughout the Black colony in which only Black colonial subjects will be allowed to participate, for the purpose of determining the will of Black people as to their national destiny.

(Accessible on various web sites [e.g., www.lib.berkeley.edu/MRC/panthers10pt.html].)

46. It is also relevant to note the ways in which the garb of the hosts and commentators was modified to express the changing times, from the traditional suits worn in the premiere to the Afrocentric garb donned a year later.

47. Smith and Carlos were remembered for their silent protest at the 1968 Olympics, with their black power salute and bowed heads. For more details on the meaning of their protest, see Amy Bass, "Race and Nation in Olympic Proportions," 8–24.

48. Other *Black Journal* episodes included segments on the liberation issue in African nations, the Poor People's campaign, the education system, African American athletes, the assassination of Martin Luther King Jr., the murder of Fred Hampton, unionization struggles, and labor disputes.

49. In his article "Documenting Social Issues: Black Journal 1968–1970," Tommie Lee Lott notes that the Black Nationalist slant of *Black Journal* at times had negative ramifications. For instance, in its coverage of labor issues, the program often ignored Black-Latino coalitions that were formed to combat mutual problems.

50. James D. Williams, "Blacks and Public TV," 31.

51. "TV's Black Journal Lacks Funds—May Close," 4.

52. Ibid.

53. "Black TV: Its Problems and Promises," 88.

54. Carol A. Morton, "For Black Viewers: Some Other Choices Besides Off/On?" 49.

55. Brown continually used the press to challenge the media and their assumptions about *Black Journal*. In 1972, an article entitled "Black Journal Charges New York Times with Attempted Assassination" covered Tony Brown's response to critiques of a *Journal* episode entitled "Black Paper on White Racism Part I." *New York Times* writer John J. O'Connor criticized the roundtable discussion involving John Henry Clarke, an associate professor of African and Afro-American history at Hunter College in New York; Preston Wilcox, head of the educational workshop of the Congress of African People, and Reverend Albert Cleage, of the Shrine of the Black Madonna, in Detroit, stating that the panelists presented "a blend of facts, half truths, myths and legends" and suggesting that "if Black racism, no less objectionable and absurd than any other form of racism, is offered as 'a tool in the struggle for dignity and pride' the program also deserves to be seriously questioned." Brown stated that the *New York Times*'s critique was "an attempt at political assassination of Black Journal." "Black Journal Charges New York Times with Attempted Assassination," 44.

56. Peter Bailey, "Black Excellence in the Wasteland," 47.

57. Williams, "Blacks and Public TV," 32.

58. Ibid., 32.

59. Ibid., 32.

60. Jacob Wortham, "In with the Big Boys," 15.

61. Richard K. Doan, "The Doan Report," A-3.

62. "Tony Brown: Television's Civil Rights Crusader," 36.

63. George Hill, *Ebony Images: Black Americans and Television,* 67.

3. What You See Is What You Get

1. The work of these black political organizations is discussed further in chapter 5.

2. For more information on these shows, see Bogle, *Prime Time Blues.*

3. Todd Boyd, "A Trip down 'Soul Train's' Memory Lane," 1.

4. Quoted in Jones (aka Baraka), *Blues People,* xi.

5. See Nelson George, *The Death of Rhythm and Blues,* 42, for this and the following quotations.

6. In his book *Imagined Communities,* Benedict Anderson suggests that during the late eighteenth and the nineteenth centuries the consumption of mass media (newspapers in particular) provided a link to other members of the nation and could be considered a nation-forming device.

Listening to black radio created an "imagined community" and reflected black nationhood and fellowship, a bond between the listening audiences.

7. The Harvard Report, cited in George, *The Death of Rhythm and Blues,* 136.

8. Norman Mailer's 1957 essay "The White Negro" described and embraced the white social outlaw who seized the style, sexuality, and music of African Americans. The stereotypical underpinnings of Mailer's arguments are clear. However, the article did reflect aspects of American society in the late 1950s. Figures such as Elvis Presley epitomized the donning of the accoutrements of black culture without understanding it, using it for profit without any benefit to the black community. This pattern would culminate when producer Alan Freid of New York radio's WINS began to disguise the blackness of R&B by calling it rock and roll and marketing it to young white teenagers.

9. For more detailed analysis of the Blaxploitation movement, see Guerrero, *Framing Blackness*; and Bogle, *Toms, Coons, Mulattoes, Mammies & Bucks.*

10. On the other hand, films of the Los Angeles School, such as Haile Gerima's *Bush Mama* (1974) and Charles Burnett's *Killer of Sheep* (1977), and films produced through the Black Filmmakers Foundation, such as Warrington Hudlin's *Street Corner Stories* (1977), although written, produced, and directed by politicized African American filmmakers, were often ensconced in academic or high art settings. These films often did not reach the everyday black person. For a detailed analysis of the Los Angeles School of Black Filmmaking, see Ntongela Masilela, "The Los Angeles School of Black Filmmakers," 107–17.

11. Del Shields quoted in George, *The Death of Rhythm and Blues,* 111–12. Evidently the inherent power of black radio also produced a level of fear among white station owners—all plans to support the growth and development of black programming were dropped. The person who best represents this transition is Gary Byrd, a black deejay personality whose style influenced up-and-coming deejays across the country. His impact diminished when he was confronted by the station managers' use of the Bill Drake format of radio. This pattern attempted to systematize radio into "time, temperature, artist, title of record" and indeed sapped the deejay of any distinct personality traits. George asserts that this was brought about by two central factors: the fear of the power of the black deejay after King's assassination and the assimilationist trend in black America. Those who desired to move into white circles were embarrassed by the sound of black radio deejays who were grounded in the oral tradition and used black vernacular.

12. Sonia Murray, "Soul Train," 4.

13. Cornelius quoted in Andy Meisler, "The Beat Goes on for 'Soul Train' Conductor," 7.

14. Cornelius quoted in Michael E. Hill, "Soul Train's Chief Engineer," Y07.

15. Rowland Barber, "Soul Train: For Rock Fans It's Right on Time," 33.

16. Hill, "Soul Train's Chief Engineer," Y07.

17. Ibid., 79.

18. Boyd, "A Trip down 'Soul Train's' Memory Lane," 1.

19. Lori Moody, "Durable Soul Train Is Pop History in the Making," 1E.

20. Murray, "Soul Train," 4.

21. Robert Feder, "'Soul Train' Host Rails against MTV," 39.

22. Boyd, "A Trip down 'Soul Train's' Memory Lane," 1.

23. Neill Strauss, "You Say Soul Train Is How Old?" 3.

24. Barber, "Soul Train," 32.

25. Ibid., 32.

26. George quoted in Murray, "Soul Train," 4.

27. White artists such as David Bowie and Elton John also made appearances on *Soul Train*. For a full list of acts that appeared on *Soul Train* in the 1970s, please see www.soultrain.com.

28. For further analysis of James Brown, his music, and politics, see George, *The Death of Rhythm and Blues*.

29. Sheila Simmons, "'Soul Train' Hails Black Artists," 5E.

30. Sonia Murray, "The Soul Train Music Awards," 1B.

31. Ibid., 1B.

32. Feder, "'Soul Train' Host Rails against MTV," 39.

33. After Cornelius withdrew as weekly host, a rotation of guest hosts followed. Mystro Clark became the first regular host followed by Shemar Moore.

34. Ann Hodges, "Ladies of Soul," 3.

35. Sonia Murray, "'Soul Train' Creator: TV Still Off-Track after 25 Years," 21P.

36. Information available on the show's web site: www.soultrain.com.

37. Bill Davidson, "Likability: That One Word May Explain Why a Sometimes Morose Young Man Named Clerow Wilson Is the Hit of the TV Season," 21.

38. Miles Corwin, "TV Comedian Flip Wilson Dies at 64," 3.

39. "Flip Wilson's Commercial Spots Go Up," 56.

40. Allen quoted in "Flip Wilson, 64; 1970s Comedian Known for 'Geraldine' Character," B17.

41. J. N. Vorobey, "Wonderful Flip," A24.

42. Redd Foxx and Norma Miller, *The Redd Foxx Encyclopedia of Black Humor*, 196.

43. For more information on the myth of the classless American society, see Donna Langston, "Tired of Playing Monopoly," 126–36.

44. Watkins, "Flip Wilson, 64, Over-the-Top Comic," 18.

45. Flip Wilson quoted in Watkins, *On the Real Side*, 518.

46. John Kiesewetter, "One of TV's Funniest Cross-Dressers Primed for a Comeback," C7.

47. Bob Henry quoted in Greg Braxton, "Flip Side: Happy Not Being Funny," 1.

48. Watkins, "Flip Wilson, 64, Over-the-Top Comic," 519. Colorless comedic material is defined as having no racial or ethnic specificity to the humor. For example, Bill Cosby's humor was often family oriented and frequently dealt with his children. Many races and ethnicities could recognize their families in his humor and relate to the issues.

49. In his article "The White Negro," Norman Mailer discusses and recommends that white mainstream society break out of the sedate middle-class lifestyle. The conservatism of the 1950s could be overcome by embracing blackness, as represented at the moment by jazz culture. The implicit racism in Mailer's article is noted in the ways in which he describes African Americans as being innately tied to animalistic and lustful emotions.

50. Henry quoted in Davidson, "Likability," 21.

51. John Leonard quoted in Watkins, "Flip Wilson, 64, Over-the-Top Comic," 18.

52. Ibid., 18.

53. Dwight Whitney, "I'm on the Case," 22.

54. "Flip Wilson: Host of TV's Hottest New Show," 62.

55. Watkins, *On the Real Side,* 519. This also explains why *The Richard Pryor Show* lasted but four episodes; Pryor's approach, which he was unwilling to curb, was simply not acceptable on mainstream television.

56. Watkins, "Flip Wilson, 64, Over-the-Top Comic," 18.

57. See the introduction and Robin D. G. Kelley's use of the term *hidden transcripts* to discuss the location of black resistant culture in everyday spaces.

58. "Famed Comedian Flip Wilson Dies in California," 14.

59. Many theorists have discussed some of the essential problems of religion and African American society. For more detailed information on this issue, see Carter G. Woodson, *Miseducation of the Negro*; Ben Sidran, *Black Talk;* and LeRoi Jones, *Blues People.*

60. Sidran, *Black Talk,* 1–29.

61. Woodson, *Miseducation of the Negro,* 73.

62. When I showed this clip in an African American popular culture course, the black students found Reverend Leroy particularly humorous and laughed at his every physical move. They commented that, although at times he is exaggerated, he reminded them of preachers they knew and themes played out in black churches, and they appreciated the congregation's response during the skits. They also understood why a black middle-class audience might have objections to his performance, as if taken literally he could give a negative impression of the black church. While students of other racial groups enjoyed characters such as Geraldine, they did not

find as much humor in the Reverend Leroy. Without the cultural context, they were unable to derive a similar pleasure in reading the text.

63. Watkins, "Flip Wilson, 64, Over-the-Top Comic," 18.

64. Mark Lorando, "You Devil, You," T9. Wilson would also say that Geraldine was based on a childhood "friend." As he relates, "Geraldine was a cute little girl who always went around in these saucy little dresses, lots of makeup and long colorful fingernails. Her false fingernails had just come out and Geraldine said, 'I'll be your girlfriend if you'll get me some of those false fingernails from the store.' But I didn't have any money. We went down to the Woolworth's, and we went by and she pointed to them. Then I had to walk her back home because she was a lady. Then I went back, and I stole those false fingernails. And I came back to Geraldine's house with them, and they were the wrong size. And so Geraldine gave those to her sister. And I went back and I got the size next to those. When I got back, Geraldine and her sister had shown them to the girl next door who was their friend. And she sent me back again. And I got caught. And Geraldine never had anything to do with me after that. So she was the girl I could never have." David Martindale, "Flip Wilson Clicked at the Right Time," 4.

65. Corwin, "TV Comedian Flip Wilson Dies at 64," 3.

66. Except that Wilson already kept his material essentially clean.

67. Jesse Jackson quoted in "Comedian Flip Wilson Dies at Age 64," B06.

68. Davis quoted in Leo Standora, "TV Funnyman Flip Wilson Is Dead at 64," 15.

69. This deal also explains why the show disappeared from television after the 1970s. It was brought back to TV Land when Flip Wilson sold the rights for one airing of the show at ten million dollars.

70. "Flip Scores Big in New Television Season," 56.

71. Jeff Wong, "Comedian Brought Black Voice to TV," A16.

72. Braxton, "Flip Side," 1.

73. Ibid., 1.

74. Bruce Britt, "Leaping Barriers with Laughter," F01.

75. Flip Wilson can be compared to Clay, the main character of film *The Dutchman* (1967), based on Amiri Baraka/LeRoi Jones's play of that title. Although very angry and resentful toward racist white society, which had no understanding of what it was to be a black person in America, Clay keeps all of this inside and maintains a middle-class, upright exterior. Unlike Clay, who by the end of the film releases what he has held in for so long, Flip is not given the opportunity. However, unlike the character of Clay, who is murdered by a white woman, the symbol of white society, Flip lived and thrived.

76. Davidson, "Likability," 23.

4. This Ain't No Junk

1. Jones, quoted in Bill Davidson, "The World's Funniest Dishwasher Is Still Cleaning Up," 29.

2. Joe X. Price, *Redd Foxx, B.S. (Before Sanford)*, 114.

3. Foxx and Miller, *The Redd Foxx Encyclopedia of Black Humor*, 238.

4. Signifying refers to a verbal challenge; by using funny or sharp comments, one person attempts to put down another. Toasts included the use of language that rejected middle-class values and thus contained obscenities and sexual innuendos.

5. The Bad Nigger character was depicted in 1920s urban black folklore. The Bad Nigger was more aggressive than the trickster and more openly confronted white society. He was therefore to be feared by mainstream America. Watkins, *On the Real Side*, 458–76.

6. Foxx and Miller, *The Redd Foxx Encyclopedia of Black Humor*, 239.

7. Redd Foxx, "LBJ," on *Fugg It!!! The Very Best of Redd Foxx*, #64.

8. Redd Foxx, "Chains," on *Fugg It!!! The Very Best of Redd Foxx*, #35.

9. Michael O'Daniel, "He's Come a Long Way from St. Louis: Still the Comedian Hasn't Found Contentment," 25.

10. Watkins, *On the Real Side*, 361.

11. Price, *Redd Foxx, B.S. (Before Sanford)*, 1.

12. Ibid., 2.

13. Ibid., 4.

14. Ibid., 85.

15. Ibid., 47.

16. Archie Bunker remains one of the most controversial figures in U.S. television history, and *All in the Family* is considered one of the most influential shows. Archie was a problematic figure. Although a bigot, he was embraced by many Americans. As Donald Bogle points out in *Prime Time Blues*, Archie was so popular that during the 1972 presidential election, stores sold bumper stickers that read "Archie Bunker for President." A CBS study also indicated that although many believed the show would instigate change in people's attitudes about race, apparently it simply reinforced long-standing racist beliefs. Bogle, *Prime Time Blues*, 185–86.

17. Dick Adler, "Look What They Found in the Junkyard—the Spare Parts of a Comedy Series That Breaks Some New Ground," 28.

18. Joel Eisner and David Krinsky, *Television Comedy Series: An Episode Guide to 153 Sitcoms in Syndication*, 720.

19. For more information on the history of this figure, see Gates, *The Signifying Monkey*.

20. Watkins, *On the Real Side,* 16–41. Also see the introduction for further delineation of African American humor.

21. This image can be seen in such films as *Hallelujah* (1929), the first major Hollywood film that featured an all-black cast, and the Paul Robeson film *The Emperor Jones* (1933). It is interesting to note that African American director Oscar Micheaux's films also used this stereotype to condemn working-class blacks who did not conform to middle-class and church-oriented lifestyles.

22. Although adapted from a *Steptoe and Son* script, the nuances of the African American performance by Foxx and other characters transform this script into traditional African American humor.

23. Watkins, *On the Real Side,* 23.

24. Davidson, "The World's Funniest Dishwasher Is Still Cleaning Up," 27.

25. Ibid., 27.

26. Pryor will be discussed in more detail in the analysis of *The Richard Pryor Show,* in chapter 6.

27. For further information on the reclaiming of the term *nigger* in contemporary popular culture, see Todd Boyd, *Am I Black Enough for You? Popular Culture from the Hood and Beyond.*

28. Cecil Smith, "Sanford & Son: It's TV's First Black-on-Black Show," 2.

29. Eugenia Collier, "Sanford and Son Is White to the Core," 1, 3.

30. Smith, "Sanford & Son," 2.

31. Alex McNeil, *Total Television,* 722.

32. Michael O'Daniel, "Everything a Performer Could Ask for . . . Except the One Thing He Wants Most: Respect," 19.

33. Ibid., 19.

34. Ibid., 20.

35. Bill O'Hallaren, "Without Sanford and without Son . . . ," 60.

5. Respect Yourself!

1. Ella Baker, quoted in Giddings, *When and Where I Enter,* 284.

2. George, *The Death of Rhythm and Blues,* 105–6.

3. Robin Kelley refers to the work of anthropologist James C. Scott.

4. I use the term *racial dictatorship* as suggested by Omi and Winant and as described in the introduction.

5. Lynn Spigel, *Make Room for TV: Television and the Family Ideal in Postwar America,* 1.

6. The quotation that serves as the heading for this section is from Diahann Carroll, quoted in Carolyn See, "I'm a Black Woman with a White Image," 30.

7. Richard Warren Lewis, "The Importance of Being Julia," 24.

8. Ibid., 24.

9. I specify *TV Guide* here and continue to use this publication as a primary source in this chapter. As a mainstream publication with a wide readership and obvious ties to television, *TV Guide* proves to be a relevant resource in understanding the narratives created around television, the interpretations of the historical moment, and eventually the power and widespread impact of the statements made by African American entertainers when featured within its pages.

10. Lewis, "The Importance of Being Julia," 24.

11. To criticize *Julia* for not portraying a realistic black person is essentializing, as the Civil Rights movement had helped to solidify a black middle class and Julia was leading a black middle-class existence.

12. Lewis, "The Importance of Being Julia," 27.

13. Ibid., 27–28.

14. Ibid., 27.

15. Ibid., 28.

16. Ibid., 28.

17. For a detailed discussion of the gender implications of *Julia,* see Aniko Bodroghkozy, "'Is This What You Mean by Color TV?' Race, Gender and Contested Meanings NBC's *Julia,*" 143–67.

18. Any citation with stage directions suggests the use of an archived script. Otherwise dialogue is taken directly from the taped episodes.

19. See, "I'm a Black Woman with a White Image," 29–30.

20. Ibid., 30.

21. Edith Efron, "What's Happening to Blacks in Broadcasting? Excluded, Distorted, Mishandled and Exploited," 44.

22. Ibid., 44.

23. *Maude* was a spin-off of *All in the Family.* Bea Arthur as Maude Finley was Edith Bunker's cousin, a strong-willed and opinionated "feminist" who challenged Archie. Maude espoused liberal views, and the show dealt with controversial issues. The episode most often cited to describe the show's edge dealt with abortion. *Good Times* was a spin-off of *Maude.*

24. Esther Rolle, quoted in Riley, "Esther Rolle the Fishin' Pole," 17.

25. Ibid., 18.

26. Bob Lucas, "Collard Greens' TV Show," 53.

27. Gaines, *Uplifting the Race,* 5.

28. Esther Rolle in an interview in *Color Adjustment,* dir. Marlon Riggs, California Newsreel, 1991.

29. Franklin and Moss, *From Slavery to Freedom,* 493.

30. Carson et al., eds., *The Eyes on the Prize,* 294.

31. I call these shows pure sitcom because they were not only devoid of politics and pedagogy but also leaned strongly toward exaggerated characterizations and meaningless story lines.

32. It is interesting to note that, although a black writer, Eric Monte, scripted the original episode and the following four scripts were by freelance black writers, the majority of the scripts thereafter were written by white writers, which was objectionable to Amos and Rolle because they believed these writers were disconnected from the issues at hand and therefore responsible for enlarging J.J.'s role.

33. John Amos quoted in Rick Mitz, *The Great TV Sitcom Book,* 318.

34. Esther Rolle, quoted in Louie Robinson, "Bad Times on the 'Good Times' Set," 35, 35–36.

35. Jimmy Walker never attained any level of consciousness and remained oblivious to the ways in which his character reflected old minstrel stereotypes and how his comedy disrupted the more relevant aspects of the series. He also did not embrace the notions of uplift evident in the words of Rolle. As he once stated, "I play the way I see it for the humor of it. I don't think anybody 20 years from now is going to remember what I said. I am not trying to have my lines etched in some archives or on a wall someplace. . . . I don't think that any TV show can put out an image to save people. My advice is do not follow me. I don't want to be a follower or a leader . . . just a doer." Robinson, "Bad Times on the 'Good Times' Set," 37.

36. Mitz, *The Great TV Sitcom Book,* 319.

37. Ibid., 320.

38. Gates as interviewed in *Color Adjustment,* dir. Marlon Riggs.

6. That Nigger's Crazy

1. Richard Pryor and Todd Gold, *Pryor Convictions and Other Life Sentences,* 72–73.

2. James McPherson, "The New Comic Style of Richard Pryor," 26.

3. "Beyond Laughter," 90.

4. In his book *Pryor Convictions,* Pryor refers to the moment as occurring in 1967, however, many magazine articles from the 1970s claim that the incident happened in 1970.

5. Pryor and Gold, *Pryor Convictions and Other Life Sentences,* 93.

6. Richard Pryor, "Super Nigger," on *Richard Pryor.*

7. Pryor and Gold, *Pryor Convictions and Other Life Sentences,* 98.

8. Ibid., 99.

9. Ibid., 115–29.

10. Bill Cosby quoted in Watkins, *On the Real Side,* 541.

11. McPherson, "The New Comic Style of Richard Pryor," 22.

12. From Richard Pryor, "Niggers vs. the Police," on *That Nigger's Crazy.*

13. Richard Pryor, "Wino and Junkie," on *That Nigger's Crazy.*

14. McPherson, "The New Comic Style of Richard Pryor," 20.

15. Ibid., 22.

16. Reggie Collins, liner notes, "Pryor Times," on *Richard Pryor: And It's Deep Too: The Complete Warner Brothers Recordings*, 35.

17. Pryor and Gold, *Pryor Convictions and Other Life Sentences*, 144–45.

18. Ibid., 144–45.

19. Collins, liner notes, "Pryor Times," 37.

20. Maureen Orth, "The Perils of Pryor," 61.

21. Ibid., 61.

22. Louie Robinson, "Richard Pryor Talks," 117.

23. "A New Black Superstar," 67.

24. Pryor and Gold, *Pryor Convictions and Other Life Sentences*, 158.

25. D. W. Griffith's film *Birth of a Nation* is considered an American masterpiece. It rewrites U.S. history to claim that during Reconstruction, the white South was held hostage by out-of-control and power-hungry blacks. In one scene, blacks have taken over the political system, and one of the first laws passed allows blacks to marry whites. The black men voting look around in a lustful manner toward the whites in the balcony. Soon thereafter is the famous sequence in which the overpowering black buck Gus chases "little sister" across the forest and toward a cliff. She chooses to jump off rather than be touched by Gus. The problems of Reconstruction are solved by the rise of the KKK. The popularity of the film is indicative of the U.S. embrace of the ideas espoused by Griffith, the primary fear of intermarriage between whites and blacks, and the eventual empowerment of the black population.

26. The sexism inherent in this skit is undeniable, and, as in *Julia*, in confronting racism, Pryor and his writers leaned toward stereotypical constructions of women.

27. Other skits include Pryor as the leader of a rock group, Black Death. Pryor performs for, and then shoots, his white audience. In the other skit, Pryor plays the owner of a pet human head.

28. Other skits in episode three include a seduction between Pryor and Marsha Warfield over food at a restaurant, Pryor as a caveman who makes fire for the first time, and a Western stand-off.

29. "Hey, man! Say, nigger, you with the cape. What you doing, peeking in them people's window? What's you name, boy? Dracula? What kind of name is that for a nigger? Where you from, fool? Transylvania? I know where it is, nigger. Yeah, you ain't the smartest motherfucker in the world, you know. Even though you is the ugliest. Oh yeah, you a ugly motherfucker. Why don't you get your teeth fixed, nigger? That shit hanging all out your mouth" (Richard Pryor, "Wino Dealing with Dracula," on *That Nigger's Crazy*).

30. In another bit, Pryor saves people from the sinking *Titanic*. While the first person thanks him, the others use increasingly racist terms, Sambo, Tar Baby, Jigaboo, Remus, and Jungle Bunny, to get his attention. They consider throwing him overboard when the boat begins to sink. But Pryor, armed with a gun, takes their jewelry and stays in the boat. Pryor also plays a disgruntled Santa Claus who, in a news clip, rails against the commercialization of Christmas; Santa is also continually censored. Other skits in episode four include a restaging of the *Psycho* shower scene; instead of Norman Bates, Pryor enters the bathroom and plays the scene as a commercial for an at-home chef. Pryor also plays a swashbuckler called El Neggro and is involved in another Western scene.

31. Smith, running on a ticket for a "whiter, brighter Rhodesia," advocated white rule. Winning the election, he served as prime minister from 1964 to 1969 (the country has since become Zimbabwe). During his tenure, an estimated thirty thousand Zimbabweans were killed.

32. In 1977 Bryant spoke out against proposed legislation in Dade County, Florida, that would allow homosexuals to hold teaching positions in private and parochial schools. Although the bill passed in Florida despite Bryant's lobbying, her statements had an impact at a national level. A gay rights bill proposing minority-group status for homosexuals was in front of Congress. With Bryant speaking against it, the bill did not pass for three consecutive years. Bryant's vocal conservatism made her the brunt of media derision, numerous protests were made against her, and her face graced many anti-Anita T-shirts and bumper stickers.

33. Pryor and Gold, *Pryor Convictions and Other Life Sentences*, 156.

34. Orth, "The Perils of Pryor," 60.

35. Louie Robinson, "Richard Pryor Talks," 117–18.

36. These shows will be discussed in further detail in the conclusion. Sherman Hemsley and Isabel Sanford, who played George and Louise Jefferson, remain recognized television figures, having become spokespersons for Denny's and Old Navy.

Conclusion

1. Lyrics of the theme song.

2. Although early on the show dealt with some serious issues such as the racial bias of standardized testing, the main focus was on the antics of Arnold.

3. Episodes included issues such as teen pregnancy, drugs, and racism.

4. For more details on all of these shows, see Bogle, *Prime Time Blues*.

5. Ibid., 239–46. For an analysis of the problematic American dream elements of *Roots*, see Leslie Fishbein, *American History/American Television*.

6. See Gray's *Watching Race* for a thorough analysis of the complexities of 1980s television and African Americans.

7. See Omi and Winant's *Racial Formation in the United States* for more details on the Reagan presidency and its effects on racial policy in the United States.

8. Sut Jhally and Justin Lewis, *Enlightened Racism: The Cosby Show, Audiences, and the Myth of the American Dream,* 132, 135–36.

9. One need only take a cursory glance at any of the many news-magazines in the late 1990s to see the number of articles that reflected this supposed concern. To mention just a few of the examples, the August 30, 1999, issue of *Newsweek* reports, "Who Needs a Fair Deal," which covers the Southeastern Legal Foundation challenge of Atlanta's affirmative action policies regarding government contracts. *U.S. News and World Report* reported on July 19, 1999, that while campaigning George W. Bush would not endorse Proposition 209, yet he "supports the spirit of no quotas, no preferences." The May 9, 1999, issue of the *Washington Post* featured an article reporting on the public availability of the files of the Mississippi Sovereignty Commission and, within that context, discussed Richard Barrett, head of the Nationalist Movement in Mississippi. Barrett speaks out against Martin Luther King Day: "The King Holiday is the only tribute ever made officially to a hostage-taker, who ravaged our cities, debased our morality and demanded surrender of our nationality as a nation and as a people. It must be abolished, so that we will be one nation, indivisible." He also runs a web site that speaks out against blacks and other minorities in the country in hopes of saving Mississippi. Many other magazines have included articles that discussed the preferential treatment of minorities, such as Mortimer Zuckerman's "Piling on the Preferences." Since the Oklahoma bombings, others magazines have sought to understand the growing militia movements and have actively discussed the white man's marginalized position in America as caused by minority groups. Articles include: Joseph Shapiro, "Hitting before Hate Strikes"; "Mainstreaming the Militia"; Peter Carlson, "A Call to Arms"; and Patricia King, "'Vipers' in the 'Burbs."

10. Gray, *Watching Race,* 148.

11. Comment made at the Guy Hanks and Marvin Miller Screenwriting Program, April 1998.

12. The National Public Radio program *Talk of the Nation* also noted that in 1999 black cable viewership was estimated at 33 percent of the audience and only 11 percent for the public networks. *Talk of the Nation,* NPR, August 25, 1999.

13. For these results, see www.emmy.tv/awards/results.asp; and www .emmys.org.

14. HBO's web site contains descriptions of its made-for-television films and upcoming productions: www.hbo.com. The Showtime series *Soul Food,* which ended in 2004, was the only black-cast drama on television. Other HBO films dealing with African American themes include: *Rebound—the*

Legend of Earl "the Goat" Manigault (1996), about the legendary basketball player; *Soul of the Game* (1996), which discusses Jackie Robinson and the Negro leagues; *Boycott* (2001), which deals with the rise of Martin Luther King Jr. as spokesperson and central figure in the SCLC and the Civil Rights movement; *Dancing in September* (2001), which tackles African American representation on network television; *Disappearing Acts* (2001), which is based on the Terry McMillan novel of that title; *Stranger Inside* (2001), directed by Cheryl Dunne, which is a story of black women inside a prison; *The Middle Passage* (2002), about the slave trade; and *Lumumba* (2002), the story of Patrice Lumumba, the first prime minister of Congo.

15. *OZ, The Sopranos,* and *Sex in the City* are examples of HBO's "edgy" programming. The HBO slogan, "It's not TV, it's HBO," also indicates the channel's cognizance of its position within the U.S. television market.

16. This is not an uncommon practice; consider *Glory* (1989) and *Cry Freedom* (1990).

17. This duality between the acknowledgment of the past and ignorance of the present is also evident in HBO's handling of documentary material. While making such pieces as *Fists of Freedom,* an in-depth analysis of the history and politics surrounding the famous protest of runners John Carlos and Tommie Smith, HBO also produced the equally infamous documentary *Pimps Up and Hos Down,* whose title is self-explanatory. However, if documentaries such as *Pimps Up and Hos Down* remain the only contemporary documentary representation, then an unsettling image of African American society remains.

18. Malcolm X, "Message to the Grassroots," 6.

19. Chuck Crisafulli, "Q&A with Chris Rock," 1.

20. Angela McManaman, "Think of Him as News, Only Funnier," 8.

21. Crisafulli, "Q&A with Chris Rock," 1.

22. The impact of *Bring the Pain* within the industry is evident, as the show earned two Emmy Awards in 1997, one for Outstanding Variety, Music, or Comedy Special and one for Outstanding Writing for a Variety or Music Program.

23. I include Chris Rock's comedy in a Black Popular Culture class at UCD. Some of my African American students have indicated that, while they initially loved and laughed at these specials, they began to believe that the white students, who also enjoyed the comedy, made negative assumptions about the black community on the basis of Rock's humor.

24. Michael Marriott, "Rock on a Roll," 116.

25. *The Chris Rock Show* also filled the void left by the cancellation of *The Arsenio Hall Show* (1989–94). The show also hosted white guests, such as George Carlin, Bill Maher, and the Red Hot Chili Peppers.

26. Connerly actually identifies himself as white, Asian, and black. In 1993, he was appointed to the University of California Board of Regents,

where he led the vote that prevented the use of race and gender as factors in UC admissions. Although this was overturned in 2001, Proposition 209 still prevents the use of race as a determining factor in UC admission policies.

27. Connerly also proposed an initiative to ban the collection of race-based data by government agencies. He believes that designating one's race on a government form is a form of segregation, and he fails to see that these data can be used as a tool in the fight against discrimination.

28. For more information on the model minority, see Deborah Woo, "The Gap between Striving and Achieving: The Case of Asian American Women," 243–51.

29. Students in my African American television course, especially the black women, were highly offended by the comment and felt that Rock played into the stereotypical views of black women as overbearing. However, his words also led to a great discussion of gender relations.

30. The incident referred to the shooting at Columbine High School on April 20, 1999, in which seniors Eric Harris and Dylan Klebold killed twelve students and a teacher before killing themselves.

31. The following is a sample of his monologue that deals with these issues: "You don't get the money [Social Security] till you're sixty-five; meanwhile, the average black man dies at fifty-four. Shit, we should get Social Security at twenty-nine. We don't live that long—hypertension, high blood pressure, NYPD, something will get ya. What the fuck is up with the police, my God. I am scared. I ain't gettin' rid of no guns—fuck that shit. I had a cop pull me over the other day, scared me so bad, made me think I stole my own car. Get out the car! Get out the fucking car! You stole this car! I'm like, damn. Maybe I did. Oh Lord, I done stole a car."

32. Defining what should be kept behind these black walls ignores the fact that other mainstream outlets have in essence taken some of the very issues that are a part of Rock's comedy to a mainstream venue in a less critical way. Talk shows have, for many years, become one of the key arenas for airing this laundry in public and in a directly exploitative way. Ricki Lake, Jerry Springer, and Jenny Jones are a few of the television programs that have used black guests for ratings in numerous episodes, for example, "My Baby's Daddy," "I'm Sleeping with Your Man," "I Need a DNA Test to Find Out the Father of My Baby." These shows expose problems without a sense of self-awareness; the guests are used simply for the value of titillation.

33. This is perhaps a reflection of the close relationship that Rock had with his father and the role he feels his father had in his life.

34. Chris Rock developed this material into a special for HBO, *Chris Rock: Never Scared.*

Bibliography

Adler, Dick. "Look What They Found in the Junkyard—the Spare Parts of a Comedy Series That Breaks Some New Ground." *TV Guide,* 13 May 1972, 28–32.

Amory, Cleveland. *The Flip Wilson Show. TV Guide,* 10 October 1970, 44.

———. Review of *Sanford and Son. TV Guide,* 26 February 1972, 47.

———. Review of *Good Times. TV Guide,* 6 April 1974, 52.

Anderson, Benedict. *Imagined Communities.* New York: Verso, 1983.

Arliss, Michael. "The Media Dramas of Norman Lear." *New Yorker,* 10 March 1975, 89–94.

Aucoin, Don. "Flip Wilson, 1933–1998." *Boston Globe,* 28 November 1998, Arts & Film, G1.

Bailey, Peter. "Black Excellence in the Wasteland." *Ebony,* 27 March 1972, 45–48.

Barber, Rowland. "Soul Train: For Rock Fans It's Right on Time." *TV Guide,* 25 May 1974, 31–33.

———. "No Time for Jivin'." *TV Guide,* 14 December 1974, 28–32.

Bass, Amy. "Race and Nation in Olympic Proportions." *Spectator* 19, no. 1 (1998): 8–24.

Berkow, Ira. "Even the Norfolk Neptunes Cut Him." *TV Guide,* 17 August 1974, 15–18.

"Beyond Laughter." *Ebony,* September 1967, 87–94.

Bianculli, David. "TV Land Proves Flip's Still Hip." *New York Daily News,* 18 August 1997, Television, 66.

"Black Journal Charges New York Times with Attempted Assassination." *Jet,* 27 January 1972, 44.

"Black TV: Its Problems and Promises." *Ebony,* September 1969, 88–92.

Bodroghkozy, Aniko. "'Is This What You Mean by Color TV?' Race,

Gender and Contested Meanings in NBC's *Julia*." In *Private Screenings,* ed. Lynn Spigel and Denise Mann, 143–67. Minneapolis: University of Minnesota Press, 1992.

Bogle, Donald. *Toms, Coons, Mulattoes, Mammies & Bucks.* New York: Bantam Books, 1973.

———. *Prime Time Blues.* New York: Farrar, Straus and Giroux, 2001.

Boyd, Todd. "A Trip down 'Soul Train's' Memory Lane." *Los Angeles Times,* 22 November 1995, Calendar, 1.

———. *Am I Black Enough for You? Popular Culture from the Hood and Beyond.* Bloomington: Indiana University Press, 1997.

Braxton, Greg. "Flip Side: Happy Not Being Funny." *Los Angles Times,* 11 March 1993, Home Edition, Calendar, 1.

———. "He Brought Us Exquisite 'Pain'; Now He's 'Bigger,' Not Better." *Los Angeles Times,* 10 July 1999, Home Edition, Calendar, F, 2.

Bright, Hazel. "TV versus Black Survival." *Black World,* December 1973, 30–42.

Britt, Bruce. "Leaping Barriers with Laughter." *Washington Post,* 28 November 1998, Final Edition, Style, F01.

Brownfield, Paul. "Flip Wilson's Comedy Transcended Era's Color Barrier." *Los Angeles Times,* 28 November 1998, Home Edition, Calendar, 6.

Carlson, Peter. "A Call to Arms." *Washington Post,* 13 October 1996, Magazine, W10.

Carson, Clayborne, et al., eds. *The Eyes on the Prize: A Civil Rights Reader.* New York: Penguin Books, 1991.

Cassese, Sid. "Spotlight: Richard Pryor: No Laughing Matter." *Ebony,* September 1969, 78–113.

Chappell, Kevin. "Chris Rock; Hot Comic Is on the Roll of His Life." *Ebony,* May 1997, 132.

Coker, Cheo Hadari. "Welcome to Rock's World." *Los Angeles Times,* 24 April 1997, Calendar, F, 1.

Collier, Eugenia. "Sanford and Son Is White to the Core." *New York Times,* 17 June 1973, sec. 2, 1, 3.

———. "TV Still Evades the Nitty-Gritty Truth!" *TV Guide,* 12 January 1974, 6–10.

———. "'Black' Shows for White Viewers." *Freedomways,* 3rd quarter (1974): 209–17.

———. "A House of Twisted Mirrors: The Black Reflection in the Media." *Current History,* November 1974, 228–34.

Collins, Reggie. Liner notes, "Pryor Times." On *Richard Pryor: And Its Deep Too: The Complete Warner Brothers Recordings,* 26–52. Los Angeles: Warner Brothers, 2000.

Color Adjustment. Dir. Marlon Riggs. California Newsreel, 1991.

"Comedian Flip Wilson Dies at Age 64." *Washington Post,* 27 November 1998, Final Edition, Obituaries, B06.

Corliss, Richard. "Pryor's Back—Twice as Funny." *Time,* 29 March 1982, 62–63.

Corwin, Miles. "TV Comedian Flip Wilson Dies at 64." *Los Angeles Times,* 26 November 1998, Home Edition, sec. A, 3.

Cripps, Thomas. "Amos 'n' Andy and the Debate over Racial Integration." In *American History/American Television,* ed. John E. O'Connor, 33–54. New York: Ungar Books, 1987.

Crisafulli, Chuck. "Q&A with Chris Rock." *Los Angeles Times,* 5 June 1996, Home Edition, Calendar, F, 1.

Curtin, Michael. *Redeeming the Wasteland: Television Documentary and Cold War Politics.* New Brunswick, NJ: Rutgers University Press, 1995.

Davidson, Bill. "Likability: That One Word May Explain Why a Sometimes Morose Young Man Named Clerow Wilson Is the Hit of the TV Season." *TV Guide,* 23 January 1971, 20 23.

———. "The World's Funniest Dishwasher Is Still Cleaning Up." *TV Guide,* 17 March 1973, 26–30.

———. "Trouble in Paradise." *TV Guide,* 6 April 1974, 4–8.

———. "The Uprising in Lear's Kingdom." *TV Guide,* 13 April 1974, 12–17.

Davis, Mike. *City of Quartz.* New York: Vintage Books, 1992.

Deggans, Eric. "'Soul' Awards Honor Artists Often Ignored." *St. Petersburg Times,* 29 March 1996, Entertainment, 2B.

———. "Rising Like a Rock." *Houston Chronicle,* 7 September 1998, Star Edition, 6.

Doan, Richard K. "The Doan Report." *TV Guide,* 11 January 1975, A-3.

Donovan, Robert J., and Ray Scherer. *Unsilent Revolution: Television News and American Public Life, 1948–1991.* New York: Cambridge University Press, 1992.

Du Bois, W. E. B. *The Souls of Black Folk.* New York: Bantam, 1989.

Dunbar, Ernest. "Black-on-White TV." *Look,* 7 September 1971, 31.

The Dutchman. Dir. Anthony Harvey. Gene Persson Films, 1967.

Dyson, Michael. *Making Malcolm: The Myth and Meaning of Malcolm X.* New York: Oxford University Press, 1996.

"Ebony Interview: Richard Pryor." *Ebony,* October 1980, 33–42.

Efron, Edith. "What's Happening to Blacks in Broadcasting?" *TV Guide,* 19 August 1972, 20–25.

———. "What's Happening to Blacks in Broadcasting? Excluded, Distorted, Mishandled and Exploited." *TV Guide,* 26 August 1972, 44–49.

———. "The License Battle Explodes." *TV Guide,* 2 September 1972, 26–32.

Eisner, Joel, and David Krinsky. *Television Comedy Series: An Episode Guide to 153 Sitcoms in Syndication.* Jefferson, NC: McFarland & Company, 1984.

Ellison, Ralph. *The Shadow and the Act.* New York: Vintage, 1995.

"Esther Rolle Returns to Good Times." *Jet,* 21 September 1978, 28–30.

"Famed Comedian Flip Wilson Dies in California." *Jet,* 14 December 1998, 14.

"Fear Redd Foxx Has Blown His Wife, TV Show." *Jet,* 9 May 1974, 14–16.

Feder, Robert. "'Soul Train' Host Rails against MTV." *Chicago Sun Times,* 19 September 1995, Late Edition, FTR, 39.

Felton, David. "Pryor's Inferno." *Rolling Stone,* 24 July 1980, 11–16.

Feran, Tom. "Revival of Old Show Gives Flip TV Bug." *Plain Dealer,* 28 August 1997, Arts & Living, 6E.

Fife, Marilyn Diane. "Black Image in American TV: The First Two Decades." *Black Scholar* (November 1974): 7–15.

Fishbein, Leslie. "Roots: Docudrama and the Interpretation of History." In *American History/American Television,* ed. John E. O'Connor, 279–305. New York: Ungar Books, 1987.

Flint, Joe. "News and Notes: Fade to White." *Entertainment Weekly,* 23 April 1999, 8–9.

"Flip Scores Big in New Television Season." *Jet,* 25 November 1971, 56–58.

"Flip Wilson: Host of TV's Hottest New Show," *Jet,* January 1971, 60–63.

"Flip Wilson Returns to Television in Spike Lee Commercials." *Jet,* 30 March 1998, 24.

"Flip Wilson, 64; 1970s Comedian Known for 'Geraldine' Character." *Boston Globe,* 27 November 1998, Obituaries, B17.

"Flip Wilson's Commercial Spots Go Up." *Jet,* 18 March 1971, 56.

Foulkes, Warren. "Perspective on Soul Train." *Black World,* February 1975, 68–71.

Foxx, Redd. *Fugg It!!! The Very Best of Redd Foxx.* Comp. and ed. Joe Reagoso. New York: Relativity Records, 1998.

Foxx, Redd, and Norma Miller. *The Redd Foxx Encyclopedia of Black Humor.* Pasadena: Ward Ritchie Press, 1977.

Franklin, John Hope, and Alfred A. Moss. *From Slavery to Freedom: A History of African Americans.* 7th ed. New York: McGraw-Hill, 1994.

Friedman, Norman L. "Responses of Blacks and Other Minorities to Television Shows of the 1970s about Their Groups." *Journal of Popular Film and Television* 7, no. 1 (1978): 85–102.

Gaines, Kevin K. *Uplifting the Race: Black Leadership, Politics, and Cul-*

ture in the Twentieth Century. Chapel Hill: University of North Carolina Press, 1996.

Gates, Henry Louis. *The Signifying Monkey: A Theory of African-American Literary Criticism*. New York: Oxford University Press, 1988.

Genovese, Eugene D. *Roll Jordan Roll: The World the Slaves Made*. New York: Vintage Books, 1976.

George, Nelson. *The Death of Rhythm and Blues*. New York: Penguin, 1988.

Giddings, Paula. *When and Where I Enter: The Impact of Black Women on Race and Sex in America*. New York: Bantam Books, 1984.

Graham, Jefferson. "'Flip Wilson Finds a Home on TV Land." *USA Today*, Life, 3D.

Gray, Herman. *Watching Race: Television and the Struggle for Blackness*. Minneapolis: University of Minnesota Press, 1995.

———. "Remembering Civil Rights: Television, Memory and the 60's." In *The Revolution Wasn't Televised*, ed. Lynn Spigel, 349–58. New York: Routledge, 1997.

Gray, John, comp. *Blacks in Film and Television: A Pan-African Bibliography of Films, Filmmakers and Performers*. New York: Greenwood Press, 1990.

Greaves, William. "100 Madison Avenue Will Be of No Help," *New York Times*, 9 August 1970, 13.

Grove, Lloyd. "Chris Rock: Stone Cold Funny." *Washington Post*, 10 April 1997, Style, B01.

Guerrero, Ed. *Framing Blackness: The African American Image in Film*. Philadelphia: Temple University Press, 1993.

Habermas, Jürgen. *The Structural Transformation of the Public Sphere*. Cambridge, MA: MIT Press, 1996.

Hamlin, Jesse. "Funnyman Flip Wilson Is Back on Stage." *San Francisco Chronicle*, 12 October 1989, Final Edition, Daily Notebook, E1.

Harry, Allister. "What's So Funny about Chris Rock?" *London Guardian*, 4 December 1998, Features, 6.

Haskins, Jim. *Richard Pryor: A Man and His Madness*. New York: Beaufort Books, 1984.

Hendrickson, Paul. "Unsealing Mississippi's Past." *Washington Post*, 9 May 1999, Magazine, W08.

Hill, George. *Ebony Images: Black Americans and Television*. Carson, CA: Daystar Publishing, 1986.

Hill, Michael E. "Soul Train's Chief Engineer." *Washington Post*, 6 August 1995, TV Week, Y07.

Hobson, Sheila Smith. "The Rise and Fall of Blacks in Serious Television." *Freedomways*, 3rd quarter (1974): 185–99.

Hodges, Ann. "Ladies of Soul." *Houston Chronicle,* 13 August 1995, Star Edition, Television, 3.

———. "Flip Wilson Travels an Eclectic Path in Life." *Houston Chronicle,* 18 August 1997, 4.

Holsendolph, Ernest, Bob Maynard, and Grayson Mitchell. "The Shame of Public Television." *Black Enterprise,* February 1979, 37.

———. "Coloring the Image of Public Television." *Black Enterprise,* March 1979, 18.

hooks, bell. *Black Looks: Race and Representation.* Cambridge, MA: South End Press, 1992.

———. *Reel to Real: Race, Sex, and Class at the Movies.* New York: Routledge, 1996.

Huggins, Nathan. *Harlem Renaissance.* New York: Oxford University Press, 1971.

Husted, Bill. "Chris Rock Shatters the Silence on Columbine." *Denver Post,* 13 July 1999, sec. A, A-02.

Imani, Dunkor. "Chris Rock Stretches the Limits." *St. Louis Post-Dispatch,* 30 August 1996, Five Star Lift Edition, Everday Magazine, 4E.

Jackson, Harold. "Humor Black and Blue." *London Guardian,* 28 December 1998, 13.

Jhalley, Sut, and Justin Lewis. *Enlightened Racism: The Cosby Show, Audiences, and the Myth of the American Dream.* San Francisco: Westview Press, 1992.

Jones, LeRoi. *Blues People.* New York: Morrow Quill Paperbacks, 1963.

———. *The Dutchman and the Slave: Two Plays.* New York: William Morrow, 1971.

Kagan, Norman. "Amos 'n' Andy: Twenty Years Late or Two Decades Early?" *Journal of Popular Culture* (Summer 1972): 71–75.

Kelley, Robin D. G. *Race Rebels: Culture, Politics and the Black Working Class.* New York: Free Press, 1994.

Kennedy, Robert, Jr. *In His Own Words: The Unpublished Recollections of the Kennedy Years.* New York: Bantam, 1988.

Kiesewetter, John. "One of TV's Funniest Cross-Dressers Primed for a Comeback." *Cincinnati Enquirer,* 18 August 1997, Metro Final, Scene, C7.

King, Patricia. "'Vipers' in the 'Burbs." *Newsweek,* 15 July 1996, 20.

Koiner, Richard B. "The Black Image on TV." *Television Quarterly* (Summer 1980): 39–46.

Langston, Donna. "Tired of Playing Monopoly." In *Race, Class and Gender: An Anthology,* ed. Margaret L. Andersen and Patricia Hill Collins, 126–36. 3rd ed. San Francisco: Wadsworth Publishing, 1995.

Lawson, Steven F. *Running for Freedom: Civil Rights and Black Politics in America since 1941.* New York: McGraw-Hill, 1997.

Leo, John. "The Texas Two-Step." *U.S. News and World Report,* 19 July 1999, 16.

Lewis, Richard Warren. "The Importance of Being Julia." *TV Guide,* 14 December 1968, 24–28.

Lorando, Mark. "You Devil, You." *Times-Picayune,* 17 August 1997, TV Focus, T9.

Lott, Tommie Lee. "Documenting Social Issues: Black Journal 1968–1970." In *Struggles for Representation: African American Documentary Film and Video,* ed. Phyllis R. Klotman and Janet K. Cutler, 71–98. Bloomington: Indiana University Press, 1999.

Lucas, Bob. "Collard Greens' TV Show." *Ebony,* June 1974, 50–53.

———. "Good Times Family Talks about Life without Father." *Jet,* 13 January 1977, 60–63.

———. "Why Black Fathers Are Vanishing in Television Families." *Jet,* 14 April 1977, 61–65.

———. "Good Times' Willona Adopts Television's Biggest Little Star." *Jet,* 10 November 1977, 56–59.

MacDonald, J. Fred. *Blacks and White TV: African Americans in Television since 1948.* 2nd ed. Chicago: Nelson-Hall Publishers, 1992.

Mailer, Norman. *The White Negro.* San Francisco: City Lights Books, 1957.

"Mainstreaming the Militia." *U.S. News & World Report,* 21 April 1997, 24–28+.

Malcolm X. "Message to the Grassroots." In *Malcolm X Speaks,* ed. George Breitman, 3–17. New York: First Grove Press, 1966.

Marriott, Michael. "Rock on a Roll." *Essence,* November 1998, 116.

Martindale, David. "Flip Wilson Clicked at the Right Time." *Houston Chronicle,* 17 August 1997, Television, 4.

Masilela, Ntongela. "The Los Angeles School of Black Filmmakers." *Black American Cinema,* ed. Ntongela Masilela, 107–17. New York: Routledge, 1993.

McCrohan, Donna. *Prime Time, Our Time: America's Life and Times through the Prism of Television.* New York: Random House, 1990.

McFarland, Melanie. "What's So Funny? Chris Rock Is." *Seattle Times,* 10 June 1999, Final Edition, Ticket, G12.

McManaman, Angela. "Think of Him as News, Only Funnier." *Milwaukee Journal Sentinel,* 29 May 1999, Saturday Final, 8.

McNeil, Alex. *Total Television.* New York: Penguin Books, 1996.

McPherson, James. "The New Comic Style of Richard Pryor." *New York Times Magazine,* 27 April 1975, 20–43.

Meisler, Andy. "The Beat Goes on for 'Soul Train' Conductor." *New York Times,* 7 August 1995, sec. D, 7.

Mendoza, Manuel. "Chris Rock Is on a Roll." *Dallas Morning News,* 27 June 1999, Final Edition, Entertainment, 1F.

Mitz, Rick. *The Great TV Sitcom Book*. New York: Perigree Publishing, 1983.

Moody, Lori. "Durable Soul Train Is Pop History in the Making." *Los Angeles Daily News,* 22 November 1995, Variety, 1E.

Morrison, Allan. "Negro Humor: An Answer to Anguish." *Ebony,* May 1967, 99–108.

Morton, Carol A. "For Black Viewers: Some Other Choices Besides Off/ On?" *Black Enterprise,* August 1971, 49.

Mullen, Jim. "Hot Sheet." *Entertainment Weekly,* 23 July 1999, 10.

Murray, Sonia. "Soul Train." *Atlanta Journal and Constitution,* 13 March 1994, Arts, sec. N, 4.

———. "The Soul Train Music Awards." *Atlanta Journal and Constitution,* 13 March 1995, Features, 1B.

———. "'Soul Train' Creator: TV Still Off-Track after 25 Years." *Atlanta Journal and Constitution,* 4 August 1995, Preview, 21P.

"A New Black Superstar." *Time,* 22 August 1977, 66–67.

"New Comedy Brings Good Times to TV." *Jet,* 23 May 1974, 58–60.

Nichols, Bill. *Representing Reality*. Bloomington: Indiana University Press, 1991.

O'Daniel, Michael. "Everything a Performer Could Ask for . . . Except the One Thing He Wants Most: Respect." *TV Guide,* 14 February 1976, 18–20.

———. "He's Come a Long Way from St. Louis: Still the Comedian Hasn't Found Contentment." *TV Guide,* 21 February 1976, 24–26.

O'Hallaren, Bill. "Without Sanford and without Son." *TV Guide,* 17 September 1977, 55–60.

Oldenburg, Ann. "Chris Rock's Wild Ride." *USA Today,* 13 October 1997, Final Edition, Life, 1D.

Omi, Michael, and Howard Winant. *Racial Formation in the United States: From the 1960s to the 1990s*. New York: Routledge, 1994.

Orth, Maureen. "The Perils of Pryor." *Newsweek,* 3 October 1977, 60–63.

Ostroff, Roberta. "I Keep Wondering If the World Is Ready for Me." *TV Guide,* 19 July 1975, 11–12.

Peters, Art. "What the Negro Wants from TV." *TV Guide,* 20 January 1968, 6–10.

Price, Joe X. *Redd Foxx, B.S. (Before Sanford)*. Chicago: Contemporary Books, 1979.

Pryor, Richard. *Bicentennial Nigger: And It's Deep Too: The Complete Warner Brothers Recordings (1968–1992)*. Los Angeles: Warner Brothers Records, 2000.

———. *. . . Is It Something I Said? And It's Deep Too: The Complete Warner Brothers Recordings (1968–1992)*. Los Angeles: Warner Brothers Records, 2000.

———. *Richard Pryor: And It's Deep Too: The Complete Warner Brothers Recordings (1968–1992)*. Los Angeles: Warner Brothers Records, 2000.

———. *That Nigger's Crazy: And It's Deep Too: The Complete Warner Brothers Recordings (1968–1992)*. Los Angeles: Warner Brothers Records, 2000.

Pryor, Richard, and Todd Gold. *Pryor Convictions and Other Life Sentences*. New York: Pantheon Books, 1995.

Radwin, Saryl T. "Julia." *Television Chronicles* 9, 33–45.

Rainwater, Lee, and William L. Yancey. *The Moynihan Report and the Politics of Controversy*. Cambridge, MA: MIT Press, 1967.

Raissman, Bob. "Refreshed by a Flip Attitude." *New York Daily News*, 8 March 1998, Sports, 83.

Report of the National Advisory Commission on Civil Disorders. Pt. III, chap. 15. Washington, DC: GPO, 1968.

Riggs, Marlon. "Tongues Retied." In *Resolutions: Contemporary Video Practices,* ed. Michael Renov and Erika Suderburg, 185–88. Minneapolis: University of Minnesota Press, 1996.

Riley, John. "Esther Rolle the Fishin' Pole." *TV Guide*, 29 June 1974, 16–18.

Robinson, Louie. "TV Discovers the Black Man." *Ebony*, February 1969, 27–30.

———. "Sanford and Son: Redd Foxx and Demond Wilson Wake Up TV's Jaded Audience." *Ebony*, July 1972, 52–58.

———. "Redd Foxx: Crazy Like a Fox, 'Sanford and Son' Star Seeks a Piece of the Action." *Ebony*, June 1974, 154–60.

———. "Bad Times on the 'Good Times' Set." *Ebony*, September 1975, 33–36.

———. "Richard Pryor Talks." *Ebony*, January 1978, 116–22.

Rosenthal, Phil. "Mouthing Off: Rock Provocative as Always in HBO Special." *Chicago Sun-Times*, 9 July 1999, Late Sports Final Edition, FTR, 45.

Sanders, Charles L. "Richard Pryor: Is He the Biggest Richest Black Movie Star Ever? *Ebony*, December 1981, 141–46.

Saunders, Dusty. "Wilson Was a Groundbreaker Remember?" *Rocky Mountain News*, 13 December 1998.

Schaefer, Stephen. "Rocking HBO." *Boston Herald*, 9 July 1999, SCE, S34.

See, Carolyn. "I'm a Black Woman with a White Image." *TV Guide*, 14 March 1970, 26–30.

Seggar, John F., et al. "Television's Portrayal of Minorities and Women in Drama and Comedy Drama 1971–80." *Journal of Broadcasting* (Summer 1981): 277–88.

Shales, Tom. "Chris Rock: In a Very Soft Place Indeed." *Washington Post*, 11 December 1997, Thursday Final Edition, Style, C01.

Shapiro, Joseph P. "Hitting before Hate Strikes." *U.S. News and World Report,* 6 September 1999, 56.

Sidran, Ben. *Black Talk.* New York: Da Capo Press, 1971.

Simmons, Sheila. "'Soul Train' Hails Black Artists." *Plain Dealer,* 29 March 1996, Arts & Living, 5E.

Sklar, Robert. "Is Television Taking Blacks Seriously?" *American Film* (September 1978): 25–29.

Smith, Cecil. "Sanford & Son: It's TV's First Black-on-Black Show." *Los Angeles Times: TV Times,* 5 August 1973, 2.

Smith, Vern E. "Who Needs a Fair Deal." *Newsweek,* 30 August 1999, 32.

Smyth, Mitchell. "Sassy Comic Takes It Easy Now." *Toronto Star,* 24 January 1993, People, D4.

Solomon, Harvey. "All the Right Moves." *Boston Herald,* 22 November 1995, Television, 045.

Sonenshein, Raphael J. *Politics in Black and White: Race and Power in Los Angeles.* Princeton: Princeton University Press, 1993.

Spalding, Sophia. "The Constable Blunders: Police Abuse in Los Angeles' Black and Latino Communities, 1945–1965." PhD diss., University of California, LA, Department of Urban Planning, 1989.

Spigel, Lynn. *Make Room for TV: Television and the Family Ideal in Postwar America.* Chicago: University of Chicago Press, 1992.

Standora, Leo. "TV Funnyman Flip Wilson Is Dead at 64." *New York Daily News,* 26 November 1998, 15.

Stevens, Gus. "CBS' Cosby Clone: Will Flip Flop or Be a Pip?" *San Diego Union-Tribune,* 9 August 1985, Entertainment, C-1.

Strauss, Neill. "You Say Soul Train Is How Old?" *New York Times,* 31 December 1995, sec. 12, 3.

Tierney, John. "The Big City; Do Daddies Get as Good as They Give?" *New York Times,* 5 August 1999, Late Edition, sec. B, 1.

"Tony Brown: Television's Civil Rights Crusader." *Black Enterprise,* September 1979, 36.

Torres, Sasha. *Black. White. And in Color: Television and Black Civil Rights.* Princeton: Princeton University Press, 2003.

"TV's Black Journal Lacks Funds—May Close." *Jet,* 12 June 1969, 44.

Varga, George. "Jokes Are Job 1." *San Diego Union-Tribune,* 10 June 1999, Entertainment, 4.

Vorobey, J. N. "Wonderful Flip." *Washington Post,* 2 December 1998, Final Edition, Op-Ed, A24.

Wallace, Michelle, and Gina Dent. *Black Popular Culture.* New York: New Press, 1998.

Watkins, Mel. *On the Real Side: Laughing, Lying and Signifying, the Underground Tradition of African-American Humor That Transformed American Culture.* New York: Touchstone Books, 1994.

————. "Flip Wilson, 64, Over-the-Top Comic and TV Host, Dies." *New York Times,* 26 November 1998, Final Edition, sec. C, Col. 1, 18.

"When Does the Pumpkin Leave." *TV Guide,* 31 July 1976, 12–13.

Whitney, Dwight. "I'm on the Case." *TV Guide,* 8 January 1972, 20–22.

Williams, James D. "Blacks and Public TV." *Black Enterprise,* January 1974, 31–33.

Williams, John A., and Dennis A. Williams. *If I Stop I'll Die: The Comedy and Tragedy of Richard Pryor.* New York: Thunder Mouth Press, 1991.

Wong, Jeff. "Comedian Brought Black Voice to TV." *Toronto Star,* 26 November 1998, A16.

Woo, Deborah. "The Gap between Striving and Achieving: The Case of Asian American Women." In *Race, Class, and Gender: An Anthology,* ed. Margaret L. Anderson, 243–51. 3rd ed. Belmont, CA: Wadsworth Publishing, 2000.

Woodson, Carter G. *Miseducation of the Negro.* Trenton, NJ: Africa World Press, 1993.

Wortham, Jacob. "In with the Big Boys." *Black Enterprise,* September 1974, 13–17.

Young, J. R. "Include Him Out." *TV Guide,* 5 October 1974, 21–26.

Zuckerman, Mortimer B. "Piling on the Preferences." *U.S. News and World Report,* 28 June 1999, 88.

Index

Christine Acham is assistant professor in the African American and African Studies Program at the University of California at Davis.